GLOBAL DEVELOPMENT IMPACT

NISHANT MALHOTRA

INDIA · SINGAPORE · MALAYSIA

Legal Disclaimer

The contents of this book are provided solely for informational and educational purposes. By accessing or reading this book, the reader acknowledges and agrees to the following terms and conditions:

Disclaimer of Liability

I, Nishant Malhotra, as the author, explicitly declare that:

- This book and its contents are provided "as is", without any warranties, express or implied, including but not limited to warranties of merchantability, fitness for a particular purpose, or non-infringement.
- No representations or guarantees are made regarding the accuracy, completeness, reliability, or suitability of any information, analysis, opinions, or data contained herein.
- Readers are solely responsible for verifying all information, data, citations, or references presented in this book.
- This book does not constitute financial, investment, legal, professional, or other advisory services, nor is it intended to substitute for professional advice or judgment.

The author shall not be liable for any direct, indirect, incidental, consequential, punitive, or special damages, including but not limited to:

- Losses arising from the use of or inability to use the information in this book
- Reliance on any content, opinions, or data provided herein
- Errors, omissions, or inaccuracies in the content

Use of Third-Party Data and References

This book includes references to data, research, and other information obtained from third-party sources, including but not limited to databases, publications, and reports. While every effort has been made to accurately cite these sources:

- The author makes no representations or warranties regarding the accuracy, timeliness, or completeness of any third-party information.
- The inclusion of third-party content does not imply endorsement, affiliation, or responsibility by the original source.
- Third-party sources are not liable for any interpretation, use, or application of their data or insights within this book.

Readers are encouraged to consult original sources for the most current and reliable information.

No Investment or Professional Advice

This book is not an offer, invitation, or recommendation to buy, sell, or hold any securities, financial instruments, or assets. It is not intended to solicit or promote any investment strategy or professional service.

Reader Responsibility

Readers are strongly encouraged to:
- Conduct independent verification of all data and claims
- Seek the advice of qualified professionals (e.g., legal, financial, tax, or investment advisers) before making any decisions
- Exercise personal judgment, discretion, and due diligence

This disclaimer is intended to be legally binding and enforceable to the fullest extent permitted under applicable law.

Reviews

Go for it

This book is a brilliant refresher for anyone in the development space who's looking to know and curious to find the financial side of Sustainable Development and the journey of financial growth till today. It touches on so many critical areas and fundamental concepts with nuances from finance, sustainable investing, carbon markets, IPCC, Article-6,9, CABM, and carbon pricing, banking, macro economy, start-ups, AI, ESG, various case studies, to business models, UN conventions and many more. It's packed with insights, yet doesn't bore you and is super convenient to read. What I really loved is how Nishant connects it all together by introducing more than two fictional characters and makes it interactive throughout with Kish and Carolina, which gives a unique touch like a novel to it. It also gives nostalgia, with smart twists, college vibes, canteen discussions where it makes the book engaging and different from the usual static reads one may find on the shelves. It doesn't feel like a textbook at all, but one may use it like. I would really recommend this book for individuals who are working in this niche sector like; NGOs, think tanks, research institutions or academics and consulting, etc., want to understand the evolution of sustainable financing. Big shout-out and congratulations, Nishant Malhotra !

– **Gaurav Sahni,**
Seasoned Climate Professional

Blending Fiction and Finance for understanding the Real-World Impact

Global Development Impact balances the narrative with technical clarity. The strength of the book lies in its innovative format of turning technical topics into relatable narratives. It's especially valuable for students, young professionals, and general readers seeking an approachable entry point into global development and social finance. The book educates and inspires by making complex development finance concepts more accessible through narrative and design. While the breadth of topics means some areas aren't explored in great depth, the book succeeds as an educational and inspiring primer. It's a creative and refreshing addition to the development literature.

– Himalay Joshi,
Seasoned Financial Services Leader

For Anyone Who Takes Sustainability Seriously

This isn't your average feel-good sustainability book — it's the real deal. Nishant Malhotra dives deep into the frameworks, policies, and financial systems that actually drive global impact. I'll admit, parts of it are dense, but in a good way. It felt like I was sitting in on a top-tier development finance lecture. What I appreciated most is how well-researched and structured it is. It doesn't just talk about "doing good" — it shows how to build real systems that create change. If you work in finance, policymaking, or international development, this book is a goldmine.

– Anu Devangan

Acknowledgements

Institutions and Data Sources

I want to share my sincere gratitude to the many actors without whom this book would not have been possible. A special thanks goes to the providers of open databases that enabled me to access and download data for visualizations and graphs—particularly the Board of Governors of the Federal Reserve System (Federal Reserve Board) and the World Bank Database, whose publicly available data was invaluable.

I am also grateful to the multilateral development banks—especially the International Finance Corporation (IFC, part of the World Bank Group)—for allowing me to reference their case studies and for making critical development finance data freely accessible. The Organisation for Economic Co-operation and Development (OECD) has been outstanding in promoting open data for global development, and I extend special thanks to the European Commission.

Thought Leaders and Institutions in Finance & Economics

My appreciation also extends to global thought leaders, and institutions advancing sustainable finance and impact investing: the Global Sustainable Investment Alliance (GSIA), the Global Impact Investing Network (GIIN), Blue Gamma, Convergence Finance, Our World in Data, the UN Climate Change, the Climate Bonds Initiative, and the International Capital Market Association (ICMA). Their work and resources have significantly enriched this book.

Organizations, Scholars and Referenced Works

Special thanks to organizations, scholars and data providers whose research and insights I have drawn upon: the International Energy Agency (IEA), European Environment Agency, ReNew, the University of Groningen, the University of California, Davis, U.S. Bureau of Economic Analysis (BEA), Dr. Joseph E. Stiglitz, Ielasi, F., Ceccherini, P., & Zito, Dr. André Perold, the Eurekahedge ILS Advisers Index, Kim Y., Tanaka K., Matsuoka S., and Artemis.

A special mention also goes to Guy Kawasaki, whose work I have referenced. I am grateful to him for permitting me to cite his insights.

Publishing and Personal Thanks

Finally, I want to extend heartfelt thanks to Notion Press for making this book possible through their support in editing and publishing. My sincere apologies if I have missed any names, as many individuals and institutions have contributed to the knowledge embedded in this book.

A special acknowledgement goes to my parents, for their patience and support throughout the research and publication process.

Note on This Edition

In this edition, errors have been rectified, with references added and selected references removed to ensure accuracy and clarity.

Contents

Summary

This book is an essential exploration of sustainable development, particularly in the realms of sustainable investing and finance. Set against the backdrop of America, it unfolds as a heartwarming fictional tale that beautifully intertwines themes of love, friendship, companionship, art, and culture with critical insights on environmental, social, and governance (ESG) factors, innovation, and sustainable finance. Crafted to inspire and educate, the narrative invites readers to engage deeply with social impact enablers while seamlessly integrating economics, finance, technology, art, and culture into the broader context of sustainable development and everyday life. Follow the journey of Kish, the central character, as you become immersed in a compelling story that reveals the intricate dynamics of the global development sector. This book is a must-read, skilfully linking ESG principles with social innovation and offering a strategic vision for the development ecosystem. Discover social and financial innovation's pivotal role in the sustainable finance landscape. You'll explore diverse social financing mechanisms, including complex structures designed to achieve positive ESG outcomes. Highlighting selected significant milestones and transformative policies, this narrative showcases the efforts reshaping the international development landscape for the better. Enriched with real-life case studies and quizzes, this book informs and entertains, making it ideal for anyone passionate about driving meaningful change in the development sector. Seize the chance to broaden your understanding and partake in the vital conversation about transforming our future. The inspiration behind this book is profoundly personal.

Author's Note

This book focuses on sustainable development, particularly on sustainable investing and finance. Written as a fictional, feel-good story set in America, it weaves a narrative of love, friendship, companionship, art, and culture, with *ESG, Innovation, and Sustainable Finance* as its central tenet. An inspirational tale, the book aims to inform and educate readers about social impact enablers, integrating the effects of economics, finance, technology, art, and culture within the context of sustainable development and daily life. The book is narrated in a fictional storytelling style; the reader follows the journey of Kish, the chief protagonist. Immerse yourself in a compelling narrative set in the United States that delves into the dynamic world of the global development sector. This book is an essential read, expertly weaving together the concepts of environmental, social, and governance (ESG) factors with social innovation, presenting a comprehensive and strategic vision for the development ecosystem. Discover how social financial innovation is critical in the sustainable finance sector. Engage with influential actors and uncover their impactful contributions while exploring diverse social financing mechanisms, including intricate financing structures that foster positive ESG outcomes. The book showcases selected pivotal milestones and impactful policies reshaping the international development landscape for the better. Through a captivating storyline enriched with real-life case studies and quizzes, this book informs and entertains, making it a must-read for anyone interested in driving change in the development sector. Don't miss the opportunity to expand your understanding and join the conversation on transforming the future. The motivation for this book has been deeply personal for a while, with tributes given to various actors and inspirations throughout the story. A special thanks to my parents for their constant motivation to write the book.

The idea of writing a book on such a serious topic in a narrative format is inspired by one of the greatest storytellers of our time, **Michael Lewis**, whose works have brought joy to readers over the years. *Liar's Poker* and *Big Short* are two of the best books I have read. A special mention goes to

Eliyahu Goldratt for his monumental work, *The Goal*, which planted the seed of thought for this book. Television shows such as *Friends*, *Seinfeld*, and *The Big Bang Theory* laid the foundation for the friendship-driven story. My time in the U.S. heavily influenced the American setting. In contrast, the portrayal of Chinese culture through martial arts and other settings draws from my experiences in China and my admiration for Bruce Lee and Jet Li. These experiences, combined with my studies in the U.S. and China, helped form the genesis of these cultural elements. Although I loosely inspired Kish, the characters are entirely fictional. Any resemblance to actual persons is purely coincidental and ludicrous.

Best
Nishant Malhotra
Solo Founder & CEO – The Middle Road

Introduction

Understanding Sustainable Development Sector

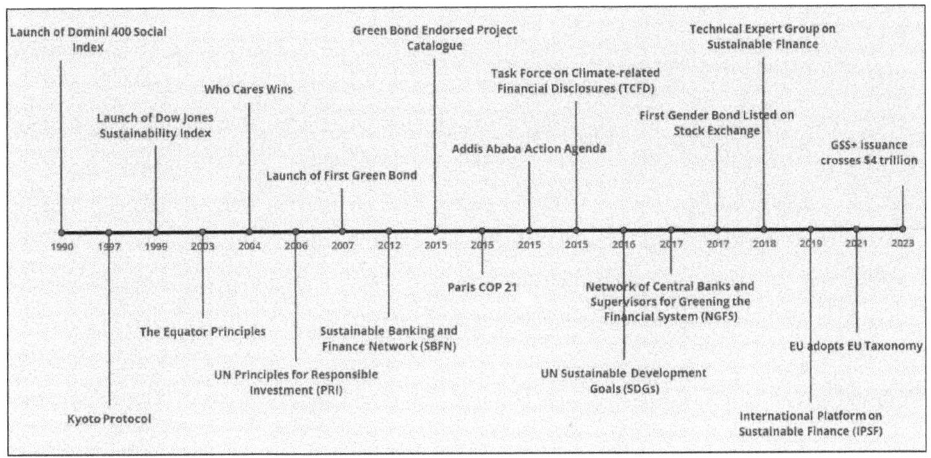

Selected key milestones within the ESG Ecosystem; **Chart:** Author

Rise of Sustainable Development Goals with a key focus on ESG (Environmental, Social, and Governance)

I reviewed the *Global Sustainable Investment Alliance (GSIA) Global Sustainable Investment Review 2022* to understand the size of the global sustainable investing market, emerging trends in sustainable investing, and the key enablers and actors governing the sector. According to the GSIA, sustainable investment assets under management (AUM) reached $30.3 trillion across key regions, including Europe, the United States, Canada, Japan, Australia, and New Zealand. However, this figure excludes significant markets such as China and India and regions like Latin America and Africa, suggesting that the actual global size of sustainable assets is more extensive than reported. Awareness of **Environmental, Social, and Governance (ESG)** factors has grown rapidly globally, with the sector experiencing significant expansion in recent years. Environmental, Social, and Governance are increasingly recognized as a framework for promoting social and environmental good. Social and climate action has become pivotal from the first **World Climate Conference** held in 1979 to the IPCC (Intergovernmental Panel on Climate Change) formation in 1988. The rise in global awareness in recent times is multidimensional. One of the primary reasons for this shift is changing demographics. Another reason is the visible adverse impact of climate change and the increase in regulations governing Environmental, Social, and Governance topics. The European Union is a leader in devising and implementing rules safeguarding consumers and promoting ethical business and social practices. With many countries having significant coastal areas, increasing global temperature leads to rising sea levels, increasing the probability of natural calamities. These, among other factors, have forced many countries to give renewed focus on *Environmental, Social, and Governance (ESG)* factors. Sustainable Finance is used interchangeably with *Sustainable Investing or ESG Investing* in the book. The innovation in sustainable finance is becoming a game-changing lever within the international development sector.

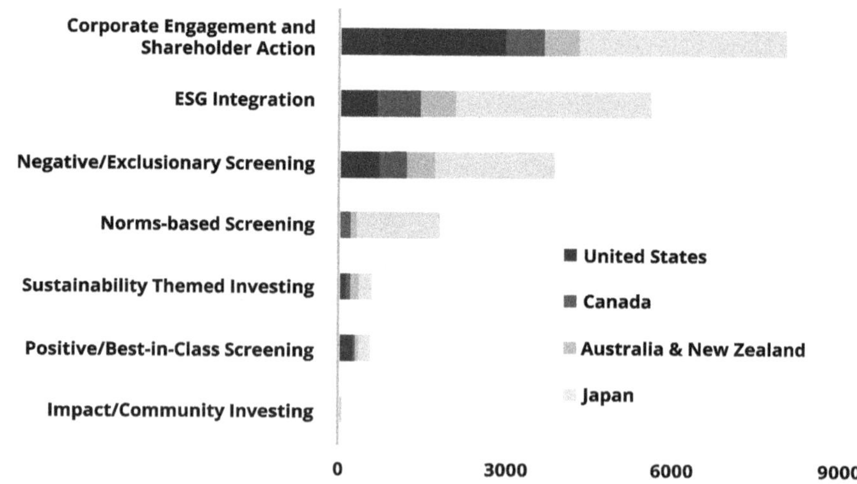

Proportion of sustainable investing assets by strategy & region 2022 in $ Billion

Data Source: Global Sustainable Investment Review 2022 (GSIA). Refer to the report for potential differences due to changes in methodology. Retrieved from *https://www.gsi-alliance.org/members-resources/gsir2022/*. **Chart Author.**

Note: European sustainable investing strategy data was not available for the reporting period and is not included in the chart. All asset values are in USD.

Global financial institutions increasingly cite Climate change and biodiversity as systemic risks. ***The density of greenhouse gases is now at its highest in over 100,000 years,*** emphasizing the urgent need to reduce fossil fuel use. There is a consensus among asset managers and investors on the material impact of environmental, social, and governance (ESG) factors on asset performance. ESG investing has become so prominent that it is now a crucial parameter in investment management. Empirical evidence shows that higher ESG integration within investment strategies leads to **lower capital costs** and **better stock performance**. While ESG integration enhances risk mitigation, asset managers also use ESG integration to generate alpha. Although there is no consensus that ESG integration will lead to better investment portfolio performance, *ESG integration is a necessity rather than a tragedy.* Although various global actors have played a pivotal role in driving the agenda of sustainable issues, the **United Nations (UN)** stands out. The United Nations plays a crucial role in global development, leading the drive for sustainable goals universally.

As a leading international organization, the United Nations is instrumental in establishing frameworks for sustainable development. *I reflect on some milestones that led to the defining focus on ESG, making it mainstream.* But first, let's examine a couple of supranational organizations that have left an indelible mark on this sector. Let's begin with the United Nations.

Supranational

United Nations
One place where the world's nations can gather together, discuss common problems, and find shared solutions.

The **United Nations** is an international organization founded in 1945, comprising 193 member states, with its headquarters in New York City, U.S. The UN operates based on the purposes and principles outlined in its founding Charter. Its main bodies include the *General Assembly, the Security Council, the Economic and Social Council, the Trusteeship Council, the International Court of Justice, and the UN Secretariat.* The United Nations is central in driving the **Sustainable Development Goals (SDGs)**, supported by various actors/stakeholders. Under its umbrella, multiple specialized agencies focus on specific objectives. The evolution from the

Millennium Development Goals (2000-2015) to the Seventeen *Sustainable Development Goals (2015-2030)* marked a significant expansion in scope and ambition. Today, the SDGs serve as a key framework for all actors within the developmental and business ecosystem to improve and achieve set environmental, social, and governance outcomes globally. As a foremost actor driving sustainable change, the United Nations must be understood for its mission and vision. However, the story of sustainable development began long ago.

Official Development Assistance (ODA) leads the way.

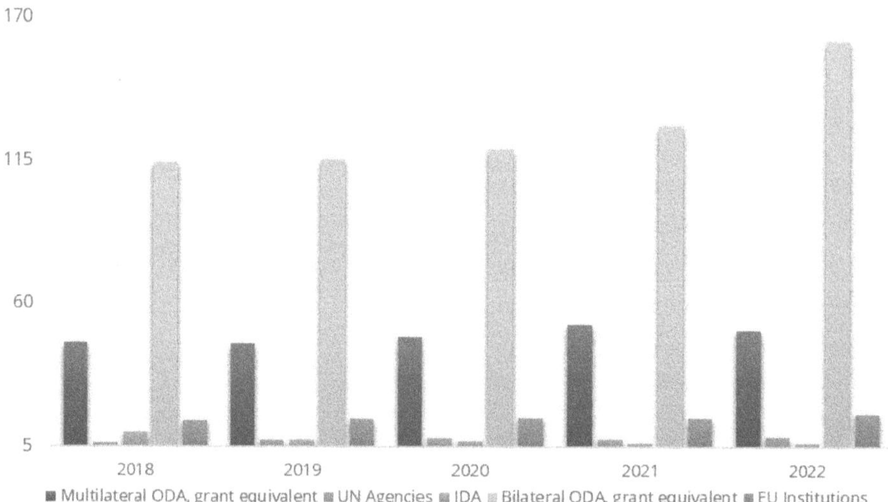

ODA, other official flows (OOF), and flows from non-governmental organizations (NGOs) or philanthropic foundations in $ Billion

Data: *https://data-explorer.oecd.org/***Data Source:** OECD Database, "Aggregates on Official Development Assistance (ODA), Other Official Flows (OOF), and Flows from Non-Governmental Organizations (NGOs) or Philanthropic Foundations." *OECD Data Explorer* (Accessed in January 2025). The chart does not include net disbursement data.

Chart; Author

OECD and Official Development Assistance (ODA)

Another key supranational whose work within the development sector is impeccable is the Organization for Economic Co-operation and Development. The Organization for Economic Co-operation and

Development (OECD), headquartered in Paris, France, comprises 38 high-income member countries. OECD plays a significant role in advancing sustainable development on a global scale. One of its key functions is to quantify international aid through Official Development Assistance (ODA), a term introduced by the OECD's Development Assistance Committee (DAC) in 1969.[2] ODA has since become the global benchmark for measuring international aid. The OECD defines ODA as government aid specifically aimed at promoting economic development and improving the welfare of developing countries.[4]

Official Development Assistance (ODA), grant equivalent 2015 to 2023 in $ Billion.Please note: from 2018 onwards, ODA is measured based on grant equivalents.

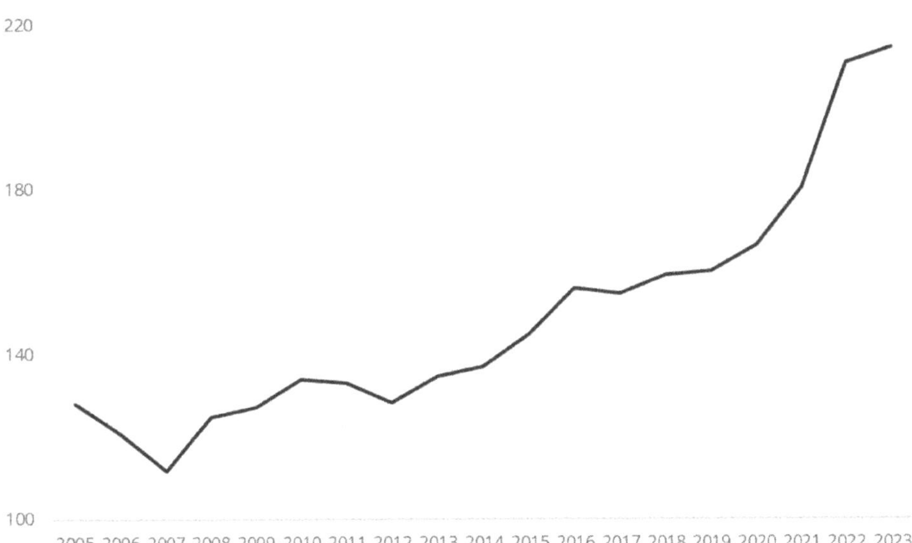

Data Sources: *OECD (2024), Flows by donor (ODA+OOF+Private) [DAC1]; https://data-explorer. oecd.org/* The data is from the OECD database that provides aggregates on official development assistance (ODA), other official flows (OOF), and flows from non-governmental organizations (NGOs) or philanthropic foundations. ODA on flows and grant equivalent measure by members of OECD Development Assistance Committee (DAC). Data rounded off to two decimals. Data also used from *https://www.oecd.org/en/topics/oda-trends-and-statistics.html*; data rounded off to 2 decimals; Note: The Development Assistance Committee (DAC) aggregate data. Chart; Author

ODA represents the largest source of external financial flows to emerging economies, funding development projects across various sectors. The definition of ODA is periodically revised and includes specific criteria, such as a minimum grant element of 25 percent (as outlined in *"Beyond ODA flows: definition and research framework"*). The United Nations stipulates that OECD countries contribute *0.7 percent of their Gross National Income (GNI) to ODA.*[2] Only a few member countries consistently meet this target, highlighting the ongoing challenges in prioritizing international development. Norway led in 2023 among these nations, contributing the highest percentage of GNI to ODA *(OECD ODA in 2023)*.[3] Beyond ODA, other primary external financing sources include foreign direct investments (FDI) and personal remittances, primarily targeting the private sector. Government borrowings, often utilized for sovereign funding, remain a core mechanism for financing national development initiatives.

DAC Members' official development assistance in 2023 on a grant equivalent basis in $ millions

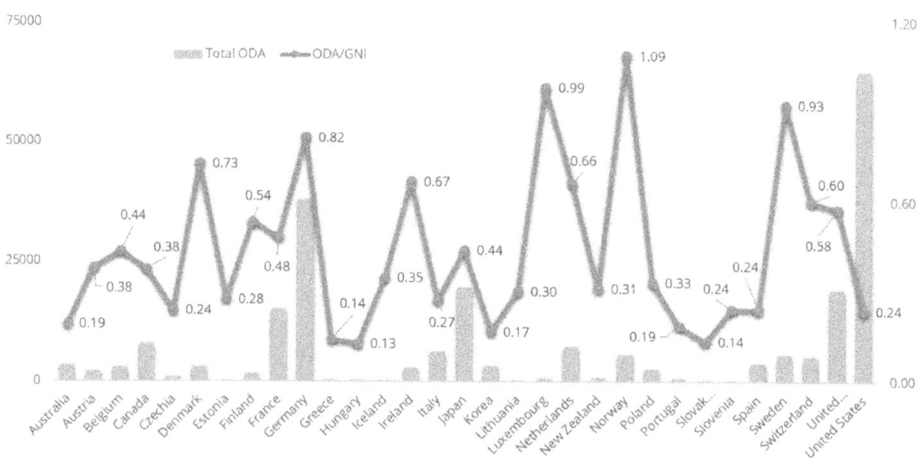

Data Source: Organization for Economic Co-operation and Development (OECD). *Development Finance Statistics: Data on Flows to Developing Countries.* Retrieved on August 2024 from *OECD Development Finance Statistics.* Chart; Author.

Data: https://www.oecd.org/en/data/datasets/development-finance-statistics-data-on-flows-to-developing-countries.html.

Notes: Total ODA is shown on the right axis, and ODA/GNI is rounded to two decimal places. Only ODA-eligible private sector instruments (PSIs) are included. In 2023, the Development Assistance Committee (DAC) agreed to revised reporting methods for measuring PSIs in ODA based on grant equivalents. Members may take up to two years to transition to these methods, with PSIs reported on a net ODA basis during the transition. Total ODA in 2023 includes USD 707 million in loans and equities provided to, and repayments and reflows from, private companies operating in ODA-eligible countries. Net flows include PSIs reported on a net disbursement basis by DAC members that have not yet implemented the new reporting rules for 2023 ODA data.

Multilateral Development Banks

Multilateral Development Banks (MDBs) are pivotal in mobilizing and channelling concessional and non-concessional capital to less-developed, low-income, and emerging economies. These institutions, such as the World Bank, Asian Development Bank, European Investment Bank, Inter-American Development Bank, Asian Infrastructure Investment Bank, and the International Monetary Fund (IMF), are established by governments to access capital markets and allocate funds for development purposes. Understanding the World Bank Group is essential to grasp the functions of its various divisions and their impact on the development sector. The World Bank Group's scale and influence are unparalleled, making it essential to comprehend its role in advancing social good. The World Bank is the largest source of development finance globally, with approximately $240 billion in loans across 77 countries. Together with the IMF, it forms a cornerstone of the international development ecosystem. Headquartered in Washington, D.C., the World Bank is owned by 189 member countries serving as its clients. Its mission is to end extreme poverty and build a livable planet. The largest shareholders include the United States, Japan, China, Germany, France, and the United Kingdom. Multilateral Development Banks (MDBs) are champions of *the SDG 17 goal, public-private partnerships (PPPs)*, playing a vital role in attracting annual capital needed to meet the Sustainable Development Goals (SDGs) goals by 2030. Key enablers within the international development sector include government-backed institutions such as multilateral organizations, bilateral aid agencies, development institutions, supranational organizations, sovereign entities, agencies, and municipalities. Additionally, foundations, impact investors, corporations, and key actors within the startup ecosystem, such as impact and impact-driven accelerator programs, are significant players in the sector. Meanwhile, civil society actors—including *non-profits, think tanks, philanthropists, activists, and social change enablers*—play a crucial role as catalysts in promoting social issues and amplifying the impact of development initiatives. These organizations drive financial innovation as key players in defining and advancing sustainable finance.

From Jimmy Carter to COP21 Paris Agreement

One name that must be mentioned for his visionary focus on the renewable sector is Jimmy Carter. **Jimmy Carter envisioned bringing renewable energy investments to the US during his presidency**. His administration invested in solar energy, established the **Solar Energy Research Institute** (later renamed the **National Renewable Energy Laboratory**), and explored alternative energy sources like synfuel production from coal and shale oil. However, these efforts did not yield the desired results for various reasons. Another significant political figure advocating for renewable energy development and action on climate change is **Al Gore**, notably through his documentary **"An Inconvenient Truth."**

Kyoto Protocol & Paris Agreement

The United Nations Climate Change is associated with climate change. COP is an acronym for the Conference of the Parties to the Convention. The Convention refers to the United Nations Framework Convention on Climate Change (UNFCCC), which was adopted in May 1992 in New York, US._a The convention opened for signatories in the landmark Earth Summit held in Brazil in June 1992. The de facto force played a critical role in adopting two of the most significant milestones within the climate action arena – *The Kyoto Protocol and the Paris Agreement.*

The Kyoto Protocol is substantial in the development sector. It marked the first time countries agreed to pursue climate action as an agenda with binding and non-binding targets. Its goal was to keep emissions in check. Sadly, the Kyoto Protocol failed. Eventually, it broke down, but it is widely credited to the COP 21 Paris Agreement that set the ball rolling by setting a target of keeping global temperatures below 2°C above pre-industrial levels. The Paris Agreement, like the Kyoto Protocol adopted under the United Nations Framework Convention on Climate Change, entered into force on 4 November 2016 and proved to be the greatest nudge for various actors to focus on climate action. It sets the ball rolling with an anchor point as a benchmark target for temperature-catalyzing pathways to attract interventions that will limit greenhouse emissions. EU Taxonomy and the European Green Deal turned out to be game changers, with the EU deciding to be carbon neutral by 2050.[5] EU Taxonomy is the region's first comprehensive and structured attempt to categorize sustainable activities to attract capital toward the sustainable development sector and prevent greenwashing. The EU and UK have been at the forefront of implementing policies emphasizing green energy. China, currently the largest investor in low-carbon technologies, has seen its electric vehicle market explode. Remarkably, despite being a developing country, China dominates the global manufacturing of renewable technologies and could achieve carbon neutrality well before 2060. Today, most EU countries derive a significant portion of their energy from clean technologies, putting Europe on an accelerated path to achieve carbon neutrality before 2050. This global leadership, particularly from advanced countries and China, has propelled the proliferation of ESG across various sectors.

Knock on ESG Door – Sustainable Finance Launches

Knockin' on Heaven's Door (initially sung by Bob Dylan and later by Guns N' Roses) is regarded by many as one of the best rock numbers of all time, but one of the top knocks on ESG's door began in 1990.

Let's go back to 1990 - the first ESG-based index had arrived. This year marks the launch of the **Domini Social 400 index now known as MSCI KLD 400 Social Index**, the first equity index explicitly favoring companies with superior track records in environmental and social factors. A cornerstone movement within the realms of sustainable investing/finance *(taking sustainable investing/finance as an umbrella term that includes ESG investing)*, the launch of the Domini 400 Social Index stands as a towering lighthouse next to a turbulent sea. For the first time, socially conscious investors could invest in companies aligned with their investment objectives, bifurcating companies on socio-environmental factors. As the world advanced, more indices were launched, keeping sustainability the central thesis. The **Dow Jones Sustainability Indices (DJSI)**, launched in 1999, stands out. These milestones, although necessary, were not a deal-breaker for driving capital within the development sector. This would change soon with the first green bond launched by **the European Investment Bank** in 2007 known as *Climate Awareness Bond,*$_c$ closely followed by another green bond by the **World Bank**. Bonds are debt instruments that fundamentally raise capital for various actors within the capital markets. **Green Bonds**, whose proceeds are designated for environmental projects, paved the way for other bonds, for example, Social, Sustainability, and Sustainability-linked bonds (collectively

> **Seed accelerators**, such as **Y Combinator** and **Techstars**, incubators, and start-up platforms like Slush are catalysts in boosting social entrepreneurship. Social stock exchanges are a step in the right direction to provide liquidity among actors within sustainable development. Angel investors, venture capitalists, and even private equity are playing an increasing role in the social impact ecosystem. Corporate social responsibility is another driver of the ESG theme globally.

known as GSS+ bonds), to raise capital for various actors within the development sector. Governments, government-backed agencies (for example, multilateral), and corporations could raise capital in international capital markets at below-market interest rates to address outcomes that benefit underserved societies. This could range from affordable housing to inclusive education and financial inclusion. The rise of these financing mechanisms fostered more financial innovation, transparency, and accountability.

Today, GSS+ issuance is about \$5.7 trillion, showcasing the rise of ESG power.$_d$ Innovation breeds innovation. In 2015, the **Addis Ababa Agenda** laid the foundation for attracting private capital through blended finance. The meeting brought new social financing tools to attract capital.

Blended Capital, not a common financing tool used in mainstream finance, has become a social financing mechanism for attracting incremental capital, especially in frontier and emerging markets.

The primary objective of blended finance is to use limited public funds to attract and leverage private capital for socio-economic interventions, particularly in frontier markets where capital is most scarce. Public investors employ various financing mechanisms, including **concessional capital**, to crowd in private investment. Sources of concessional finance include **foundations, charities, impact investors, religious institutions**, and government-backed entities such as **multilateral organizations**. The social financing innovation is designed to transform the lives of underserved communities through impact-driven outcomes while addressing funding gaps. Financial innovators like *financial institutions, insurance funds, pension funds, and impact investors* foster incremental capital in the development sector. IFC is the champion among major actors, including multilateral, in using blended finance through structured finance mechanisms, among others, to enhance private capital using limited public capital. *For every \$1 of concessional capital, IFC mobilizes \$8 from the private sector, a multiple of 8 for capital deployment.* Separately, *pay-for-success* bonds, known as impact bonds, started the race for performance-based grants. The birth of enablers like **Principles for Responsible Investment (PRI)** brought accountability and transparency to sustainable finance. The *Principles for Responsible Investment (PRI)* is a global market leader promoting ESG integration among asset managers.

Suddenly, all the ticks clicked.

Various taxonomies exist for sustainable bonds apart from national taxonomies like the European Union taxonomy for enhanced capital for sustainable activities. Renewable energy received a significant boost, especially from China, which invests more in this sector than any other country. Clean tech was boosted through various global initiatives, for example, the startup ecosystem. The startup ecosystem across many countries has become more robust in the last decade. Impact investors and major startup ecosystem enablers provide incremental capital to startups innovating across various environmental and social outcomes. Prolonged low interest rates in the US led to a global glut of capital. As responsible investment rose, the appetite for investments linked to ESG factors proliferated.

Rise in Sustainable Investing

Proportion of Global Sustainable Investing Assets by Region 2022

The rise of regulations addressing ESG concerns is also reshaping the investment management sector, driving the adoption of governance frameworks prioritizing environmental and social outcomes. The GSIA report comprehensively analyzes this evolving landscape, shedding light on the various ESG investment strategies employed globally. Among the many initiatives propelling the move toward sustainable investing, the **Glasgow Financial Alliance for Net Zero (GFANZ)**, a coalition aimed at aligning financial institutions with net zero emissions goals, is noteworthy. According to the **Global Sustainable Investment Alliance (GSIA)**, sustainable investment assets under management (AUM) reached a remarkable $30.3 trillion across key regions, including *Europe, the United States, Canada, Japan, Australia, and New Zealand*.[1] This milestone underscores the increasing recognition of ESG factors as integral components of sound investment and portfolio management practices. As awareness of ESG principles spreads worldwide, investors and asset managers incorporate these factors as material considerations in their strategies. Between 2020 and 2022, the AUM of Japan increased by 59 percent, the highest for any region. During this period, the US registered the worst growth, with the investment corpus declining by 51 percent. *(This marked drop reflects shifting regulatory landscapes and evolving definitions of sustainable investing in the U.S).* Canada registered a negative growth rate of 5 percent during this period. Sustainable Investing evolved significantly from its origins in negatively screening controversial sectors like gambling and tobacco. Rather than rules-driven investment analysis like exclusionary strategy, sustainable investing became more sophisticated, driven by fundamental analysis, thematic, or fostered by activism. These investing strategies include *best-in-class screening, ESG integration, sustainable themed investing, norms-based investing, impact/ community investing, and corporate engagement and shareholder action.*[1] According to the GSIA report, the dominant strategies have shifted over time: from negative/exclusionary screening in 2018 to ESG integration in 2020, reflecting the growing maturity of responsible investment approaches. In 2022, Corporate engagement and shareholder action are the most dominant strategies, with ESG integration as the second most used strategy. However, *ESG integration* is the most robust, employing both quantitative and fundamental-driven strategies. The emergence of financial materiality factors by the Sustainability Accounting Standards Board (SASB) has significantly driven fundamental investment strategies. For example, a material factor for energy companies would be their CO_2 footprint. A horizontal material factor across companies will be human capital, which differs in intensity depending on the type of business. Incorporating double materiality is highly relevant rather than measuring the impact of ESG factors on companies' financial performance. This requires understanding how your organization or activity underscores ESG globally.

Multiple factors have driven the rise in sustainable investment, including significant adoption by institutional investors globally, with Japanese pension funds playing a notable role in this growth.

Sustainable Investing Assets by Strategy, 2016–2022 in $ Billion

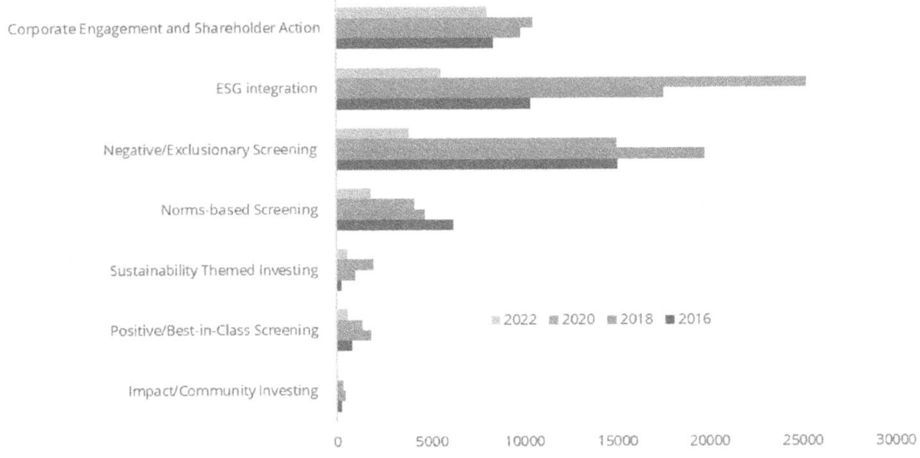

Data Source: Global Sustainable Investment Review 2022 GSIA; Chart Author. Refer to the report as there are differences in data due to a change in methodology. Retrieved from *https://www.gsi-alliance.org/members-resources/gsir2022/*.

The Mega Green Deal and Regulations

Between 2020 and 2022, Europe and the United States remained the two largest regions for sustainable investment. During this period, Europe's share of global sustainable assets rose significantly—from 34% to 46%—according to the GSIA. This growth reflects the strength of Europe's regulatory environment, including initiatives like the Sustainable Finance Disclosure Regulation (SFDR), while the decline in reported U.S. assets is primarily due to a methodological shift that narrowed the definition of sustainable investing. At the same time, key reforms, such as the adoption of **EU Taxonomy**, have contributed to sustainable investment growth in Europe. According to the *European Commission's staff working document impact assessment report*, the *European Union (EU) Taxonomy* has significantly influenced the growth of sustainable European investments.

The Taxonomy has established clear criteria to classify sustainable economic activities that align with the objectives of the EU Green Deal and, along with the EU Green Deal, limit greenwashing and market fragmentation.[5] These regulations turned out to be a decisive factor in attracting capital toward themes such as biodiversity, climate finance, circular economy, and nature-based solutions.[5]

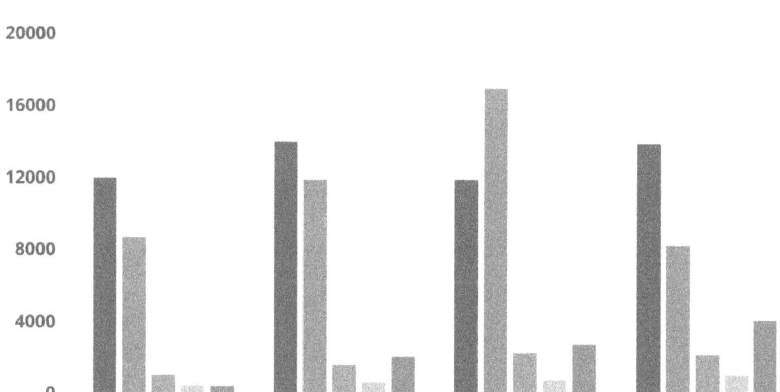

Data Source: Global Sustainable Investment Review 2022. Retrieved from *https://www.gsi-alliance. org/members-resources/gsir2022/*.

Chart Author. Note: For the US, 2022 figures are not directly comparable due to a change in methodology. However, the US figures are included in this chart.

More data is available on ESG now than ever before. While a universal sustainability standard is still lacking, the **EU** has mandated the **Corporate Sustainability Reporting Directive (CSRD)** for companies. The EU Taxonomy has been instrumental in defining and categorizing sustainable activities. On *5 January 2023*, the **Corporate Sustainability Reporting Directive (CSRD)** requirements came into force in the EU as part of the **European Green Deal** to strengthen sustainability standards across the region. The directive mandates large companies and listed entities— excluding micro-enterprises—to disclose both opportunities and adverse impacts of social and environmental issues, along with their effects on people and the environment. This legislation significantly enhances transparency for all actors within the business ecosystem. Alongside the **Sustainable Finance Disclosure Regulation (SFDR)**, which contains similar provisions regarding sustainable finance, CSRD represents a critical step toward creating a level playing field for investors, regulators, and asset managers to assess risks and opportunities. These requirements apply from 2024, with the first reports expected to be published in 2025. The **Sustainable Finance Disclosure Regulation (SFDR)** is a transformative piece of legislation that has revolutionized how financial

The **EU** implemented a novel mechanism of limiting greenhouse emissions through its cap-and-trade mechanism known as the **ETS (Emissions Trading System)**– the first international carbon emissions trading system. This is an innovative approach to enforce and mitigate carbon emissions rather than using other carbon pricing strategies like carbon taxation. Today, this kind of carbon emissions trading system is deployed globally in many countries.

market participants and advisers report sustainability risks. The regulation ensures that adverse sustainability impacts are properly accounted for and communicated transparently, particularly through mediums such as websites.

SFDR defines sustainability risk as: "An environmental, social, or governance event or condition that, if it occurs, could cause a negative material impact on the value of the investment, as specified in sectoral legislation, in particular in Directives 2009/65/EC, 2009/138/EC, 2011/61/EU, 2013/36/EU, 2014/65/EU, (EU) 2016/97, (EU) 2016/2341, or delegated acts and regulatory technical standards adopted pursuant to them."[6]

This regulation is the first genuine attempt to quantify sustainability risks within investment management. Among its key provisions, SFDR requires financial advisers' performance-based remuneration to align with full disclosure of *adverse sustainability risks* to their clients. SFDR also mandates that financial market participants disclose their methodologies for assessing sustainability risks, helping all stakeholders understand the key performance metrics employed to measure sustainability factors within their portfolios. This level of transparency greatly improves the due diligence of investments concerning social, environmental, and governance factors. The **Sustainable Finance Disclosure Regulation (SFDR)** serves as a universal beacon for showcasing ESG-related risks and opportunities within investment decisions, while curbing malpractices associated with misrepresenting investment products based on sustainability claims. A forward-looking piece of legislation, SFDR marks the first comprehensive effort to recognize sustainability risks and establish a robust set of guidelines for evaluating risks and opportunities in the investment management sector. The introduction of the **Sustainable Finance Disclosure Regulation (SFDR)** in the EU has been a game-changer. In India, sustainability disclosures are on the rise. The *Business Responsibility and Sustainability Reporting (BRSR)* aligns with global reporting standards like GRI and

TCFD, requiring the top 1,000 companies by market capitalization to report on ESG standards. Task Force on Climate-Related Financial Disclosures (TCFD) reporting is now compulsory in the EU and UK. As of now, IFRS Foundation has taken over monitoring the progress of companies' climate-related disclosures. [b]

To address the challenges and opportunities in ESG investing, the GSIA report underscores the need for greater global alignment through initiatives like the *Sustainable Finance Regulatory Convergence Taskforce.* It also commends the work of key organizations such as the *International Sustainability Standards Board (ISSB), the European Sustainability Reporting Standards (ESRS), the International Organization of Securities Commissions (IOSCO), the Network for Greening the Financial System (NGFS),* and GFANZ. The emergence of sustainable accountability standards has greatly enhanced the acceptability of sustainability reporting by companies. ISSB owns the Sustainability Accounting Standards Board (SASB) and recently developed IFRS S1 and S2 standards.

We don't realize the role of ESG factors in our lives, from our well-being to investment and portfolio management. Understanding global sustainable development is crucial to making a meaningful difference in our world and our lives.

Chapter 1

The Story Begins

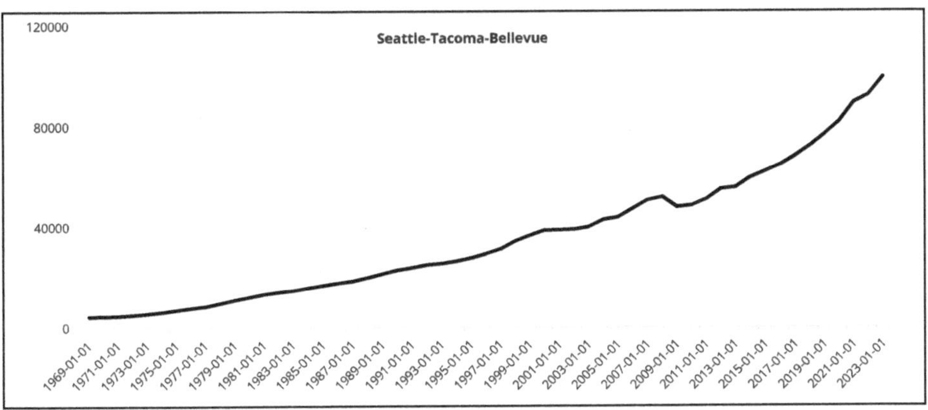

Per Capita Personal Income in Seattle-Tacoma-Bellevue

Data: U.S. Bureau of Economic Analysis, Per Capita Personal Income in Seattle-Tacoma-Bellevue, WA (MSA) [SEAT653PCPI], retrieved from FRED, Federal Reserve Bank of St. Louis; https://fred.stlouisfed.org/series/SEAT653PCPI, February 20, 2025. Data frequency is annual, Dollars, Not Seasonally Adjusted. Chart Author.

I am eagerly waiting for the leading social impact-driven event in Seattle to begin. It is misty outside, which is typical of the climate in Seattle. Seattle, the commercial hub of Washington state, is one of the wealthiest cities in America, with a median household income of $92,113 (as of 2022, Seattle-Tacoma-Bellevue).[a] Seattle is rated as one of the most affluent and educated cities in the US. Seattle is the hub of business activity in the state, and Olympia is the capital. Seattle and its suburbs are known for their vibrant culture and natural beauty. Washington has it all, with splendid biodiversity. An American powerhouse, Washington state is the headquarters of **Starbucks, Expedia, and Microsoft**. The state has one of America's better higher education systems, a key driver of its thriving high-tech society. Washington is known for its inclination toward fitness and well-being. Seattle, with an active lifestyle and wondrous landscape, is one of the best cities in America. Built like a typical American city, Seattle and its surroundings house some of the most historic and creative cultural places. The region is known for its globally iconic sites, such as the famous Space Needle, Chihuly Garden and Glass, Museum of Pop Culture, Ballard Locks, and world-class hiking trails. Birthplace of grunge music, the city is home to the late Kurt Cobain of Nirvana fame and the rock band Pearl Jam. Seattle houses the Museum of Pop Culture with its significant Jimi Hendrix exhibit.

Seattle is surrounded by magnificent places like Kirkland and Issaquah, which have stunning landscapes, and a city with high-tech and architectural marvels, Bellevue, which houses the headquarters of global technology companies like T-Mobile. Redmond, another town close to Seattle, houses Microsoft and scenic hiking trails. The University of Washington, based in Seattle, is highly regarded (Bruce Lee attended the university and is an alumnus of the university).

Enter Kish

It had been a tough week for me. My startup, a social impact-driven edtech startup, is struggling to increase its paid subscribers. My educated parents encouraged top-notch learning for personal and professional growth. I graduated with a master's degree from a leading US university and took a consulting job. I grew up watching Hollywood movies and listening to Western music, becoming well-tuned to American culture. America, a dream destination, became a cornerstone of human achievement. I love the American people, their way of life, and their cities. The unique blend of nature, art, history, and architecture in American cities is vitalizing and refreshing. With considerable work experience in India and after a brief consulting stint, I started my venture. During this time, I met the love of my life. Just like in movies. First 2015. It is a landmark year for the sustainable sector.

2015 – A Landmark Year in the Global Development Sector

2015 and early 2016 marked a landmark period for the global development sector. On January 1, 2016, the United Nations officially launched its 17 Sustainable Development Goals (SDGs), which outlined a comprehensive set of social, economic, governance, and environmental objectives to be achieved by 2030. These SDGs were adopted in September 2015 at the United Nations Sustainable Development Summit held in New York, but came into effect in 2016. 2015 also witnessed the adoption of the Paris Agreement, a pivotal milestone in climate action, and the **Addis Ababa Action Agenda (AAAA)**, which spearheaded social financing innovation. Additionally, the **Task Force on Climate-related Financial Disclosures (TCFD)** was established in 2015, although its recommendations were released afterward. This year also saw the launch of the **"Green Bond Endorsed Project Catalogue"** in China—the first taxonomy for green bonds aimed at providing better guidelines for sustainable investments.

Selected Key Milestones in Climate Action & Sustainable Finance Sector

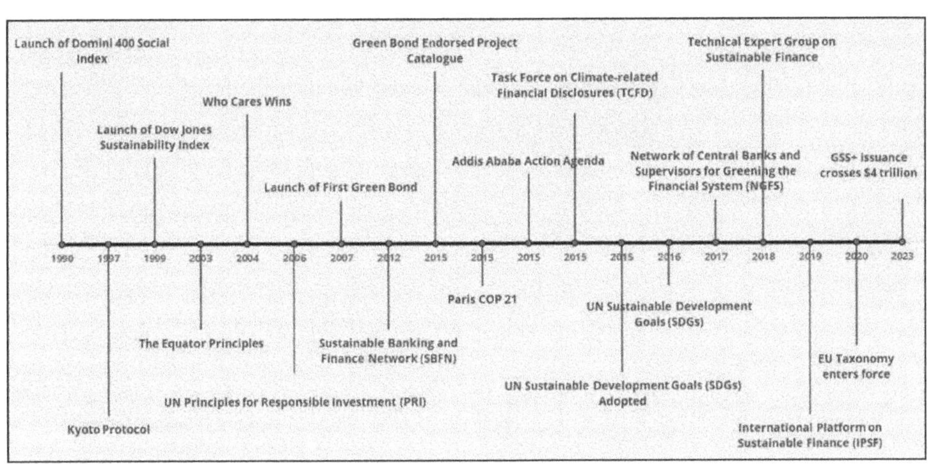

Selected Key Milestones in Climate Action and Sustainable Finance Sectors, Chart Author.

In **2015**, the **Addis Ababa Action Agenda (AAAA)** meeting set the framework for incorporating financial innovation through various financial instruments to enhance private capital via public-private partnerships. The **Addis Ababa Action Agenda (AAAA)** is a game-changer in sustainable finance. The event bolstered the role of public sector actors, especially *multilateral development banks (MDBs)* like the **World Bank, the IMF, and the European Investment Bank**. A key multilateral within the social financing domain is the **International Finance Corporation (IFC)**. One approach is to attract private capital through blended finance instruments, such as catalytic finance, targeting social, economic, and environmental outcomes that private actors might not typically fund. This would create a new financing source for the social sector, leveraging existing public sector funding. Another measure emphasized using data analytics and technology for projects and interventions for various social and environmental-driven outcomes. The meeting also set pathways to fortify domestic economies through fiscal and taxation prudence, reinforce the commitment of advanced economies toward concessional funds for less developed and emerging countries, and enhance international co-operation, among other objectives.

Meeting Caroline

An American, Caroline, is a triumph of humanity. A yoga instructor and an economics graduate, Caroline dazzled everyone with her *beauty, charisma,* and *intellect.* Our paths crossed during my master's program at a prestigious American university. The first yoga class where I met her remains etched in my memory—a surreal encounter. Caroline is the epitome of a yoga instructor; her graceful poses and gentle guidance are almost otherworldly. Her presence is transformative, turning that initial session into a dreamlike experience. Despite my grueling academic schedule, I eagerly attended every class she taught. Under her expert tutelage, my physical fitness flourished, making me more flexible and complementing my gym regimen perfectly. We kept running into each other at various social events, including a wedding and, coincidentally, a funeral, which reminded me of a romantic comedy plot, **"Four Weddings and A Funeral"**. One thing led to another, and I fell hopelessly in love with her. Caroline's stunning beauty and passion for life that grew without bounds attracted me to her. With her southern roots in America, Caroline embodied a unique blend of spirituality that transcended her Christian upbringing.

Her Catholic father and Jewish mother, a British immigrant, had cultivated a loving family environment that welcomed me warmly during our visits to New Orleans, Louisiana, for Thanksgiving and Christmas. Those deep blue eyes of hers could make me forget all worldly concerns. She playfully called me "Kish," a nickname that stuck. Our connection deepened as we discovered shared passions for *economics, arts, mindfulness, fitness,* and *social good.* We were outdoors people; we frequently visited the gym together, and, on her motivation, I started power training routines. Road trips across America, hiking, camping, and the theater are regular features for both of us. With her striking white complexion and red hair, Caroline exuded vitality and empathy. Her contagious smile showcased a childlike innocence about her, a quality that rubbed off on me. The **United Nations** is pushing the seventeen Sustainable Development Goals, a set of goals that loosely inspired my work. We both loved to discuss how these sustainable development goals facilitate social change and good. Our particular interest is the intersection of finance, economics, and the international development sector. The World Bank Group drove some of the best social financing instruments to drive private capital to enhance social outcomes, alleviate poverty, and bring about defining change within the social sector. As our relationship blossomed, Caroline became my pillar of support, encouraging me to pursue my dream of launching a social impact venture. Her work as an ESG analyst at asset management kept her busy and happy. Caroline is a mainstay at her company and is well-liked by her supervisors and peers. We periodically discussed the latest financial and future trends within the ESG sector. Her enthusiasm for ESG investing is contagious and understandable. No doubt, the rise in ESG awareness is translating into ESG investing.

Multilaterals, especially IFC, a member of **The World Bank Group**, use innovative social financing instruments to drive private capital to target projects and interventions that achieve social and environmental outcomes. The difference between these new financial mechanisms and ubiquitous grant-based funding is that they aim for long-term change by making outcomes sustainable through performance-based incentives and results. The **United Nations** pursues the seventeen **Sustainable Development Goals (SDGs)**, which loosely inspired my work. These UN goals are objective-driven, with the aim to standardize and quantify **Environmental, Social, and Governance (ESG)** outcomes. Popularly known as ESG, these issues have become mainstream over the years. From the first **World Climate Conference** held in 1979 to the formation of the **IPCC** in 1988, social and climate action has become of pivotal importance. The proliferation of technology, advancement of development economics through evidence-based statistical techniques, empowerment of the youth, and the prominent role played by activists have led various global organizations to take serious action on ESG factors, especially climate. Global warming has become a central tenet among many people globally, with its adverse impacts clearly visible. From heat waves that devastate nature and kill many, leading to a loss of biodiversity, to the increase in global temperatures, climate action is pivotal for universal well-being. Global warming not only impacts environmental issues, including biodiversity, but also has deep socio-economic implications. Heat waves and rising global temperatures have led to an increase in deaths, inequities, and migration. Although land use is the primary reason for the loss of biodiversity, climate change is one of the biggest causes of altering biodiversity. For example, peatlands like swamps and marshes constitute only 3 percent of the world's land but work as superlative carbon sink powerhouses. Sadly, climate change affects marginalized and less privileged societies the most. Extreme poverty and migration of marginalized communities are on the rise. The United Nations had to act, and it did through a series of initiatives. Two events to remember are the **Kyoto Protocol** and the **Paris Agreement**.

Rise of ESG

The market size of sustainable investing must exceed $32 trillion, as many key regions are not part of the analysis in the GSIA report. With the size of the global asset management sector expanding globally, it is not surprising that investment products feature ESG as a theme. We were both passionate about ESG and investing, making these topics a significant focus of my work. Our discussion led to an understanding of the impact of ESG ratings on the valuation of companies. Caroline, a researcher at heart, started discussing various findings on the positive impact of better ESG ratings on company valuations.

"Kish, you know I've read various research reports, and there's a positive correlation between the two."

"Sure, my love, share your research with me. I'm interested."

"Well, I'm still reading reports on the impact of ESG on various financial measures. The research is usually done using regression analysis," Caroline mentioned.

Our discussion turned to regression analysis.

A Brief About Regression Analysis

Regression analysis is a statistical technique used to find relationships between variables. It is commonly used in econometrics to quantify these relationships. Regression is one of the techniques used in econometrics. In a simple linear regression, only one independent variable (a regressor or predictor variable) and one dependent variable. In multivariate analysis, there are multiple independent variables. Here is a simple estimated regression equation.

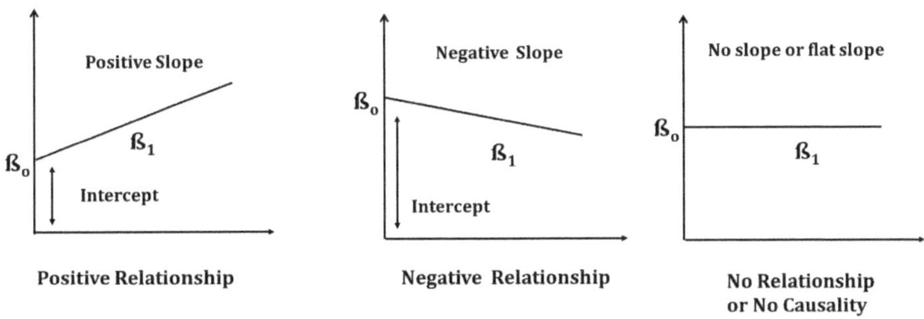

A simple estimated regression equation; Chart Author

X is the independent variable, or Regressor Variable, or Predictor Variable. Y is the dependent variable. β_0 is the intercept, β_1 is the slope of the equation. Regression helps approximate the functional relationship between variables. The error term represents the difference between observed values and the regression line.

Multivariate analysis is increasingly used in the development sector to evaluate the impact of interventions. Regression analysis helps understand the marginal change in the dependent variable for a unit change in the independent variable(s), keeping other factors constant. However, it does not establish causality between dependent and independent variables.

Example of Simple Regression Types

Chart: Author

Caroline continued discussing the origins of ESG within the investment management sector.

MSCI KLD Domini 400 Social Index

ESG investing has come a long way since the launch of **MSCI KLD Domini 400 Social Index,** she said, explaining in detail about the index. **(KLD 400 Social Index** was **created by KLD Research & Analytics** and is **now maintained by MSCI**). A cornerstone for the intersection of *Environmental, Social, and Governance* and financial markets. 1990 is the year when sustainable investing got an excellent thrust. It's the year **Environmental, Social and Governance (ESG)** got a major boost in the financial markets. This would be the first step in the transformative journey of sustainable finance. In May 1990, **KLD Domini 400 Social Index** was listed. This is the first socially responsible index in the world. The index consists of the largest 400 US companies by market capitalization with outstanding Environmental, Social, and Governance (ESG) ratings.

True, even the share of ESG in Smart Beta has increased.

Caroline is a champion of motivation. Despite the constraints of student loans and limited capital, her unwavering faith in me fueled my determination. My venture's dual focus on social and financial returns posed fundraising challenges. This led me to explore the growing realm of impact investing—a sector that had burgeoned over the past decade, supporting startups driving sustainable societal change through innovative solutions. Caroline's influence on my life and career has been profound. Her encouragement has been the cornerstone of my journey, enabling me to navigate the complex landscape of social entrepreneurship with confidence and purpose. Her encouragement encouraged me to attend this global compact event to get a better perspective by meeting various actors within the sustainable development ecosystem.

Adriana and Social Impact

I came out of my thoughts when I heard Adriana call out my name. I recalled my most recent discussion with Caroline. Adriana is doing wonderful work in a for-profit social impact-driven healthcare organization. Her organization aids less privileged sections of society through affordable healthcare. Leveraging technology, the startup administers health check-ups, including various blood tests, at highly affordable prices. Dark-haired, tall, and voluptuous, Adriana is a bit of a stunner, standing at 5'8. During her college days, she briefly modeled; her love for science led her to pursue an undergraduate degree in engineering.

After working for a few years in a leading global engineering company in California, Adriana decided to work at the intersection of science, social impact, and public policy. Building on her ambition, Adriana completed her master's from a leading global policy school, intending to work in the public administration sector in her home country, Peru. However, she got a dream offer from a leading global consulting company to work in the social impact space and decided to stay in the US and work. Her job at the consulting firm gave Adriana the flexibility to work on projects globally, especially in South America, that she could not resist. However, after seven years, Adriana quit her job and joined as the head of a venture-backed startup. She frequently shuttled between Seattle and Washington DC for work. Her company is acquiring a crowdfunding company based in Bellevue that would give the startup a global footprint in the affordable healthcare sector. Amidst a Beta rollout of the crowdfunding product in Chile and Peru, Adriana had little time to socialize. We met after a couple of months, and we were looking forward to meeting impact investors, especially our friend Peter.

"Lovely meeting you, Adriana, it's been such a long time," I said. We hugged and exchanged pleasantries.

Soon, our conversation drifted to the adverse impact of climate change on emerging countries. We both agreed that despite positive steps, much needed to be done.

I started discussing the latest insights shared by IEA to understand the achievements in the green energy sector. Some of them are striking and noteworthy. Some of the steps taken by the EU and China are helping the growth of the renewable sector over the next few years. The US is also using various policies to boost the renewable sector, along with India, Brazil, and Mexico, to name a few among the emerging markets. The future projections are based on estimates and policy decisions that can change over time.

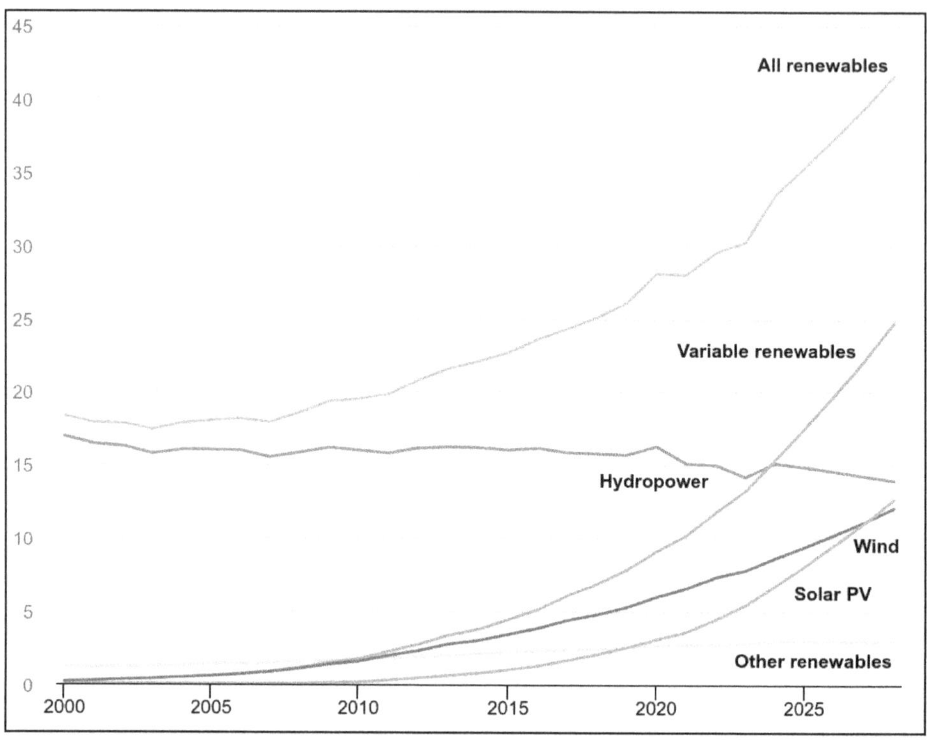

IEA (2024), *Renewables 2023*, IEA, Paris, https://www.iea.org/reports/renewables-2023, License: CC BY 4.0
Refer to the disclaimer in the annexure.

Notes: Electricity generation from wind and solar PV indicates potential generation including current curtailment rates. However, it does not project future curtailment of wind and solar PV, which may be significant in a few countries by 2028.

According to the **International Energy Agency (IEA),** global annual renewable capacity additions increased by almost 50 percent to nearly 510 gigawatts (GW) in 2023, the fastest growth rate in the past two decades. Of this capacity, China is likely to have almost 60 percent of the new renewable capacity expected to become operational globally by 2028. [b] The fact that renewable sources were the largest contributor to power in the EU in 2023, and more capital has been invested in the renewable sector compared to fossil fuels in 2023, is positive for the sustainable economy. Yet the world is far from achieving the UN sustainable development goals by 2030.

Adriana interrupted to mention that millions live on less than $2.15 daily. I nodded and said, "Ah, yes, very true." I elaborated. Based on data from the United Nations, we are still far from achieving the *Sustainable*

Development Goals (SDGs) by 2023. Only a tiny fraction of the targets are expected to be met. Challenges such as lack of political will, data limitations, and the debt burden in low- and emerging economies have made achieving the stated UN development goals difficult. In recent years, various stakeholders in the development sector have taken steps to innovate financing mechanisms for socio-economic interventions. However, much more needs to be done.

> We were interrupted by another acquaintance. Brad is pursuing a bachelor's in public policy and working as an intern with my company. A smart and sharp kid, Brad aims to work at a development financial institution or other leading actors like impact investors within the development sector.
>
> "Great to meet both of you, Kish and Adriana. What's the discussion about?" I explained our chat about the progress of SDGs. "Cool. Isn't the Paris Agreement a game-changer?" Brad asked. Both Adriana and I nodded.

Climate change was a significant impetus during the COP21 event in Paris, France. Popularly known as the **Paris Agreement**, it set the pathways of work in climate action among countries. The Paris Agreement is a more considerable success than the Kyoto Protocol. Held in 1997, the **Kyoto Protocol** is another significant milestone within the climate change narrative. The **Kyoto Protocol** and the **Paris Agreement** are game changers in defining the way forward within the sustainable development sector. I suggested we know more about greenhouse gases before exploring climate change. I let Adriana talk about various climate change initiatives. However, I shared my analysis before Adriana spoke on climate change.

Greenhouse Gases (GHGs)

The greenhouse gases (GHGs) are composed of **carbon dioxide, Nitrous Oxide (N_2O), Methane (CH_4), Fluorinated Gases (F-gases - Hydrofluorocarbons (HFCs), Perfluorocarbons (PFCs),** and Sulfur hexafluoride (SF6)), and **Water Vapor.** Water vapor does not directly contribute to human-caused greenhouse gas emissions, but enhances the impact of other greenhouse gases. Carbon dioxide is by far the most ubiquitous greenhouse gas. Although it's less potent than other gases, its impact on our environment is long-lasting, as its atmospheric lifetime is much longer than that of many other greenhouse gases.

> **Net Zero** is an important concept that is used often today. For example, EU wants to be net zero by 2050. Net Zero is the difference between carbon emissions emitted and the amount of greenhouse gas removed from the atmosphere. Net zero pertains to a geography example a country or region.

Greenhouse gases are often expressed in carbon dioxide equivalent (CO_2e) or (CO_2eq) as all gases are converted to equivalent units of carbon dioxide based on their global warming potential. It's not that carbon dioxide is unimportant. CO_2 helps to warm the climate and make it more habitable. Otherwise, our planet would be too cold to live on. However, since the dawn of the industrial age, the rise in greenhouse gases has been unprecedented. The global temperatures have been rising.

I added an interesting fact and analysis that both Adriana and Brad would love to hear.

Roaring 60s and Rise in GHGs

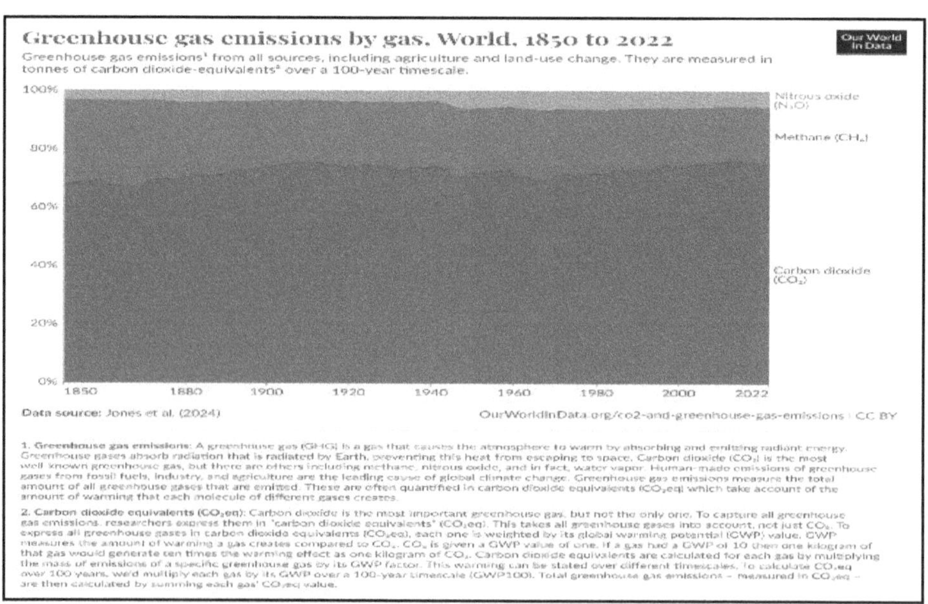

After World War II, infrastructure rebuilding started in Europe and the US. Under the **Marshall Plan (1948-1952),** Americans provided economic aid to Europeans to rebuild their infrastructure. In 1956, President Eisenhower initiated one of the biggest infrastructure projects in history with the **Interstate Highway System.** The 50s, 60s, and 70s were the era of building roads, bridges, dams, and much of the infrastructure in the US. With excellent transportation came automobiles. This period is also considered a period of business and economic expansion. Technology grew by leaps and bounds; man landed on the moon. Humans were on a high. Rock 'n' Roll was the thing. Elvis Presley and the Beatles became global brands. With music came drugs and substance abuse, especially psychedelic drugs. And the world got more prosperous. This economic growth led to wage growth and new avenues to grow your talent. This led to the birth of the middle class. This time saw a boom in traveling with growth in the automobile sector. Brands emerged with cars driven by *speed, style, and looks.* A rise in automobiles, especially passenger vehicles, and the dream American family and European resurgence gave rise to an increase in greenhouse emissions unlike anything seen before. Life was easier for many with the support of free speech backed by a strong constitution. The increase in economic growth and the level of technology led to an unprecedented rise in air pollution and greenhouse gas emissions.

Below observed trends in total greenhouse gas concentration levels between 1860 and 2021, considering all greenhouse gases and other forcing agents (including aerosols) and percent change over the previous period. The data recorded over a five-year interval starting from 1860 until 2020.

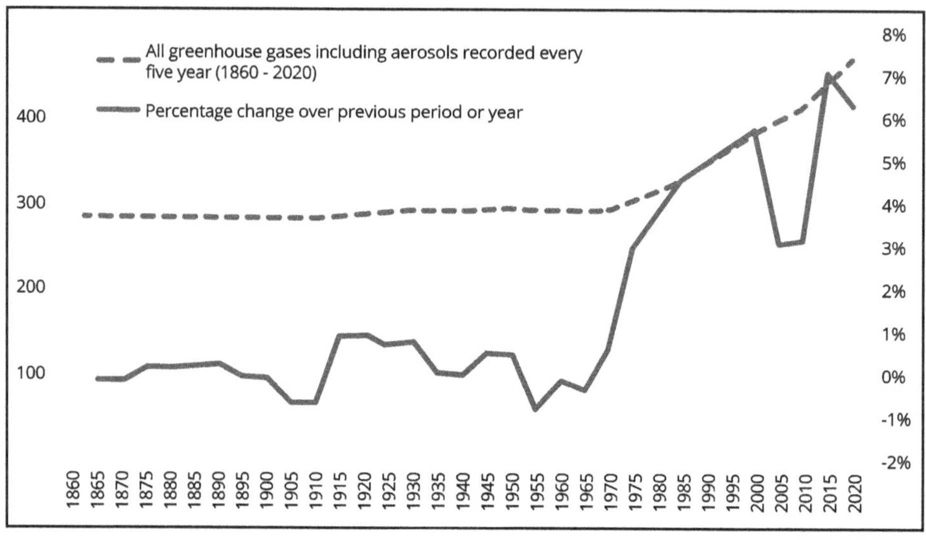

Data Source: EEA.Europa.eu; Chart and Analysis Author

The above chart shows that the percentage increase in greenhouse gas concentration has been steep since 1965. The maximum percentage increase over the previous period occurred between 2010 and 2015, followed by the period between 2015 and 2020. Averaging out the percentage increase over the previous periods, the average percentage increase between 1965 and 2020 is 3.97 percent, compared to 0.15 percent between 1865 and 1960. There is a significant relationship between the increase in the concentration of greenhouse gases and other forcing agents and urbanization, which began in what are now advanced nations and later continued in emerging markets, keeping other factors constant. A consistent and significant increase in percentage increments every five years between 1990 and 2020.

Urban Population (% of Total Population)

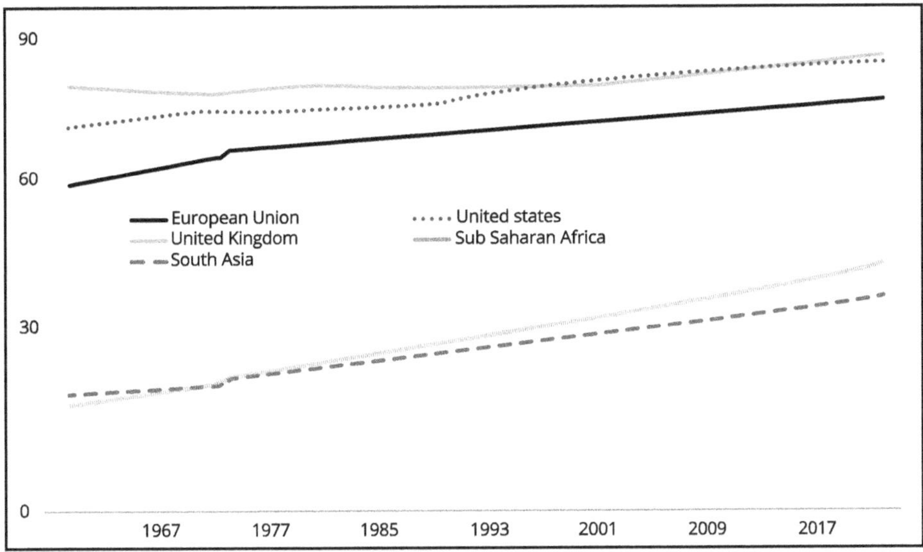

About the data: Urban population refers to people living in urban areas as defined by national statistical offices. The data is collected and smoothed by the United Nations Population Division. World Development Indicators. Data downloaded from the World Bank Link- *https://data.worldbank.org/indicator/SP.URB.TOTL.IN.ZS*; Chart Author

However, many countries face the growing challenge of increasing dependency ratios, a trend observed in several advanced economies. This shift presents structural economic problems, burdening the working population to sustain economic development. Additionally, it pressures asset managers, particularly pension funds, to focus on risk mitigation while simultaneously delivering alpha on their assets under management. Today, ESG is emerging as a critical driver, forming a key part of the **double materiality** concept—i.e., addressing both financial returns and societal impact.

Age dependency ratio (% of working-age population)

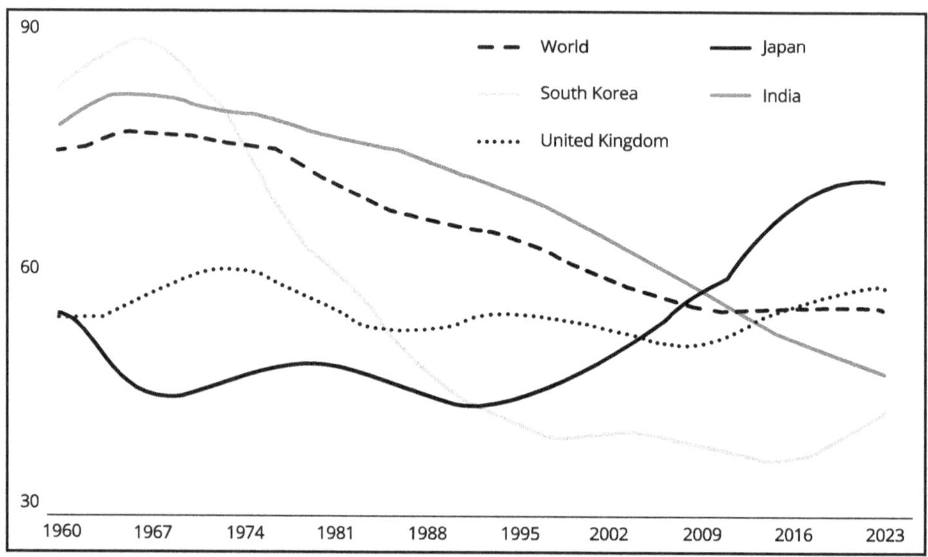

About the Data: Age dependency ratio is the ratio of dependents—people younger than 15 or older than 64—to the working-age population—those aged 15-64. Data are shown as the proportion of dependents per 100 working-age population. World Bank staff estimates are based on age distributions of the United Nations Population Division's World Population Prospects: 2022 Revision. Data downloaded from the World Bank Link - https://data.worldbank.org/indicator/SP.POP.DPND; Chart Author.

Peter Walks In

When I finished, there was a stunned silence. Adriana and Brad tried to fathom the depth of my insightful articulation of the topic. Amidst my eloquent take on emissions, Peter joined us. Peter, the founder of an impact investment company, is a dear friend of Adriana and me. Peter said, "Bravo, well done!"

I introduced Brad to Peter, having already mentioned how Brad could be an asset to his organization. Peter said he would look into it, as they had plans to hire an analyst at their new office in Chicago. I nudged Adriana to discuss climate initiatives.

"Adriana began explaining animatedly."

"Ok, now on the two key initiatives within the climate change sector," mentioned Adriana.

Kyoto Protocol

Knowing more about the UN Climate Change is essential to understanding the Kyoto Protocol. The United Nations Framework Convention on Climate Change came into effect in 1994 to stabilize greenhouse gas concentrations in the atmosphere at a level that would prevent dangerous anthropogenic (human-induced) interference with the climate system. The UN Climate Change has 198 members and is the parent treaty of the 1997 Kyoto Protocol and the 2015 Paris Agreement. The convention organizes the world-famous Conference of Parties (COP) annually, the world's largest United Nations conference. The Conference of the Parties means the Conference of the Parties to the Convention. The convention refers to the United Nations Framework Convention on Climate Change, adopted in New York on 9 May 1992.

The work done by the **Montreal Protocol** to bind countries together to phase out chlorofluorocarbons (CFCs) that deplete the ozone layer is much lauded. During the 1990s, there was an emerging scientific consensus about the anthropogenic nature of climate change. Later, the *IPCC's Fourth Assessment Report (2007)* presented more apparent evidence linking human activities to global warming. The UN Climate Change led to the formation of investment funds for climate solutions through grants and loans. There is a particular focus on climate adaptation to build climate resilience projects. This is the first serious attempt to hold developed countries responsible and make a collective action plan to invest in developing countries with the aim of emissions mitigation or adaptation through the participation of non-state actors. The **Kyoto Protocol** turned out to be a trailblazer for climate change initiatives. The convention led many developed countries to group on a platform for addressing positive climate change actions. The central tenet was to limit and mitigate emissions, a process quantified through commitments. Although the protocol was a game-changer in terms of its objective, it did not turn out to be a significant success. The ratification took some time, and the US withdrew support before ratification as China and India were not part of the agreement. The exception given to emerging countries is the extension of the **UN Climate Change principle, "common but differentiated responsibilities and respective capabilities"**.

Therefore, the major signatories to the event were industrialized economies listed in Annex I, which listed countries that were part of the OECD bloc and those that were transitioning to a market economy. Over the next decade, China would undergo unprecedented nation-building, leading to large-scale urbanization and the building of infrastructure projects.

> I added to the conversation how various market-based mechanisms led to the formation of carbon markets. I will not go in-depth about carbon markets, but will discuss the various initiatives in this sector here.
>
> Adriana clapped. "Sure, I would love to know your analysis," Peter nodded. "I enunciated."

The protocol boosted global clean technologies, including in the US, emphasizing sectors not covered by the Montreal Protocol. At the same time, it provided incentives for developed countries to help developing countries in climate mitigation and adaptation activities. One prominent thought leadership feature is the introduction of market-based mechanisms. This led to the foundation for the formation of carbon markets. The initiative proposed the establishment of **International Emissions Trading** for carbon pricing with *two project-driven mechanisms* - the **Clean Development Mechanism** and **Joint Implementation**. The Clean Development Mechanism is focused on developing countries, wherein developed countries can invest in projects that lead to the mitigation of carbon emissions. These projects that lead to a reduction in greenhouse emissions have salable **Certified Emission Reduction credits (CERs)**, each equal to one ton of CO_2. These can be used to meet Kyoto targets by selling and trading certificates among industrialized nations. This feature enhances the use of these instruments for investing capital in less developed countries. This landmark improvisation is a significant feature of carbon markets. Major regions, including EU ETS, have this feature, which will be discussed at length.

Mechanisms and Initiatives for Building the Carbon Market

Brad asked, "What about the impact of the Kyoto Protocol on environmental and economic effectiveness?"

I mentioned that there is a lot of debate on that, though it is agreed that the Kyoto Protocol produced many forward-looking initiatives.

"True, but I can reference research I've read," said Peter.

"Sure, Peter, we would love to hear about it."

How much did the Kyoto Protocol change the world?

According to *"environmental and Economic Effectiveness of the Kyoto Protocol by Yoomi KimID, Katsuya Tanaka, Shunji Matsuoka,"*, the first analysis on both environmental and economic effectiveness, the authors use two techniques in statistical analysis: difference-in-differences and propensity score matching methods for impact assessment. The research includes country-wise panel data from 1997 to 2008 and from 2005 to 2008. Using advanced statistical methods, the study found the impact of the Kyoto Protocol on Annex 1 countries concerning economic growth, measuring the GDP of the parties involved and environmental conditions, using the reduction of CO_2 as a measure. To understand this research report, we first need to introduce the term "counterfactual." A counterfactual is a hypothetical "what if" scenario that explores what would have happened if a specific event or condition had occurred differently from what actually happened.

The research uses **gross domestic product (GDP), population, CO_2 levels, and factors of production—capital, labor, and human capital** as variables to consider various countries' socio-economic and environmental conditions. This research uses panel data from 209 countries from 1997 to 2008. The Annex I members signed the treaty in 1997, which came into effect in 2005. Two models were employed for environmental and economic impact assessment using logarithmic regression. CO_2 is the dependent variable for the environmental model, while GDP is the dependent variable for the economic model. The base years are 1997 and 2005, while the target year is 2008.

The counterfactual concept is widely used to measure the impact of interventions in the development sector. This concept was made popular by the medical industry, specifically to understand the effect of medicines during clinical trials using randomized controlled trials. In such trials, two groups are randomly chosen: one receives the intervention (known as the **Experimental Group**), in this case, the medication; the other group, known as the **Control Group**, usually receives a placebo. To avoid biases, it is best to conduct a **double-blind test**, where neither the participants nor the researchers are aware of which group is experimental or control. The **Control Group is called the counterfactual group** as it does not receive the intervention. The difference in outcomes between the two groups is the **measure of impact**. The evaluation is conducted over time, and for better results, no one is aware of which group receives the intervention and which receives the placebo.

The above process is used to simplify the results and methodology employed. Although no randomized controlled trial was established, as there are two counterparts – one with the Protocol intervention and the other without- it's possible to measure the difference in the **marginal damage cost of carbon emissions**. In this case, the reduction in emissions by participants is long-term, keeping other factors constant. The research uses various statistical measures to remove selection bias. In the context of the Kyoto Protocol, the intervention is the protocol itself. The Annex I parties represent the experimental group, given the intervention of mitigation targets and limits on greenhouse gas emissions. The non-Annex I parties serve as the control or counterfactual group without obligations to reduce emissions. The difference in emissions reduction between these two groups could be considered a measure of the Protocol's **impact on environmental and economic effectiveness**.

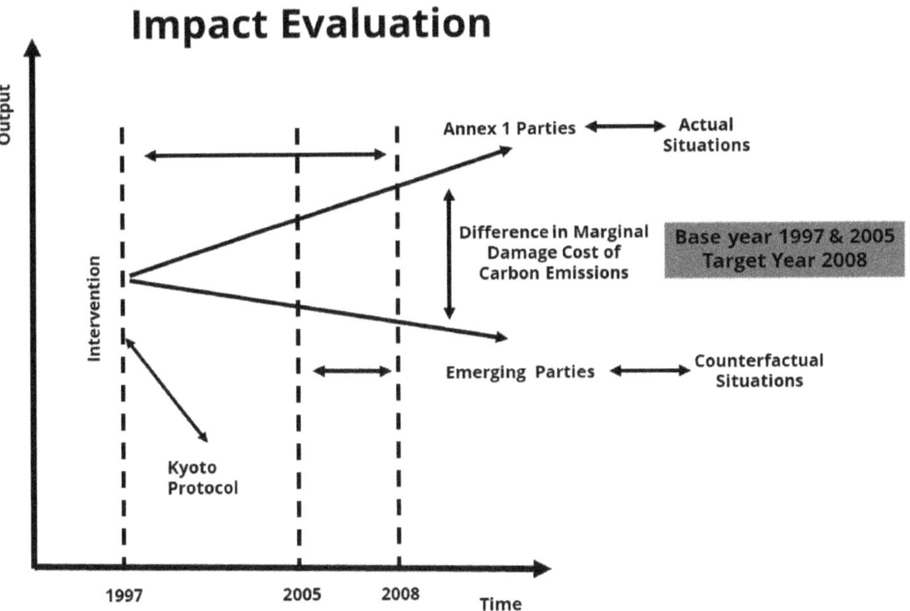

Image Author

> Impact Evaluation = Marginal Damage Cost of Carbon Emissions at time t+1 – Marginal Damage Cost of Carbon Emissions at time t+0

> Impact Evaluation = Marginal Damage Cost of Carbon Emissions at time t+2 – Marginal Damage Cost of Carbon Emissions at time t+1

The findings show that emissions reduced between 2005 and 2008 for Annex I parties, suggesting that lowering emissions takes time, considering the ratification process. The results show that a rise in GDP is associated with a rise in emissions. The multivariate regression analysis shows a relationship between increased GDP and emissions. *For a one percent increase in GDP, there is a one percent increase in emissions, keeping other factors the same for multivariate analysis.* The findings also showed that economic performance was reduced by approximately 7 percent between 2005 and *2008 for Annex I* countries. The results showcase that Annex I parties had a positive impact on emissions mitigation but a negative impact on economic growth during the period covered in the report. The authors recommend a more nuanced and balanced approach toward environment and economic growth for sustainable development, especially for developing countries. The report's authors noted the effect of external shocks on carbon emissions reduction and a trade-off between economic growth and emissions reduction over the long term due to technological advancement and structural changes within the economy. The report cites a significant decrease in emissions from the former countries of the Soviet Union. However, there have been research studies that mention the use of less stringent methodologies for registering emissions, which makes the accuracy of reported reductions in emissions questionable.

Climate Watch Historical All Greenhouse Gas Emissions in MtCO2e

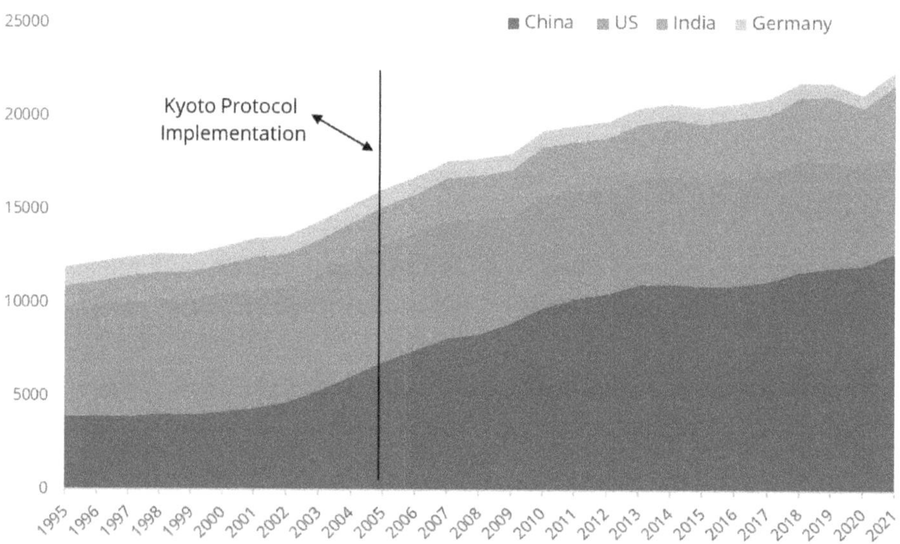

Data Source: Climate Watch; Greenhouse Gases including LUCF: Land Use-Change and Forestry. Climate Watch Historical GHG Emissions. 2022. Washington, DC: World Resources Institute. Available online at: *https://www.climatewatchdata.org/ghg-emissions*. Climate Watch Historical GHG Emissions data (previously published through CAIT Climate Data Explorer) are derived from several sources. FAO 2021, FAOSTAT Emissions Database. CO_2 Emissions from Fuel Combustion, OECD/IEA, 2021. As of March 2020, emissions from **the European Union (27)** for all years no longer include emissions from the United Kingdom on Climate Watch. **MtCO2e** is million metric tons of carbon dioxide equivalent. This is the standard measure used to measure greenhouse gas emissions.

COP 21 Paris Agreement

The primary aim of the Paris Agreement is to limit this increase in greenhouse gases through a multi-collaborative effort using actors at both the public and private levels. The COP 21 Paris Agreement enhanced the global impetus of coalescing various global actors toward climate action. The **COP 21, held in 2015 in Paris, France, turned out to be** a landmark event for climate change. 196 parties adopted the agreement; it came into force on 4 November 2016. The event marked the Paris Agreement, wherein a commitment was made to limit global temperature increase to well below 2°C above pre-industrial levels and to pursue efforts to limit the rise to 1.5°C by the end of the century. The meeting was a success as it developed a collaborative stance.

A bottom-up approach lets the member countries decide on their commitment to reduce greenhouse gas emissions through **Nationally Determined Contributions (NDCs).** While the Paris Agreement is legally binding, Nationally Determined Contributions (NDCs) are voluntary and vary by country. This limits the accountability of member countries, unlike the European Union. The European Union, however, has implemented a legally binding 'EU Climate Law' to reach net zero by 2050. The NDCs of many countries are not enough to impede the rise of greenhouse gas emissions; carbon emissions have been on the rise. Despite a resurgence in climate action activism, there has been only marginal performance improvement. Another positive side effect of the Paris Agreement is the impetus given to nature-based solutions. **Nature-based solutions** emerged during the first **International Union for Conservation of Nature (IUCN)** around 2009-2010. **UN Climate Action Summit** held in 2019 made nature-based solutions a force to reckon with. Nature-based Solutions are a cost-effective method of reducing global carbon emissions. Forest and ocean ecosystems are among the largest sequesters of carbon dioxide. Forests, peatlands, and mangroves are key to preserving biodiversity and must be nurtured and expanded in various capacities. Along with mangroves, peatlands play a significant role in the natural ecosystem as climate mitigation agents. The pandemic caused by COVID-19 has increased awareness of the dangers of zoonotic diseases. Preserving nature and biodiversity reduces the probability of the rise of zoonotic diseases, and nature-based solutions are one of the most optimal ways of reducing GHG emissions. Reducing Emissions from Deforestation and Forest

Degradation (REDD+) is one of the cheapest options for reducing carbon emissions. Nature-based solutions are increasingly being used for climate action, creating numerous jobs.

Forest area (% of land area)

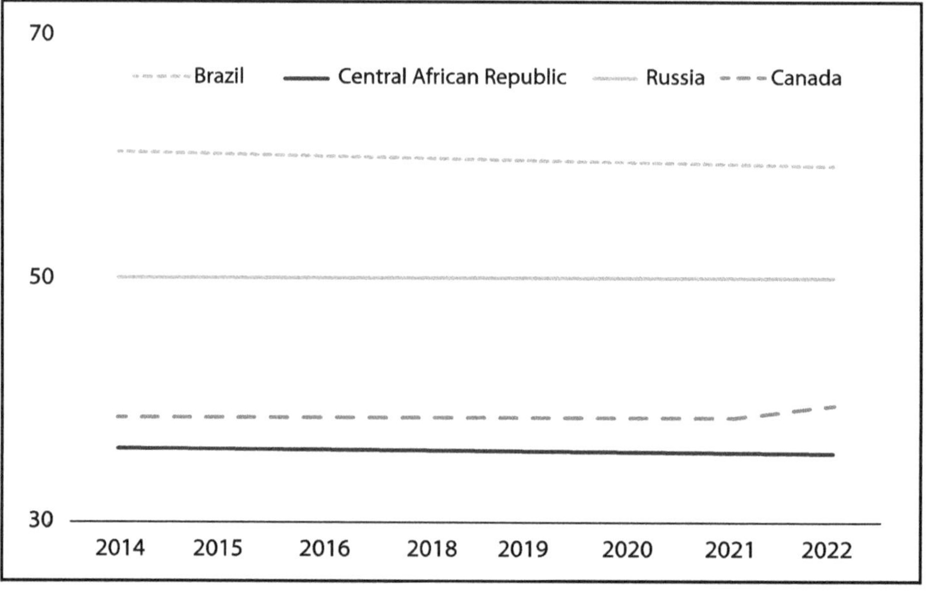

Data Source: Food and Agriculture Organization, electronic files and website. World Bank Group; Chart Author. Periodicity: annual, aggregation method: weighted average. Data can be downloaded from here: *https://data.worldbank.org/indicator/AG.LND.FRST.ZS*

Forest is determined both by the presence of trees and the absence of other predominant land uses. The trees should reach a minimum height of 5 meters in situ. Areas under reforestation that have not yet reached but are expected to reach a canopy cover of 10 percent and a tree height of 5 meters are included, as are temporarily unstocked areas, resulting from human intervention or natural causes, which are expected to regenerate. The Food and Agriculture Organization (FAO) provides detail information on forest cover, and adjusted estimates of forest cover. The survey uses a uniform definition of forest. Although FAO provides a breakdown of forest cover between natural forest and plantation for developing countries, forest data used to derive this indictor data does not reflect that breakdown. Total land area does not include inland water bodies such as major rivers and lakes. Variations from year to year may be due to updated or revised data rather than to change in area. The indictor is derived by dividing total area under forest of a country by country's total land area, and multiplying by 100. FAO has been collecting and analyzing data on forest area since 1946. This is done at intervals of 5-10 years as part of the Global Forest Resources Assessment (FRA). FAO reports data for 229 countries and territories; for the remaining 56 small island states and territories where no information is provided, a report is prepared by FAO using existing information and a literature search. The data are aggregated at sub-regional, regional and global levels by the FRA team at FAO, and estimates are produced by straight summation. The lag between the reference year and the actual production of data series as well as the frequency of data production varies between countries. Deforested areas do not include areas logged but intended for regeneration or areas degraded by fuelwood gathering, acid precipitation, or forest fires. Negative numbers indicate an increase in forest area. Data includes areas with bamboo and palms; forest roads, firebreaks and other small open areas; forest in national parks, nature reserves and other protected areas such as those of specific scientific, historical, cultural or spiritual interest; windbreaks, shelterbelts and corridors of trees with an area of more than 0.5 hectares and width of more than 20 meters; plantations primarily used for forestry or protective purposes, such as rubber-wood plantations and cork oak stands. Data excludes tree stands in agricultural production systems, such as fruit plantations and agroforestry systems. Forest area also excludes trees in urban parks and gardens. The proportion of forest area to total land area is calculated and changes in the proportion are computed to identify trends.

After Adriana finished her discourse, we all felt educated on many topics. We dispersed to the network. Following an initial address by the chapter head, a long discussion on social innovation with various thought leaders from the development industry is scheduled. The discussion involves people from multilateral development banks, impact investors, impact finance and advisory firms, and social impact consulting organizations.

This roundtable discussion is to last about two hours, followed by lunch. Post-lunch, multiple events are planned, featuring various actors from the development industry discussing their work globally. The key focus for their projects is **Latin America, Africa, and Asia**. I attended the event on implementing quality education in Nepal, while Adriana spoke about her work in Chile in the Health Tech session. Peter taught a master class on impact investment, discussing the enablers for successful and practical impact, both socially and financially. Brad left for work after lunch. I exchanged business cards with everyone I met, an excellent practice I developed for effective networking in the US. This approach makes it much easier to contact people and remember their names.

We would regroup - Adriana, Peter, and I during tea and continue our conversation.

Chapter 2

Understanding Asset Classes and Asset Managers

Peter: "Adriana, how was the session?"

Adriana: "Excellent! I spoke about crowdfunding," she went on to share in-depth about her session.

Impact Investors and Crowdfunding

Our discussion soon turned to the value added between technology and the development sector. Financial inclusion, education, nature-based solutions, and healthcare are our favorite themes to discuss. Adriana, vociferous and passionate about this topic, started discussing crowdfunding. Her discussion about affordable healthcare outlined her organization's strategy of using crowdfunding to raise funds for various projects in the healthcare sector. Crowdfunding is an avant-garde invention that operates at the intersection of philanthropy and technology. It has exponentially increased retail participation in philanthropic outreach with small ticket sizes of giving.

Kish, do you know about **Muhammad Yunus**?

Yes, I do. **Muhammad Yunus** practically invented micro-funding. He and C.K. Prahalad are two well-known names we use when articulating innovation for underserved communities.

I was gifted two books: **"The Fortune at the Bottom of the Pyramid"** by C.K. Prahalad and **"Clay Water Brick: Finding Inspiration from Entrepreneurs Who Do the Most with the Least"** by Jessica Jackley (with a foreword by Jeffrey Sachs). Jessica is one of the founders of Kiva, and her book contains an excellent collection of stories about social entrepreneurs.

Adriana mentioned **Muhammad Yunus** of **the Grameen Bank** fame, who spearheaded microfinance for marginalized entrepreneurs in Bangladesh. In microlending, small ticket-size loans are disbursed at variable rates that can be below- or above-market rates. The idea was successful in Bangladesh and gained popularity globally. Thought leaders like C.K. Prahalad made selling to the less affluent sections of society a sustainable business model. **"The Fortune at the Bottom of the Pyramid"** by C.K. Prahalad became a top management book. Listening to her talk, I remembered Kiva, an innovative peer-to-peer marketplace. I told them how Kiva reinvented the wheel using crowdfunding to enhance financial inclusion. Adriana agreed, and we started our conversation on Kiva.

Kiva

Sustainability, transparency and efficiency are at the core of our work, our mission and our financial model.

Kiva Marketplace

Taking a leaf from the explosive potential of microloans for funding marginalized business people and leveraging peer-to-peer technology, two Stanford alums, Jessica Jackley Flannery and Matt Flannery, pioneered a business model for raising micro-capital for aspiring entrepreneurs. Jessica, author of the book *Clay Water Brick*, is a Professor of the **Practice of Social Entrepreneurship** at **the Marshall School of Business at USC** and co-founder and General Partner at Untapped Capital. *Clay Water Brick* is a collection of stories on social innovation and entrepreneurship. These are inspirational stories of people who, despite hardship, succeed through their inventiveness and determination.

Kiva uses an innovative marketplace model. There is no interest rate on loans to entrepreneurs (but field partners might). The nonprofit has evolved into a major micro-funding platform globally and added more revenue streams to its initial offering. Peer-to-peer technology, made famous by **Napster**, cemented Kiva as the world's first online peer-to-peer microfinance marketplace.

Returning to my conversation with Adriana and Peter, I mentioned how impact investors make a difference in the development sector.

Many top impact investors like **Acumen, Omidyar Network,** and **Accion** are renowned within the social impact sector. But first, Peter's story.

Life was difficult; Peter's father worked in the automobile sector, and his mother, a nurse, doubled as a homemaker. With four siblings, life was challenging while growing up. His ancestors had emigrated from Scandinavia about a century ago. Standing tall at 6'5" and athletic, Peter gained prominence in sports. An injury during his teens forced him to transition from sprinting to American football, where he excelled as a quarterback. Excelling in both studies and sports, he earned a scholarship to a top-ranked business school, leveraging his football skills. He pursued a bachelor's degree in business and philosophy. This became a turning point for Peter. Not only did he lead his college to the finals in the football league, but he also developed a strong interest in business, particularly in valuation. Peter is remembered for his iconic touchdown, where he broke through the competitors' defense, running 20 yards for a touchdown before three defenders brought him down. His passion for business led him to pursue an MBA. Known as the "king of valuation," Peter chose a career in finance over becoming a professional footballer.

Married with two children, Peter found the certainty of the investment management sector more fulfilling after repeated injuries. After years in investment management, Peter and a couple of friends established an impact investing company focusing on fintech, life sciences, education, and clean tech. Peter raised $100 million in their first fundraising outreach and recently invested in four companies. Most investments are in life sciences, and Peter is considering investing in one of my friends' startups. Peter and I were introduced at a university event, where Peter addressed a small gathering of students and industry practitioners about the future of impact investing. We instantly connected, frequently discussing finance and fitness. Peter invited me a couple of times to barbecue with his family and requested that I become a godfather to his youngest son, which I happily obliged. Peter's wife worked in a leading global private equity firm. We often discussed how various asset classes and asset managers performed over time. Peter had started his career on the buy side of an investment banking investment management vertical. Involved in valuing companies for mergers and acquisitions, Peter had also looked at distressed companies. He quit to join a hedge fund with assets under management of $1 billion and rose to the position of Chief Investment Officer.

Impact Investing: Rise of Patient Capital

According to the 2024 figures from The **Global Impact Investing Network (GIIN)**, impact investing assets stood at $1.571 trillion worldwide, growing at a compound annual growth rate (CAGR) of 21 percent since 2019. The research covered 1,593 organizations, with the average investment portfolio exceeding the median. The average portfolio size is $986 million, compared to a median value of $42 million (outliers above two standard deviations were excluded from this analysis). For a sample size of 920 organizations, investment managers account for 59 percent of all impact investing organizations but rank second to pension funds in terms of their share of global impact assets under management. Pension funds stood second in the percentage of all impact investing organizations at 14 percent. Refer to the report for all analysis. A significant milestone for the industry, but compared to the size of capital markets that exceed $200 trillion (both equity and debt), the impact sector has a way to go. Compare this to the **World Bank (IBRD)** financing of projects through sustainable development and green bonds. As of FY 2023, there are $266.8 billion in bonds outstanding, with $42.2 billion in bonds issued. (World Bank, IBRD FY23 Impact Report)[a]

> **Impact investing** often includes **patient capital**, usually investing in for-profit companies and projects that solve complex problems within the development sector. Jacqueline Novogratz, founder of Acumen, popularized "patient capital." Patient Capital refers to the long-term horizon required for generating financial returns while creating social impact, particularly in the social and environmental sectors. Impact investors look for a balance between economic and social returns, funding social impact-driven initiatives that address market failures. In recent years, there has been a significant increase in the use of private capital to build solutions targeting underserved sections of society. One approach is through the development financial institutions and multilaterals, such as the IFC, that use leverage to enhance public funding, especially concessional financing, to support development sector interventions. The World Bank Group focuses on the sustainable development sector. It regularly issues sustainable development bonds wherein the proceeds of these debt securities, either bonds or notes, fund

developmental and environmental projects or interventions with quantifiable outcomes.

Another technique is funding organizations and projects that primarily serve the underserved sections of society. Rather than working solely with non-profits and relying on grant funding, the new approach is to build sustainable businesses and project structures that address solutions for those at the Bottom of the Pyramid or use disruption to be more cost-effective. Examples include *affordable healthcare, financial inclusion, quality education, and clean tech projects*. These initiatives plan to be self-sustaining once their revenue models are established. Many operate in clean tech, healthcare, fintech, and education sectors, often building technology platforms or products with longer gestation timelines. Since they primarily operate in less privileged sections of society, it takes time to become profitable. Impact investors are early-stage investors who fund initiatives with little revenue to show. However, in recent years, due to high inflation, the interest rates have climbed up, and the cost of funding has become more expensive; many impact investors prefer revenue-generating companies and projects before investing. Nonetheless, impact investors like Accion continue to fund very early-stage ideas.

Electronica Finance Ltd. and Green Finance Initiatives

Electronica Finance Ltd., part of the SRP Electronica Group, is a pioneering Pune-based non-banking financial company in green finance and microlending for small and medium-sized enterprises (SMEs). The company has raised capital from impact investors through a Green Masala Bond in partnership with the *Climate Fund Manager* and *responsAbility*. Under Shilpa Pophale's leadership, the company has emphasized the importance of the MSME sector, which contributes 40 percent of jobs in India. Small businesses play a crucial role globally. In the US, they have created two-thirds of all new jobs, pay high wages, and account for 98 percent of identified exporters, according to the Office of the US Trade Representative (USTR). Electronica Finance Ltd. has partnered with SIDBI and maintains non-performing assets below 2 percent through innovative risk management practices.

Masala and Green Masala Bonds

Masala bonds, similar to the dim sum bonds in China or bulldog bonds in the UK, are issued in foreign countries but denominated in the issuer's domestic currency. The IFC issued the first global Masala Bond in 2014, followed by a **Green Masala Bond** in 2015.[b] The proceeds from the Green Masala Bond were used by Yes Bank for renewable energy and energy efficiency projects in India, particularly in the solar and wind sectors. Green Masala Bonds are categorized as sustainable finance instruments due to their ***ESG (Environmental, Social, and Governance)*** factors. These bonds could have lower coupon rates compared to non-ESG bonds. They expose foreign investors to Indian currency, transferring currency fluctuation risks to investors. They could help reduce the **weighted average cost of capital** for issuers due to interest rate differentials between advanced and developing countries and improve ESG ratings for companies. Offshore bonds are part of the external bond markets. These bonds can be issued in either domestic or foreign currencies. **Eurodollar Bonds**, for example, are issued in foreign countries but denominated in U.S. dollars. Similarly, Euroyen bonds are issued in foreign countries using the Japanese yen. The first Euro bond in 1963 by **Autostrade** in Italy, a $15 million Eurodollar issue. Global bonds, such as those issued by the World Bank, are distributed across multiple countries simultaneously and underwritten by an international syndicate. In the onshore market, entities raise capital in domestic currency. For example, Yankee bonds in the US or Bulldog bonds.

Coming back to impact investors, let's discuss an example of a social impact-driven company based in Africa.

We were joined by **Xu Wenjun** (徐文俊**)**, whose name means "cultured and talented." Xu embodied all the qualities of his name. Born in *Beijing*, Xu graduated with top honors in engineering from a leading university in China. He won the Math Olympiad and pursued his Ph.D. in Materials Science from a leading university in the US. An expert in Wing Chun, Xu also practiced various forms of martial arts. He worked at prominent semiconductor firms before launching his startup in chip design. Xu's startup had recently received Series A funding. Invited to speak on the evolving semiconductor sector, Xu met all of us. I met him in one of the **Wing Chun** classes, and we have become friends over time. I knew Xu's French girlfriend **Élise** before I met Xu. Élise worked for a global development organization in the sustainable finance department. Élise is Caroline's dear friend, a batchmate from a leading US university. Both connect vehemently over the latest social financial innovations, cudgeling their minds with key financial innovation mechanisms.

We all greeted Xu. "Where is Élise? I haven't seen her in a while," I asked. Xu replied, "She is traveling. Now in Miami, launching a financially innovative structure." We discussed how Florida had risen recently as one of the most attractive destinations for investment management and entrepreneurship. I briefed Xu about our discussion, especially on the impact investing sector. Xu wanted to share his experience in dealing with venture capitalists. After an animated debate between Xu and Peter, we all decided to walk nearby for ice cream and shakes. Once we had ordered, we went back to our conversation.

"Adriana said, 'I have a few questions.'"

Adriana: What is **the weighted average cost of capital**?

Peter mentioned that a company can raise capital through equity and debt. He added that understanding the basics of fixed income, especially bonds, would be necessary. Sustainable finance increasingly deploys various kinds of bonds to fund social and climate outcomes. I agreed. However, it is better to have an overview of different asset classes before discussing debt instruments. I started a brief overview of asset classes.

Understanding Various Asset Classes in a Nutshell

Asset classes are divided into three main categories: **equity, fixed income (debt),** and **alternatives**. Special equity investments, such as warrants and options, are hybrid instruments. Valuing listed equities and fixed income securities is generally straightforward, but alternatives can be more challenging due to their often illiquid nature and non-normal return patterns. Listed equities are shares of companies traded on public stock exchanges globally. In contrast, unlisted equities represent ownership in private companies that have not offered their securities through an initial public offering (IPO). For listed equities, valuation methods often include the **discounted cash flow (DCF)** model, though there are other ways of valuing companies. This involves concepts such as cost of debt and equity, *weighted average cost of capital (WACC)*, and analysis of financial statements. These statements primarily consist of the balance sheet, income, and cash flow statement. These statements primarily consist of concepts incorporate the **Capital Asset Pricing Model (CAPM),** a single-factor model for determining a theoretically appropriate required rate of return.

Before I go ahead, which trade asset class is larger globally, equity or debt?

Xu chimed in – equity man. Adriana replied, "Absolutely.". Peter smiled as I explained that although I thought equity markets would be bigger, global debt markets are the biggest asset classes. Xu, an avid stock investor, seemed disappointed.

Market capitalisation of listed domestic companies (current US $) in $ trillion

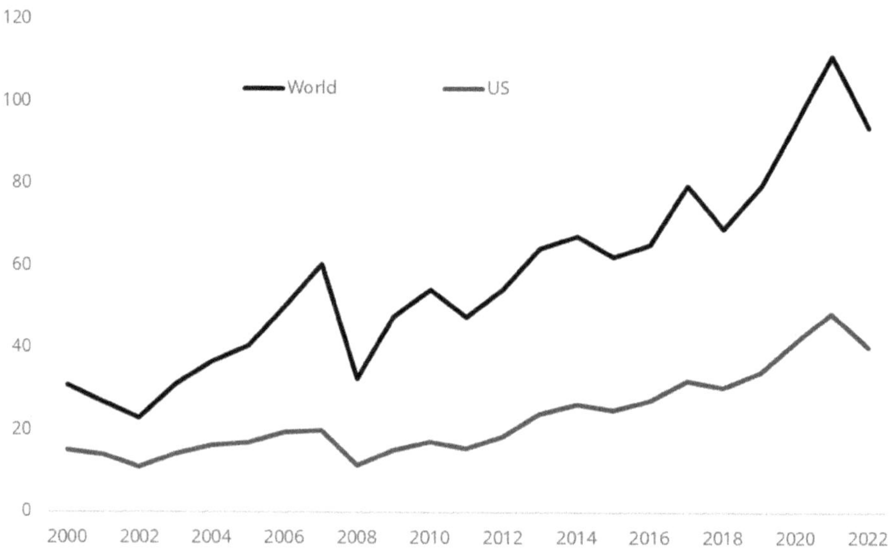

Data Source: World Federation of Exchanges database; World Bank Group. Link: *https://data.worldbank.org/indicator/CM.MKT.LCAP.CD*

Chart; Author. Market capitalization (also known as market value) is the share price multiplied by the number of shares outstanding (including their several classes) for listed domestic companies. Investment funds, unit trusts, and companies whose only business goal is to hold shares of other listed companies are excluded. Data is end-of-year values converted to U.S. dollars using corresponding year-end foreign exchange rates. Stocks traded, total value (current US $). Figure rounded off to two digits.

The chart above shares an excellent overview of globally traded stocks. The value of globally traded stocks stood at 93.69 trillion in 2022. The size of US traded stocks, the highest among all the countries, stood at $40.3 trillion for the same year, roughly less than half of the global size at 43.01 percent. This shows the depth of the traded equity and capital markets in the US.

What is WACC i.e. weighted average cost of capital?

Valuation using the discounted cash flow (DCF) method is based on two key parameters: expected future cash flows and the appropriate discount rate. The discount rate calculation is crucial, as it determines the present value of an asset by discounting future cash flows. Consider a firm with no debt. In this case, equity valuation involves discounting free cash flows to equity at the cost of equity. This is where the future projection of earnings (future cash flows) and the appropriate discount rate are important. Since the returns accrue only to equity holders, the cost of equity is the discount rate. However, if a firm has equity and debt, a different approach is used to calculate cash flows and the discount rate. The cost of debt has to be included. By considering both the cost of equity and debt, we arrive at the weighted average cost of capital (WACC). Herein, the future cash flows are discounted by WACC instead of the cost of equity to account for debt. The discount rate used is WACC, which represents the weighted average of the cost of equity and the cost of debt, based on their respective proportions in the firm's capital structure. Since debt has an associated cost, it must be factored into the discount rate calculation. Preferred stocks are hybrid securities, differing from common stocks, representing company ownership. Some preferred stocks are convertible and can be treated as equity.

Cost of Capital = Cost of equity (Proportion of equity used to fund business) + pretax cost of debt (1-tax rate) (Proportion of debt used to fund business)

Value of the firm = $\sum$CF to firm/ (1+WACC)^t

t = time periods; WACC= weighted average cost of capital, CF is cash flows.

This should be fine for now. I am keen to cover the basics of fixed income, which would connect the dots on our discussion of masala bonds.

Caroline had made a presentation on the basics of bonds for undergraduate students. I had helped her develop the presentation, which discussed some intermediate topics on fixed income with ease. It is derivative of an online course I had designed, but Caroline wanted to keep it simple and sweet. I encouraged her to teach a course in finance as a visiting faculty member, but she did not have the time. Caroline has had a meteoric rise within her firm, heading one of the verticals for ESG in the US. I shared a few points from the presentation I had designed; I begin with basics before graduating to various actors in the global fixed income sectors and types of bonds.

Basics of Bonds in a Nutshell

A bond is a debt instrument, typically secured, and a significant source of funds for corporations, especially in advanced countries like the US. In developing countries, loans still serve as corporations' primary funding source. The issuer of a bond is called a debtor or borrower. A plain vanilla bond has the following characteristics:

- **Fixed period of borrowing:** The bond is issued for a set duration.
- **Coupons or Interest Payments:** The interest amount on the face value is paid to the lender periodically.
- **Principal repayment:** The principal is repaid at the end of the tenure.
- **Interest rate:** The rate can be fixed or floating. In floating rate bonds, the coupon rate is linked to a reference rate, such as the prime lending rate or SOFR.
- **Coupon rate:** The nominal interest rate paid on the bond's par or face value.
- **Par value:** The principal amount of the bond.

Bonds have various maturities: this could vary.
- **Short-term:** 0 to 5 years.
- **Medium-term:** 5 to 12 years.
- **Long-term:** Over 12 years.

Bonds are a major source of debt funding, alongside bank loans, commercial paper, and lease agreements in the US. Countries issue sovereign bonds to raise capital for their spending needs. They are also a significant means for central and state governments to fund budget deficits and are an essential asset class for diversifying risk in investment portfolios.

➤ Peter interrupted. Now, tell me when the first US bond was offered.

Adriana guessed the Revolutionary War.

Yes, correct," Peter mentioned. Now, Kish, when and who issued the first modern government bond?

Fortunately, I knew the answer. I read about the Napoleonic Wars. The first government bond was issued by the Bank of England in 1693 to raise money to fund a war against France. Peter clapped, delighted to hear the answer.

I continued with an explanation of bonds, just briefly explaining the basics.

Major Actors in the Bond Market

1. **Governments (Sovereigns):** Issue treasury securities, which have short—to long-duration durations. The 10-year government security is the most liquid bond.
2. **Corporates:** Issue domestic and foreign bonds, including medium-term notes, structured notes, and commercial paper. These bonds are categorized as investment grade or non-investment grade (speculative/high yield/junk bonds). Corporate bonds are also known as the credit sector.
3. **Agencies:** Issue securities for development purposes, owned by the central/federal government or government-sponsored enterprises (GSEs) like Fannie Mae and Freddie Mac.
4. **Supranational:** Formed by two or more central banks, such as the World Bank, the IMF, the European Investment Bank, the Asian Development Bank, and the African Development Bank. They issue Global and Sustainable Development Bonds for development purposes.
5. **Municipalities:** Issue bonds to fund local government projects.

Bond Characteristics and Provisions

➤ **Secured and Unsecured Bonds:** Bonds can be backed by collateral (secured) or not (unsecured).

- ➢ **Callable and Non-Callable Bonds:** Callable bonds can be redeemed by the issuer before maturity, while non-callable bonds cannot. These bonds will be covered in depth later to understand some of the financial innovation within the development sector. They are a major part of structured products that are increasingly being employed by multilaterals within the sustainable sector.
- ➢ **Coupon/Accrued Interest Payments:** Interest is typically calculated on a 360-day calendar year basis for corporate bonds.

Peter mentioned Michael Milken. Michael expanded and popularized the market for junk or high-yield bonds. Junk bonds are issued by volatile companies that find it difficult to tap any other form of funding. These companies have weak balance sheets or structural problems leading to financial difficulties. This increases the probability of default, limiting their access to capital. These bonds have a higher probability of default, so they have a higher coupon to compensate for the risk. The general rule is that the higher the risk, the higher the risk premium investors require to adequately compensate for the risk. Risk Averse investors require a higher premium for any expected risks.

The topic led me to start discussing credit agencies. Fitch, Moody's, and S&P are among the premier credit rating agencies in the world. They rate various kinds of debt instruments and products. Companies with ratings of BBB-/Baa3 or higher are considered investment grade, with AAA/Aaa as the top credit rating. Bonds rated below BB+/Ba1 are considered speculative, with bonds in the C category classified as high-yield or junk bonds. Bonds within this category have the highest risk and offer the highest returns regarding interest payments or higher yields. However, junk bonds also have the highest default rates. The rating agencies also assign ratings to individual loans, bonds, and preferred stock issues, providing a probability assessment of the recovery of these loans. It's challenging to have a definitive opinion on the default amount as it's difficult to predict the legal outcomes that drive bond covenants when issuers default on their interest or principal payments. Recently, ESG has played an increasing role within the credit rating ecosystem. ESG issuer profile scores and carbon transition indicators are included for issuers or certain sectors of companies. A company with a strong credit rating **may** have better ESG scores than peers, keeping other factors constant. They may also access more investors with flexibility in paying lower coupons, securing longer bond tenures, etc.

Default loss rate = Default rate * (100% - Recovery rate)

Recovery Rate = (1 − loss given default) where LGD i.e. loss given default is the loss of an asset value when a borrower defaults.

There are other types of bonds, such as zero-coupon bonds, mortgage-backed securities securitization, and others, that I do not want to discuss in detail. Zero-coupon bonds do not pay any coupon and are issued at a discount to the face value.

Peter thoughtfully asked me an excellent question. He knew the answer but asked to make the conversation more insightful.

Peter: What's the difference between Mortgage-Backed Securities (MBS) & Asset-Backed Securities (ABS), and Covered Bonds? Isn't the covered bond market more prominent in Europe?

Kish: Yes, that's true. Covered Bonds are a significant sector in the European bond market, especially in countries like France, the UK, Denmark, and Germany. **Covered Bonds** are debt securities issued by a bank or mortgage institution and backed by a cover pool of assets, typically residential mortgage loans, commercial mortgage loans, and public sector loans.

Dynamic Asset Pool: The pool of assets backing covered bonds is dynamic, meaning the assets remain on the issuer's balance sheet and can be replaced over time to maintain the cover pool's value. Covered bonds are particularly prominent in Europe, with well-established markets in countries like Denmark and Germany. Mortgage-Backed Securities (MBS) & Asset-Backed Securities (ABS): MBS and ABS are securities created by pooling various types of loans (mortgages for MBS and other loans like car loans and credit card receivables for ABS) and selling them to investors. The pool of assets in MBS and ABS is static and transferred to a Special Purpose Vehicle (SPV), meaning the assets are removed from the issuer's balance sheet. This makes them riskier for bondholders as the assets are offloaded to the SPV. Securitization is more prevalent in the US, where agencies, governments, and corporations issue these securities. MBS and ABS are also utilized within the sustainable development sector.

Collateralized Mortgage Obligations include structuring the cash flows into bonds of varying risk types and tenures. Another type of bond commonly used within the development sector is the floating rate bond. In these bonds, the coupon rate is linked to a reference index, such as SOFR (Secured Overnight Financing Rate). Since the SOFR rate is variable, the coupon rate is not fixed. The coupon rate is calculated as the sum of the reference rate and a quoted margin. These bonds are part of structured products and can include various features, such as bonds having a minimum coupon (floor) or bonds where the payout is capped. Investors prefer these types of bonds when they anticipate increasing interest rates. These bonds are frequently issued as floating-rate notes.

In 2024, the World Bank (International Bank for Reconstruction and Development, IBRD, Aaa/AAA) priced a $1.25 billion Sustainable Development Bond linked to the SOFR Index, maturing on February 23, 2027. The bond pays a coupon of compounded daily SOFR plus 28 basis points. For reference, 100 basis points equal 1 percent. Listed on the Luxembourg Stock Exchange, most investors in this bond were banks, bank treasuries, and corporates. I will cover more on sustainable bonds ahead.

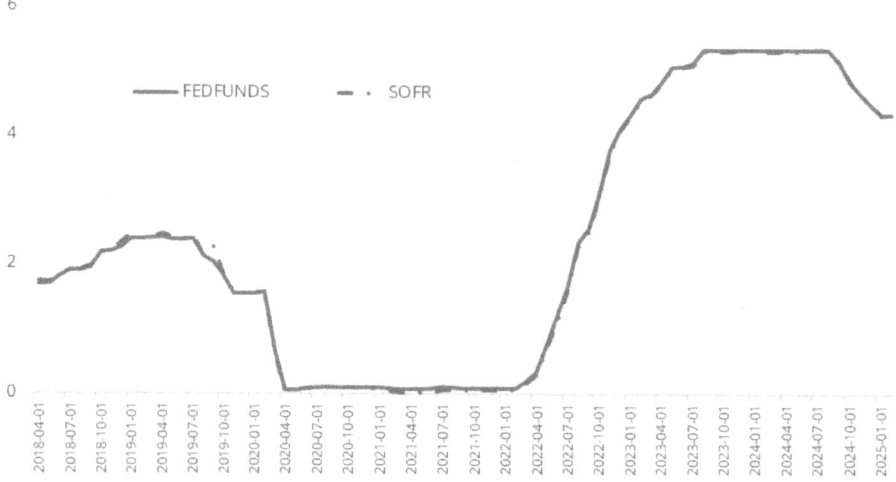

Data: Board of Governors of the Federal Reserve System (US), Federal Funds Effective Rate [FEDFUNDS], retrieved from FRED, Federal Reserve Bank of St. Louis; *https://fred.stlouisfed.org/series/FEDFUNDS*, Federal Reserve Bank of New York, Secured Overnight Financing Rate [SOFR], retrieved from FRED, Federal Reserve Bank of St. Louis; *https://fred.stlouisfed.org/series/SOFR*, Chart Author Data Monthly, Not Seasonally Adjusted, Percent

The federal funds rate, or FED rate, is one of the most important policy rates to watch globally. This rate serves as a barometer of liquidity within the US economy and influences global liquidity. It's the rate at which banks in the US borrow from each other overnight. During a liquidity crunch, the Fed funds rate jumps, as seen during the credit crisis.

The **Federal Open Market Committee (FOMC)** sets the federal funds target rate. The Federal Reserve (Fed) uses open market operations to influence the effective federal funds rate. The Fed rate is crucial for understanding inflation expectations and economic growth. The Fed uses many variables to decide on interest rates, following a dual mandate to manage inflation around 2 percent and maintain maximum sustainable employment. The People's Bank of China follows a dual mandate of focusing on economic growth and maintaining financial stability, which includes stabilizing the currency. Following a dual mandate is usually unusual. The ECB, Bank of England, and Riksbank follow a hierarchical method that prefers price stability by monitoring inflation. The Fed rate is highly correlated with inflation expectations. The Fed has recently increased the federal funds rate to contain and reduce inflation. A higher rate increases the cost of borrowing within the economy. Many mortgage coupon rates are benchmarked to the **Secured Overnight Financing Rate (SOFR)**, which closely mirrors the federal funds rate. SOFR is a broad measure of the cost of borrowing cash overnight, collateralized by Treasury securities. For monthly data from January 4, 2018, to Feb 1, 2025, the correlation coefficient is 1 when rounded off to two digits.

> Peter mentioned that I must first explain what reserves mean and the repo rate.

> Ah! Excellent idea.

Repos, or repurchase agreements, are short-term secured loans where the party buys back the securities from the other party at a specific price at a particular time. The repo concept is more or less universal. Banks can hold cash with central banks or as currency in their vaults. To increase liquidity within an economy, central banks buy securities. This mechanism increases the central bank's balance sheet (asset side) and increases currency in the economy, leading to higher price levels. You should look at the Quantity Theory of Money by economist Milton Friedman, who won the Nobel

Prize in Economic Sciences in 1976. His work has considerably influenced monetarism and the role of money supply in controlling inflation. In Milton's words, "Inflation is always and everywhere a monetary phenomenon." However, there has been recent debate on this subject.

The Quantity Theory of Money is expressed as:

$$M * V = P * T \qquad \text{or} \qquad M * V = P * Y$$

M = Quantity of Money, V = Rate at which money circulates in the economy,

Y = Real GDP, P = GDP deflator or price of a fixed quantity of goods and services, PY = Nominal GDP

Over the long run, money's velocity is usually constant, implying that the money supply impacts nominal GDP. According to the equation, printing too much money generates inflation. Adriana raised her hand. "I have a question. What is an open market operation?" Excellent question, I said. I am coming to it. The central bank's action to modulate liquidity within economies is done through Open Market Operations.

Open Market Operations (OMOs) are either permanent or temporary. The Fed uses Repo and Reverse Repo Rates to regulate short-term rates, such as the effective fed funds rate or overnight lending rates between banks. Outright purchase or sale of assets is a permanent open market operation. Asset purchases increase the aggregate supply of reserves, i.e., the money supply. Buying assets boosts liquidity within the economy and encourages lending and investment. During the credit crisis and the recent pandemic, the Fed used quantitative easing to foster economic credit growth. To absorb liquidity from the system, central banks sell bonds. They also increase interest rates in the economy. Unwinding bonds by central banks is known as quantitative tightening.

And what is quantitative easing?

Quantitative easing is a tool used by central banks to purchase assets to boost liquidity in the markets when interest rates are near zero.

Remember from Econ 101: **Nominal Interest Rates = Real Interest Rates + Expected Inflation**, a simplification of the Fisher equation.

Buying assets boosts liquidity within the system and could increase inflation. Nominal Interest Rates are the interest rates banks charge on deposits or the return on bonds. They include the price effect and are considered the opportunity cost of capital. Real interest rates define the purchasing power of households and are adjusted for expected inflation.

Ex-ante real interest rates = nominal interest rates − expected inflation. Expected inflation is crucial as central banks consider this aspect carefully when taking corrective policy measures. Higher expected inflation will induce central banks to increase policy rates; there is an outside lag between the time taken for policy action and its influence on the economy. That's why it's always better to look at the real GDP growth or real wage growth over the long run. This explains the change in the purchasing power of consumers.

Peter and Xu both smiled. We discussed the effectiveness of quantitative easing and left the analysis for another day.

To learn more about bonds, let's look at interest rate yield and term structure. Bond pricing follows the concept of the time value of money. "Let's continue," I said.

Peter interrupted and mentioned that it is advisable to first discuss concepts such as personal savings rate and disposable income to fully comprehend the macroeconomic cycle that leads to borrowing. I agreed and digressed to discuss the consumption function.

Let Y be the economic output of an economy.

GDP is the most commonly used economic variable to denote Y.

$$GDP = Y = C + I + G + NX$$

GDP is calculated in both **Real** and **Nominal** terms. Real GDP is calculated at constant prices using a base year to filter out the rise in GDP due to increases in price levels. For example, if an economy only sold bananas, and it sold 50 dozen of them in both 2018 and 2023, then the economic value added is the same. However, if the price of bananas increases due to inflation in 2023 compared to 2018, it will seem as if the economic value added is greater in 2023, which is not the case. If the price of bananas is $3 per dozen in 2018 and $5 per dozen in 2023, the correct way of calculating GDP in 2023 would be to multiply 50 dozen bananas by $3 rather than $5.

For an open economy, **NX** represents net exports, which are exports minus imports. A positive value of net exports indicates the country is a net exporter of goods and services. For a closed economy, the net export is zero. **C stands for Personal Consumption, G for Government Purchases, and I for Private Domestic Investment.** Government purchases include expenditures by federal, state, and local governments, and these can be divided into defense and non-defense spending. Gross private domestic investments include investments in residential, equipment, intellectual property among others. Households save their income for a rainy day, and this savings rate is denoted as the personal savings rate. Income is divided between savings and consumption. Let Y here be the total income of households. If T is the tax rate within this economy, the disposable income is given by Y–TY = Y(1-T).

This disposable income is divided between *personal savings and consumption.* The personal savings rate is a function of a variable known as the **marginal propensity to consume.**

MPS (marginal propensity to save) = 1 – MPC

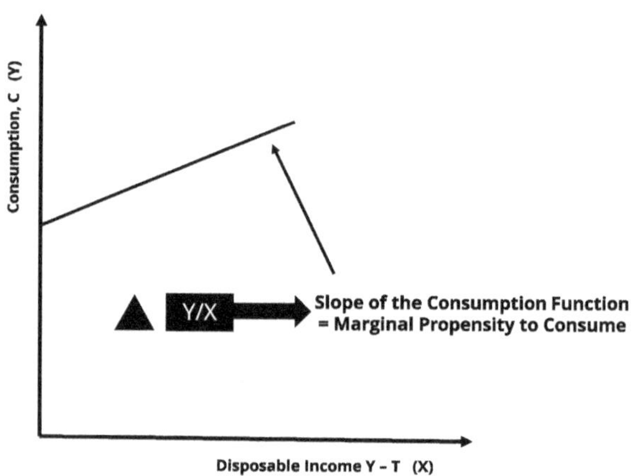

The consumption function is plotted with consumption on the Y-axis and disposable income on the X-axis. The personal savings rate is a barometer of consumer spending behavior as it reflects the disposable household income not spent on the consumption of final goods.

The personal savings rate in the US has declined in recent years. The personal savings rate stood at 3.6 percent on January 1, 2023, revolving consumer credit owned and securitized, increasing to $1.32 trillion. Since the beginning of January 2020, the personal savings rate has drastically decreased from 12 percent to 3.4 percent, a drop of approximately 72 percent in three years. Meanwhile, revolving consumer credit has increased by about 35.3 percent during the same period. One reason could be high inflation and interest rates, which lead to a decrease in the savings rate and an increase in consumer credit. With high inflation and interest rates, the real purchasing power of households reduces while the cost of borrowing increases, putting increased pressure on the personal savings rate. Advanced countries often have lower personal savings rates compared to emerging markets. When analyzing this data, it is essential to keep all factors affecting consumer spending constant.

Personal Savings Rate vs. Revolving Consumer Credit Owned and Securitized

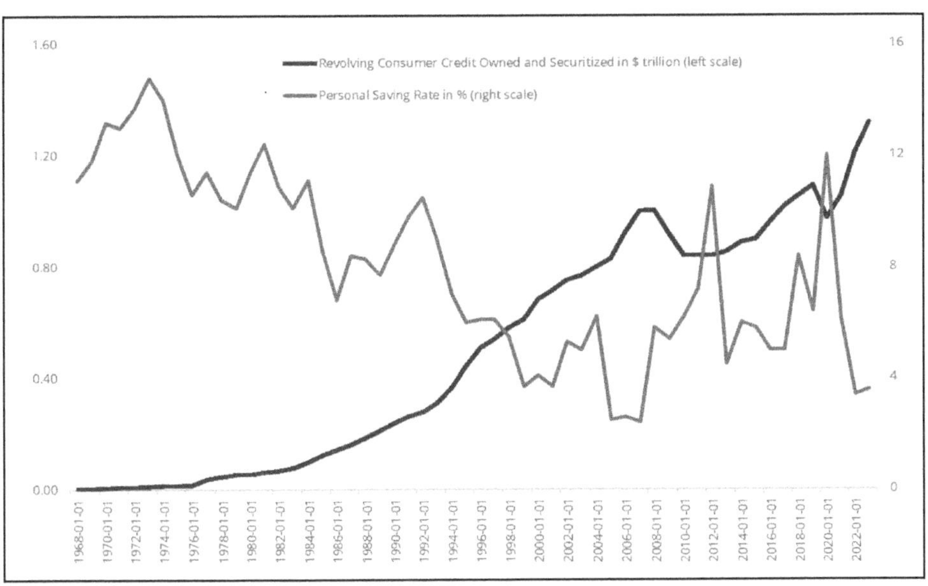

Data Source: U.S. Bureau of Economic Analysis, Personal Saving Rate [PSAVERT], retrieved from FRED, Federal Reserve Bank of St. Louis; https://fred.stlouisfed.org/series/PSAVERT, August 8, 2024. Board of Governors of the Federal Reserve System (US), Revolving Consumer Credit Owned and Securitized [REVOLSL], retrieved from FRED, Federal Reserve Bank of St. Louis; https://fred.stlouisfed.org/series/REVOLSL, August 8, 2024. Chart Author. Fig rounded off. Yearly, end of period. Seasonally adjusted.

Adriana added to my discussion. With high borrowing costs, consumers' revolving credit should increase, as the borrowers now have higher borrowing costs and interest payments. This will also eat into their personal savings rate. I get the idea of keeping other factors that drive credit the same. Correct, I am impressed. Precisely, I mentioned.

Xu mentioned there are other ways of categorizing bonds. We all came back to our discussion on bonds. Bonds can also be classified based on the priority of cash flows. Bondholders of senior secured bonds have a right to some property of the issuer in case of default, for example, mortgage bonds backed by real estate assets. Second in line with secured senior bonds are unsecured or unsecured debentures, which promise to pay interest and principal but are not backed by assets. These bonds are riskier than senior secured bonds and have a higher coupon rate. Senior unsecured bonds are preferred over senior subordinated bonds. Last are subordinated junior debentures, wherein bondholders are only paid interest when it is earned. The coupon rate for subordinated junior debentures would be the highest among these bonds.

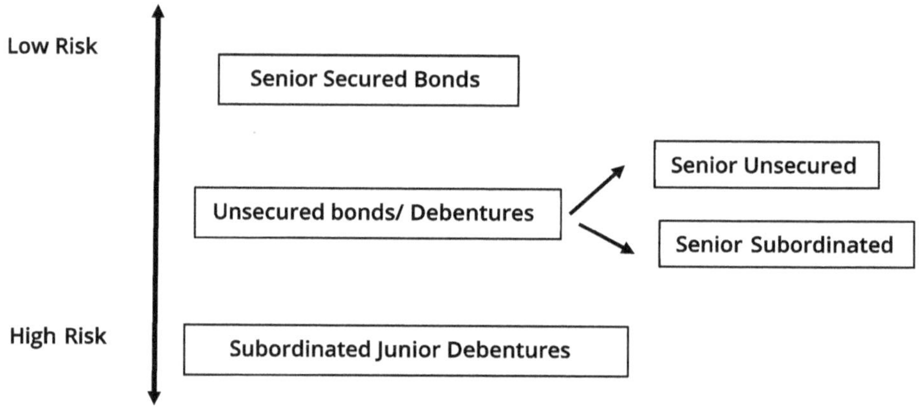

Price and Yield of a Bond

The price of a bond is inversely related to its yield. Bond prices are quoted based on yield. The current yield of a bond is calculated as the annual coupon interest divided by the bond's price. The price of a bond represents the present value of its expected cash flows. An increase in the required yield leads to a decrease in the present value of cash flows and, consequently, a reduction in the bond's price. The coupon rate, maturity, prevailing market interest rates, and comparable bonds with similar credit profiles influence the bond's price.

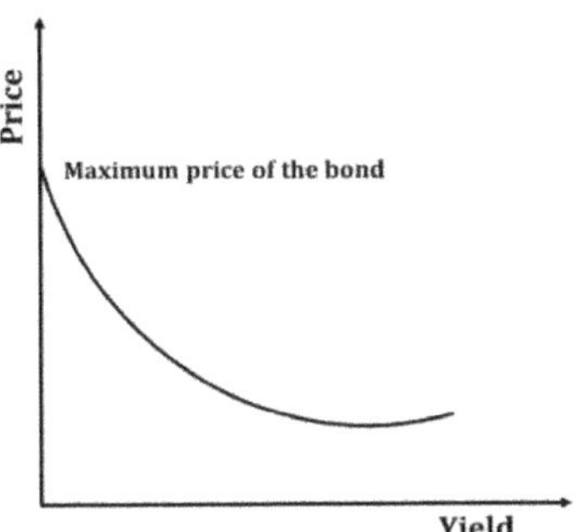

10-year Benchmark Yields – United States, Canada, Euro Area

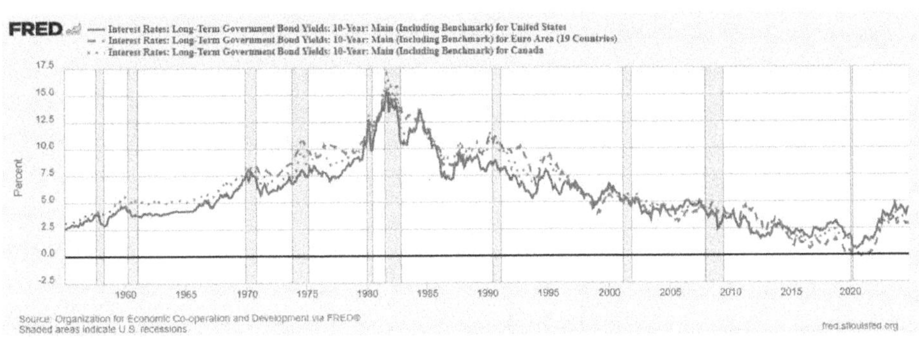

Chart: Organization for Economic Co-operation and Development, Interest Rates: Long-Term Government Bond Yields: 10-Year: Main (Including Benchmark) for the United States [IRLTLT01USM156N], retrieved from FRED, Federal Reserve Bank of St. Louis; *https://fred.stlouisfed.org/series/IRLTLT01USM156N*, Organization for Economic Co-operation and Development, Interest Rates: Long-Term Government Bond Yields: 10-Year: Main (Including Benchmark) for the Euro Area (19 Countries) [IRLTLT01EZM156N], retrieved from FRED, Federal Reserve Bank of St. Louis; *https://fred.stlouisfed.org/series/IRLTLT01EZM156N*, Organization for Economic Co-operation and Development, Interest Rates: Long-Term Government Bond Yields: 10-Year: Main (Including Benchmark) for Canada [IRLTLT01CAM156N], retrieved from FRED, Federal Reserve Bank of St. Louis; *https://fred.stlouisfed.org/series/IRLTLT01CAM156N*.

Percentage, Not Seasonally Adjusted, monthly.

A popular term often used is *yield to maturity or YTM*. YTM is the interest rate that will equal the present value of the bond price. It estimates the rate of return of the bond held to maturity or the rate that acts as a discounting factor to value the present value of cash flows. Consider cash flows that are irregular from a project. One way to calculate the yield to maturity of the project is the internal rate of return.

> To understand portfolio theory, it's imperative to have an understanding of what we mean by efficient markets. Random Walk Theory, Efficient Market Hypothesis (EMH) and an overview of Brownian motion is important to understand the portfolio theory.

Bond Valuation

Price of a bond = Present value of all the cash flows

➢ CF_n = Last coupon + Principal Amount

➢ CF = Cash Flows

$$\text{Present Value of the bond} = \frac{CF_1}{1+y} + \frac{CF_2}{(1+y)^2} + \cdots \frac{CF_n}{(1+y)^n}$$

Let n be the number of periods for coupon payout. For a bond of maturity of 4 years, for annual payment, the periods would be 4; for semi-annual payment, the time period would be 8, and so on. Peter mentioned another type of bond: *convertible bonds*. These bonds are hybrid instruments with embedded options, typically allowing conversion into equity under predefined terms. The floor value is a straight fixed bond with equity kickers, meaning they can be converted into predetermined equity shares based on specific metrics. Options provide the right, but not the obligation, to buy or sell an underlying asset at a predetermined price. For this right, the holder pays the issuer a premium.

Let's not go into the valuation detail I mentioned. This would take time. I suggested to Peter to discuss the evolution of the single-factor Capital Asset Pricing Model. That would be an excellent discussion for anyone who wants to know more about the origins of quantitative finance on Wall Street. Peter agreed and, taking a cue from Peter Bernstein's book "Capital Ideas", he started tracing out the origins of mathematical finance.

> "A market where there are a large number of rational, profit-maximizing participants actively competing to predict future market values of individual securities, and where important current information is almost always available to all participants."
>
> **— Eugene Fama on Efficient Markets**

The Theory of Random Walk laid the foundation for the **efficient market hypothesis (EMH)**. Eugene Fama, often considered the father of modern mathematical finance and a Nobel Laureate, is one of the most influential economists of the modern era. His work on EMH and asset pricing is crucial to modern portfolio theory. The efficient market hypothesis asserts that markets are informationally efficient, meaning that current security prices fully reflect all available information. The Theory of Random Walk underpins this hypothesis, suggesting that stock prices move randomly and are unpredictable.

Selected Key Milestones in the Story of CAPM 1900 to 1969

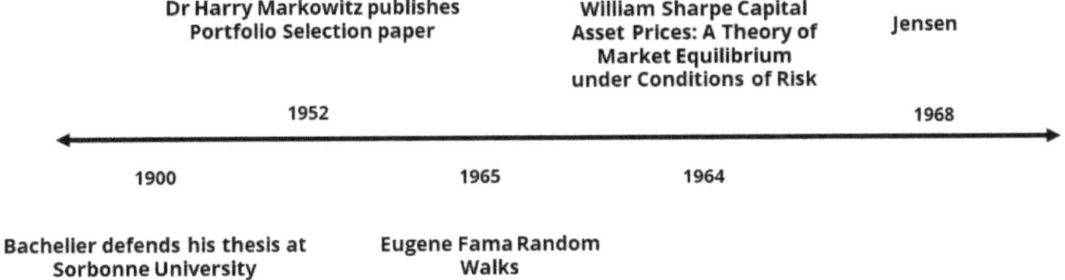

Image: Key Milestones in the story of CAPM 1900 to 1969 Author; **Reference:** Capital Ideas by Peter Bernstein

The book "Capital Ideas" by Peter Bernstein is a highly recommended read on the origins of finance on Wall Street. Written by the Wall Street guru Peter Bernstein, the book traces the advent of mathematical finance, leading to the evolution of models in risk, valuation, portfolio management, and capital market pricing that define investment management today. The book captures the role of various actors within the business ecosystem—economists, mathematicians, statisticians, professionals, and technicians—in understanding and quantifying capital pricing models. The story begins in 1900, when French mathematician **Louis Bachelier** wrote a seminal paper titled *"Théorie de la Spéculation,"* marking the inception of mathematical finance. Bachelier structured a mathematical model of price movement, which we now understand as **Brownian motion**. This concept, later known as a random walk, is popularized by Nobel Laureate Eugene Fama. Bachelier was the first to develop a stochastic process to analyze the random movement of stock prices. His theory posited that any variable whose price changes unpredictably over time follows a stochastic process. These variables can be continuous in time, like stock market prices. He is famous for his analysis, which states that "the mathematical expectation of a speculator is zero." Bachelier also noted that the range within which stock prices tend to fluctuate increases as the square root of the time interval.

Random Walk Theory

The efficient market hypothesis (EMH) is a cornerstone theory in finance that attempts to explain how financial markets work. Eugene Fama set the ball rolling with his groundbreaking work in the paper "Random Walks in Stock Market Prices". Fama discovered that the future path of the price level of a security is no more predictable than the path of a series of cumulated random numbers. He deduced that the successive changes in individual securities will be independent. The theory means that the past prices of a stock or security have no bearing on the future price pattern of the stock. He believed markets are efficient and are priced based on all the available information. The efficient market theory assumes markets are informationally efficient. Current security prices reflect all the available information. Investors want to maximize profits; they are large and independent of each other. Information comes out in a random, independent, and unpredictable fashion, and markets adjust rapidly to the information available or adjust over a short time. The efficient market hypothesis can be categorized into three forms of efficient markets.

In the weak form of the efficient market hypothesis, current stock prices fully reflect all past trading information on the security market. The theory proposes that the past rate of return has no bearing on future returns. "I remember chatting with Caroline and telling her that the technical analysis is no good for picking stocks. Although there is a debate on the usefulness of this analysis, according to a weak form of an efficient market hypothesis, this type of analysis will not yield a higher risk-adjusted return since the analysis focuses on patterns of stocks' previous returns to predict future returns. Caroline laughed and replied that, by that logic, even fundamental analysis would be ineffective under the semi-strong form of the Efficient Market Hypothesis. In a semi-strong form efficient market hypothesis, current stock prices rapidly adjust to all public information. For example, the market reacts immediately to an earnings report. The stock prices would reflect the quality of the earnings report after the announcement. In the strong form of efficient market hypothesis, current stock prices in these markets reflect both public and private information. For example, Insider trading. Efficient Market Hypothesis shares a framework of understanding investor behavior depending on the type of market hypothesis."

It is important to understand **Stochastic and Markov Processes**. Any variable whose price uncertainty changes over time follows a Stochastic Process. These processes are continuous or discrete. The trading of the stock market over time is continuous, whereas the payoff of options is discrete. The Markov process is a type of stochastic process where only the current value of a variable is important for predicting the future. Brownian motion is a continuous-time stochastic process with independent increments. It is a particular **Markov Process** with independent increments. The process is normally distributed over a finite time, and variance increases linearly over time.

I asked Peter if the US equity markets exhibited any of these forms. Usually, there is a consensus that the semi-strong form of the Efficient Market Hypothesis applies. Peter agreed that this would be the most likely scenario. Peter is the best person to explain **Modern Portfolio Theory**.

Dr. Harry Markowitz, the Father of Modern Portfolio Theory, published the breakthrough paper "Portfolio Selection" in the March 1952 issue of the Journal of Finance. Dr. Markowitz proposed focusing on the selection of portfolios rather than individual securities. The premise of the portfolio theory is that investors make decisions based on expected return and risk, i.e., the variability of the portfolio. Variance is the measure of the risk of a portfolio; the higher the risk, the higher the expected return. Investors will need extra compensation for an additional unit of risk. One key concept in portfolio management is the efficient frontier, a collection of superior portfolios. Portfolio diversification is so important to remove unsystematic or diversifiable risk. One way would be to increase securities from various asset classes as part of the portfolio. The lower the correlation between assets, the more diversified the portfolios. That's why asset managers hold shares of many companies to diversify the risk. However, systematic risk cannot be diversified. For example, global recessions, exposure to interest rates, especially in the US, or the global pandemic.

COVID-19 is an excellent example of how the pandemic has impacted various economies globally.

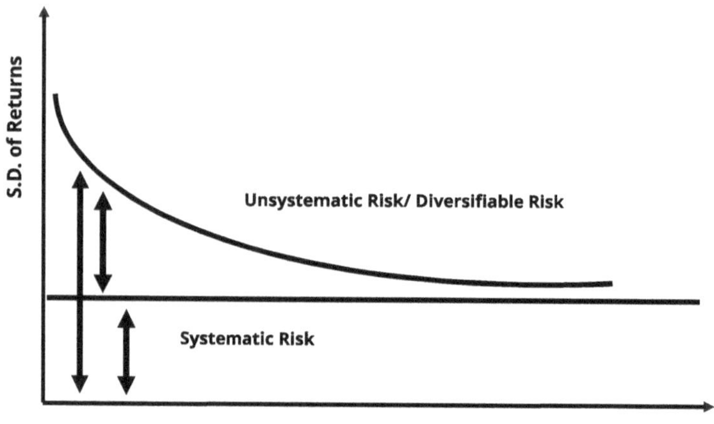

Image: Author

Efficient Frontier: Includes Most Efficient Portfolios

I knew that at one point, Peter was involved in customizing portfolios using the technique of the efficient frontier to pick the best securities. I asked Peter how he would define an efficient portfolio. He explained, "First, you must understand the risk and return trade-off. Risk is measured as the standard deviation of the portfolio. It can also be designated as variance, the square of the standard deviation. For a given measure of risk, the portfolio that provides the highest return would be efficient. Any asset or portfolio is efficient if it offers higher expected returns for the same or lower risk, or the same or higher expected return for lower risk."

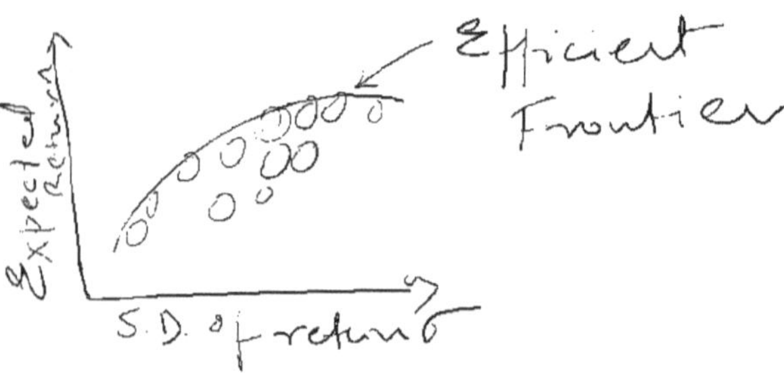

Peter took his pen and drew a diagram of an efficient portfolio. He pointed to the portfolios on the efficient frontier. These are the ones you need in your portfolio. Financial assets are those assets that deal in money and have better liquidity than real assets. Real assets like real estate, precious metals, and art are usually illiquid. **REITs (Real Estate Investment Trusts)** are examples of tradable assets with real estate as the underlying asset. Today, private equity funds have art and precious metals as the underlying assets.

Understanding Capital Asset Pricing Model

We started discussing the CAPM model in an accelerated manner. The standard capital asset pricing model is a single-factor Capital Asset Pricing Model. The one-factor **Capital Asset Pricing Model (CAPM)** is innovative in its simplicity, predicting a company's valuation using only a few variables. The CAPM builds on the work by Harry Markowitz on diversification and modern portfolio theory. The CAPM model was introduced independently by Jack Treynor (1961, 1962), William F. Sharpe (1964), John Lintner (1965), and Jan Mossin (1966). The model primarily relies on Beta, a key measure of systematic risk, along with the risk-free rate and the market return, to estimate the expected return of an asset. Beta is calculated through regression analysis using historical asset data and a benchmark index. The relationship between the expected required market rate of return plotted with *Beta (a standardized measure of systematic risk)* is defined as the security market line, graphically representing the **standard capital asset pricing model**. The model relies on one factor, i.e., Beta, to predict expected return. According to the model, diversifiable risk is not rewarded; assets are valued based on systematic risk. By adding more securities, the diversifiable risk can be eliminated. The less correlation between securities, the less diversifiable the risk. That's one reason investors look for various asset classes within their portfolios to diversify risk. This model simplifies the expected return of asset prices given the measure of systematic risk, herein Beta. Although the one-factor CAPM is not a perfectly accurate predictor of asset prices, it effectively indicates whether an asset is underpriced or overpriced using the **Security Market Line (SML).**

William Sharpe, in his seminal paper "Capital Asset Prices: A Theory of Market Equilibrium Under Conditions of Risk," defined investor return as a factor of the ***price of time and risk.*** This is true, but in recent years, many investors have started adding another variable as a factor: ESG.

The price of time is the price of pure interest rates given by return on risk-free interest rates. As risk-free interest rates have zero standard deviation, any expectation of returns less than the risk-free rate is unacceptable. The price of risk is very intuitive. An expectation of additional return on an asset comes with a further acceptance of risk. This is the key tenet that defines investment management theory. The underpinning of the utility theory is that investors would like to maximize their returns on investments given the same amount of risk, keeping other factors the same. Risk can be divided into *diversifiable or unsystematic risks and non-diversifiable or systematic risks.*

Diversifiable risk, or unsystematic risk, can be reduced by using more securities in the portfolio. Firm risk is a unique risk pertinent to business and strategy. Non-diversifiable risk is a global macro risk, such as recession and interest rate risk, that cannot be eliminated. The single-factor Capital Asset Pricing Model uses riskless assets with a market portfolio. Riskless assets have zero variance; these securities are shorter-term government securities of advanced countries, such as the United States T-bills. The market portfolio includes tradable assets, both financial and real. Examples of financial assets include stocks and bonds, while tangible assets include commodities, land, art, and more.

The market portfolio is crucial in calculating Beta, a key variable used to determine an asset's expected return. Beta measures the covariance or correlation of an asset or security with its benchmark index or market. However, a true market portfolio is unobservable because many assets are illiquid, unlisted, or unavailable for trade. Therefore, a proxy index is used to represent the market portfolio.

The utility function is upward-sloping when the expected return is plotted on the y-axis and the standard deviation (risk) on the x-axis. This upward slope signifies that investors require additional returns for every extra unit of risk they take. The assumptions behind the Capital Asset Pricing Model (CAPM) are rigid and, at times, unrealistic. First, it assumes that investor preferences are homogeneous, meaning all investors base their decisions on the same utility function. Another key assumption is that investors have similar investment horizons, are risk-averse, and share identical risk and return expectations. However, investors often have diverse risk-return expectations due to differences in financial situations, investment goals, behavioral dynamics, and demographic factors. Second, the CAPM assumes that short selling is allowed, a practice prevalent in advanced and selected emerging capital markets. Third, the model assumes no transaction costs or taxes, which are significant factors in real-world portfolio management and vary across different geographies. Additionally, the CAPM assumes that investors can borrow at a risk-free rate, an assumption that rarely holds, especially for retail investors in many countries. Despite these assumptions, the CAPM remains widely used for its practicality and simplicity.

Let's build the standard capital asset pricing model.

Capital Market Line (CML) & Security Market Line (SML)

The *Capital Market Line (CML)* is an important concept. The portfolio theory advances when risk-free assets are combined with risky assets. This fusion of using a mix of risk-free assets with efficient portfolios led to a capital allocation line. The Capital Market Line is the most efficient among the capital allocation lines. The CML represents the combination of the risk-free asset, typically shorter-dated Treasuries, with the market portfolio. The market portfolio is the most optimal or efficient portfolio, and by combining risky assets with risk-free assets, the standard deviation used to measure portfolio risk is linearly proportional to the weight of the risky portfolio. It is important to note that risk-free assets have zero correlation with risky assets. An assumption here is that the market portfolio includes all tradable risky assets within an economy and is the most mean variance efficient portfolio. The market portfolio is completely diversified and only includes **systematic risk** or risk related to macro variables.

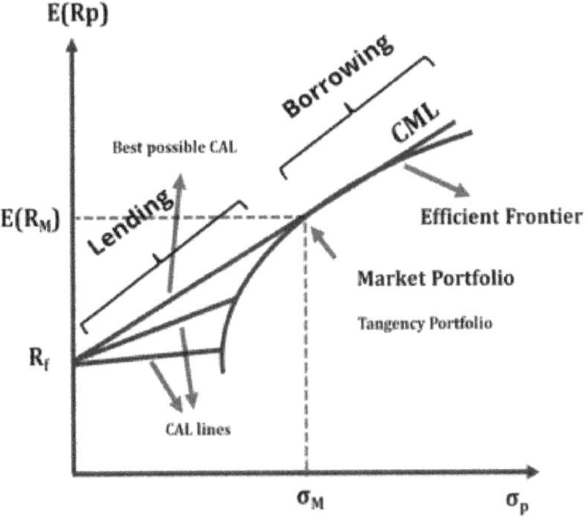

Although a market portfolio is not theoretically possible, the S&P 500 is an excellent approximation or proxy for a market portfolio in the context of the US market. A more global proxy index would be the MSCI All Country World Index. The CML also aids in understanding **Tobin's Separation Theorem**, which explains how investors can use leverage to magnify their investments. Investors can borrow at the risk-free rate and invest in the optimal or efficient portfolios or the market portfolio, representing the tangent point between the efficient frontier and the CML. The efficient frontier is a set of optimal or efficient portfolios that offer the best return for their respective risks or the lowest risk compared to other portfolios for similar expected returns (Risk captured through standard deviation).

SML is plotted using expected return and Beta to understand the price valuation of securities. The Beta of the market portfolio is 1. Here, the SML line is important to understand the returns of the stocks or whether asset prices are fairly valued.

This is key to understanding *Jensen's Alpha*, which is calculated as the difference between the return of the portfolio and the required return of the portfolio. Inset diagram, SML line.

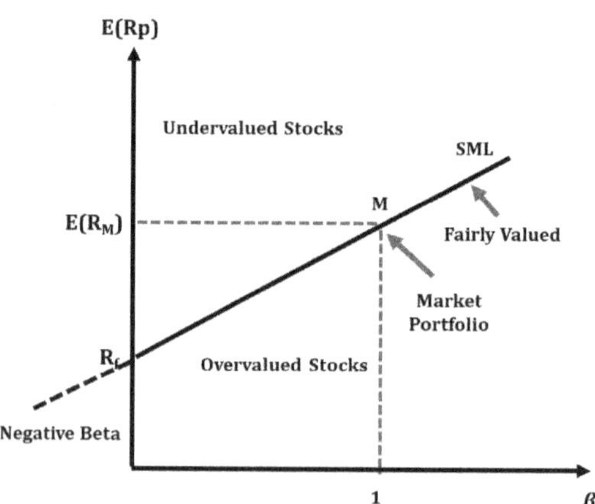

If the expected return of securities lies on the SML, then the alpha is zero. An asset manager can understand if the asset prices are under or overvalued. Undervalued assets will lie above the SML while overvalued assets will lie below the SML. An asset manager will buy undervalued stocks while selling overvalued ones, balancing the portfolio. The standard capital asset pricing model shares an excellent financial model for understanding the valuation of securities based on *Beta and market premium* - a financial model that, along with other valuation models, can aid asset or portfolio managers in the fundamental analysis of securities.

Negative Beta stocks are negatively correlated with the overall market movement. Certain asset classes, such as gold, have historically negatively correlated with the stock market index. Short selling also results in a negative beta. For simplicity, investors can borrow company shares when they expect the stock price to decline. By borrowing and selling the stock at its current price, the investor can repurchase it at a lower price and profit from the difference. For example, if a stock price falls from $20 to $15, an investor who shorted the stock at $20 and repurchases it at $15 makes a $5 per share profit (excluding transaction costs, margin, brokerage fees, interest cost, etc). By leveraging the trade, the investor can further magnify potential gains and increase risk.

Market Portfolio & The Capital Market Line

Risk-Free Asset developed Portfolio Theory into Capital Market Theory. When a risk-free asset is combined with a risky asset, the standard deviation of the portfolio is the linear proportion of the standard deviation of the risky asset portfolio. A risk-free asset has zero variance and zero correlation with risky assets. Usually, risk-free assets are short-term government securities, such as US T-bills. **Market Portfolios** are the most efficient mean-variance portfolios. They are completely diversified, have no unique risk, and include all tradable risky assets within an economy. The portfolio only includes **systematic risk** or risk related to macro variables. The slope of the CML, i.e., the risk's market price, is the market portfolio's risk premium.

Beta is the covariance of an asset's return with the market return, divided by the variance of the market return. A market portfolio is practically impossible, so proxies are used instead. S&P 500 is the best proxy for large capitalization stocks in the US. Unlisted securities are typically more challenging to value.

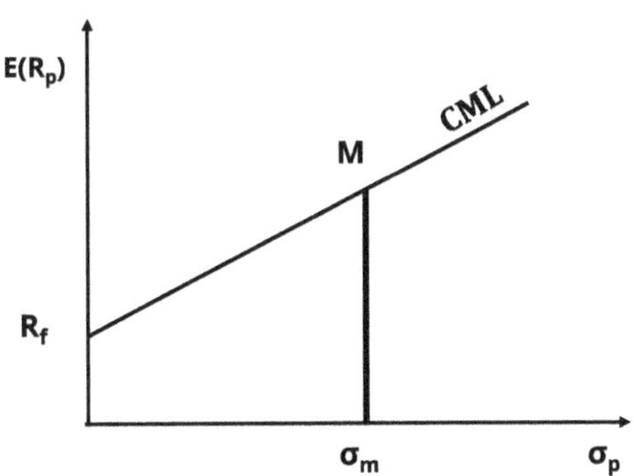

Analysts often employ various methods, including comparable company analysis and leveraged buyout (LBO) models. The asset management industry encompasses various types of firms employing diverse investment strategies. Traditional asset managers like mutual funds, pension funds, and insurance companies primarily invest in listed securities. Hedge funds may invest in both listed and unlisted securities, often using more complex strategies. Hedge funds are not regulated by the SEC in America and are therefore less transparent. Unlike mutual funds that focus on retail participation, these types of asset managers target high or ultra-high-net-worth individuals for building assets under management. Given the higher minimum investment amounts, hedge funds use various sophisticated investment strategies, including cutting-edge algorithmic trading, global macro, and arbitrage trading, among others. **Renaissance Technologies** is one of the most quant-based hedge funds globally. Some well-known hedge funds include Citadel and Bridgewater, among others. Top investment banks like *JPMorgan, Morgan Stanley, and Goldman Sachs* also have their proprietary trading desks that use quantitative trading methods to generate profits.

One of the best books written on the hedge fund industry is **"The Quants"** by Scott Patterson.

One way of calculating inequalities within economies is through the Gini coefficient.

Measuring poverty and inequality is essential for understanding socioeconomic disparities and formulating effective policies. One measure that is ubiquitous globally and used often in research is the **Gini Coefficient**. Two measures, the Kuznets ratio, and the Gini Coefficient, are discussed briefly: The Gini Coefficient ranges between 0 and 1; 0 signifies absolute equality, while 1 represents absolute inequality. Another measure, the **Kuznets ratio**, calculates inequality by comparing the income received by the top 20 percent to that obtained by the bottom 40 percent of the population.

I had in the back of my mind the idea of opening a hedge fund with Peter and Xu. Xu mentioned that he is nowadays reading Ray Dalio's "Principles: Life & Work", the book by the man who launched Bridgewater Associates, the world's largest hedge fund.

Venture capital and private equity funds typically focus on unlisted companies in early-stage or more mature private businesses to make money by appreciating the company's value over time. Generally, the mode of exit is the sale of a stake during the IPO of the acquired company or a strategic sale of the stake to another actor, such as private equity. Venture Funds, for example, **Sequoia Capital** and **Kleiner Perkins**, invest in early-stage startups, while private equity focuses on more mature companies. Listed securities are usually considered less risky than unlisted securities due to greater liquidity and regulatory oversight, and thus typically offer lower potential returns. Information on listed securities is more readily available, transparent, and frequently updated due to regulatory requirements and market demand. In contrast, investments in unlisted securities by venture capital and private equity firms often have less publicly available information and lower liquidity but may offer the potential for higher returns to compensate for these additional risks. It's important to note that while these generalizations hold in many cases, there can be significant variations in risk and return profiles within each category depending on specific securities, market conditions, and other factors. A good-natured fellow, Peter sounded very upbeat about the prospects of impact investors within the milieu of the global development sector.

The single-factor **Capital Asset Pricing Model (CAPM)** has several limitations. Constructing an actual market portfolio is practically impossible. The model only captures systematic risk as the covariance of securities with the benchmark index. Research has shown that multiple factors affect asset prices beyond just market risk. Stephen Ross developed the **Arbitrage Pricing Theory (APT)**, incorporating various factors. However, the model does not explicitly identify these factors. The APT is based on the law of one price, with arbitrage theory as its fundamental tenet. Among the various models, one worth discussing is the Fama-French five-factor model, an enhancement of their earlier three-factor model. After a full day of information, we agreed it was time to wrap up. Some of the discussions turned out to be information overload. I said farewell as I needed to pick up Caroline for personal errands, mentioning plans to organize a gathering soon. The event proved invaluable—I reconnected with friends, networked with business leaders, and had enriching discussions before heading home. Peter had a business meeting, while Adriana, Xu, and Élise went to a nearby lounge bar with others from the event for an informal gathering.

Chapter 3

Artificial Intelligence, and Startups – Innovation, Productivity and Economic Growth

I had to pick up Caroline and her grandmother. **Caroline** had flown in from **New Orleans** to spend quality time with us. The event was refreshing; I learned about the latest social financial innovations through case studies and met several people from diverse backgrounds within the development and technology sector. Eager to set up a get-together with *Peter and his family, Brad, Adriana*, and other friends at my place, I left the event a bit early to meet Caroline and discuss my plans. I had to rush but be mindful. The social scene in Bellevue is superlative, with regular events organized by leading companies. Bellevue is a paradise with fine dining, multicuisine places, a 21-acre downtown park, and many public spaces. Its downtown reminds me of Pittsburgh. Though small in area for a city, the place packs quite a punch. I had to meet Solomon, an acquaintance I met during my visit to Austin, Texas. My trip to Austin was both personal and business-oriented. I attended a major social impact conference and visited several academic institutes and organizations in the development and business sectors to seek partnerships for my startup. I had designed a special B2B and discussed it with various prospective clients.

Austin, Texas

Austin is one of the most beautiful cities in the US. As the capital of Texas, a dynamic southern state, Austin is popularly known as the "**Live Music Capital of the World.**" Austin is the tech and cultural hub of Texas, a state traditionally known for its businesses in the oil and gas sector. Texas has Dallas and Houston, two well-known cities worldwide. Music is the lifeblood of this city, much like **Nashville**, Tennessee, is the **heart**

of country music. Austin has multiple academic institutions, including the University of Texas, which is rated among the best public universities in the world. With world-class universities and a burgeoning startup ecosystem, Austin aids its startups in commercializing their products through a lab-to-market model. The city houses **Capital Factory**, a well-known accelerator enabling startups in Texas through various initiatives. The city is fast emerging as a melting point for startups in Texas in clean tech, life sciences, and fintech. Austin is famous for its cafes lining the river, often featuring live music. The city boasts one of the best tech startup ecosystems globally. As a cultural bliss, Austin hosts the annual **SXSW (South by Southwest),** an enlightening, collaborative, multifaceted, and multidimensional festival that brings together technocrats, musicians, and artists on a single platform. This cultural and artistic festival with a difference is part of the many events that propel America into a different league.

Solomon

During my visit, I met Solomon at the social impact event. Solomon has an interesting and creative background. He holds a PhD in life sciences. He is the founder of a startup in genetic engineering. He and his girlfriend, Ayana, had recently shifted to Bellevue. Solomon got invited to speak at an upcoming event on entrepreneurship on the synergies between technology, economics, and startups. He called me for help, and I suggested we meet at Starbucks to fine-tune his presentation on this topic. At the same time, I could comment on his startup's pitch deck. Solomon planned to apply to Slush, a global startup event held in Finland, on my suggestion, and I felt confident that his startup would be shortlisted for a live pitch in front of the audience.

En route to meet Solomon, I started listening to **Kenny Rogers's "The Gambler"** and Tom Petty's **"Free Fallin'"**

As I drove my new Tesla Model 3, I hummed the Tom Petty song.

Jerry Maguire, a **Tom Cruise** movie, is considered by many to be one of the best feel-good Hollywood films. This motivational movie showcases the power of ethics in business through a sports comedy-drama and a love story. The movie stars the talented **Renée Zellweger** as a single mother, Jerry's love interest, struggling to make ends meet. The movie earned **Cuba Gooding Jr** the Academy Award for Best Supporting Actor for his role as a wide receiver in American football. The film features the memorable song "Secret Garden" by Bruce Springsteen, one of the best love songs as part of the movie's soundtrack. A huge box office hit and a cult classic, the movie includes a supporting role by **Kelly Preston**, the late wife of **John Travolta**. The film was inducted into the National Film Registry by the Library of Congress in 2019. Jerry Maguire explores the pitfalls of sugarcoating business relationships by emphasizing the value of building long-term connections through genuine camaraderie in service-oriented industries. The emphasis on mutual respect and the power of a personalized approach to clients as crucial elements for long-term personal and professional success resonated well with audiences worldwide. The movie also presents a philosophical perspective on the merits of doing business, highlighting the trade-off between maximization of profits and client interest. I highly recommend this movie to everyone; it's a complete package that stands out in cinema. The radio station started playing one of my favorite songs, "The Gambler".

"The Gambler" is one of my favorite country music songs. Set on a train, it's about a conversation between strangers, a metaphor for the transient nature of life. A motivational song about wisdom and advice, shared by a gambler, the song has a strong philosophical message on how to deal with the vicissitudes of life using poker as an analogy. Written by **Don Schlitz** and sung by many artists, including Johnny Cash, who is widely regarded as one of the greatest country artists of all time. However, Kenny Rogers' version is the most well-known. The song won Kenny a Grammy for Best Male Country Vocal Performance in 1980 and is rated among the greatest country songs ever.

Seattle Central Library

I met Solomon near Seattle Central Library. A multi-storeyed masterpiece, Seattle Central Library is an intellectual powerhouse that would make Newton proud. Blessed with countless books, a video library, and many places to read and study, Seattle Central Library is a place to research and delve into a treasure trove of books. Caroline and I visited the library on weekends, picking up books and videos and visiting other downtown places.

> **Bellevue**
>
> Bellevue is one of the best-kept secrets in the US. A magnificent, high-octane, high-tech city, it is well connected through transportation networks and features skyscrapers that house some of the most important technology companies globally. About 10 miles (16 kilometres) east of downtown Seattle, Bellevue is clean and immaculate in appearance. Proximity to Seattle, a world class hub of technology and life sciences, enhances the attractiveness of Bellevue. Seattle houses the world class **Seattle Hub for Synthetic Biology. T**he **Allen Institute**, the **Chan Zuckerberg Initiative,** and **the University of Washington** launched the **Seattle Hub for Synthetic Biology**. Founded by philanthropist Paul Allen, the Allen Institute is renowned for its contributions to the life sciences. The Seattle Hub for Synthetic Biology represents an innovative collaboration between academic institutions and leading philanthropic organizations, aiming to explore the genomic cycle and understand cellular history for the treatment of diseases. Bellevue boasts one of the most vibrant and well-educated communities in America. The city houses headquarters of companies such as *Expedia, Symetra, Puget Sound Energy, T-Mobile*, and major offices of Amazon and Microsoft, to name a few. There is a multifaceted exchange of ideas with a dynamic entrepreneurship mindset.

Hello, "My boy, what's up?" I greet Solomon, and we sit down and order coffee.

Sipping an Americano, we started discussing how the global startup ecosystem is evolving, especially in the deep tech and life sciences sectors. Understanding Solomon's deep interest in economics and taking cues from productivity, I began discussing the Solow Model. I used artificial intelligence and the semiconductor industry as examples to illustrate the connection between technological advancement and productivity.

"Solomon, you need to know more about the **Solow and Endogenous Growth Models**," I said. This will connect productivity to economic growth with the startup ecosystem as an enabler. "Isn't it something to do with the production function?"

"Yes, I want to discuss how productivity changes over time. Let's begin," I said, enunciating key concepts.

Productivity, ChatGPT, and Steady State

Startups are the life and vitality of economies. A well-developed and vibrant startup ecosystem is the bedrock of innovation, economic growth, and development. Many of the working population is employed in micro, small, and medium enterprises, even in advanced countries. This statistic is even more pronounced in emerging and frontier markets. A full-fledged startup ecosystem is a powerhouse for building sustainable businesses, leading to increased productivity and well-being over the long run. In recent years, social impact-driven startups focusing on social and financial returns have become increasingly popular. The rise in global awareness of ESG issues, the development ecosystem's focus on nurturing deep-dive startup ecosystems, and the abundance of investor capital have spurred a wave of innovation.

The **US, Europe, China, Israel, Singapore, Japan,** and **South Korea** are prime examples of economies that have achieved sustained innovation and increased productivity through world-class startup ecosystems. I read **Startup Nation by Dan Senor and Saul Singer**, a riveting account of how Israelis built one of the most dynamic startup ecosystems in the world. This startup ecosystem is the backbone of Israel's economic growth and well-being. The fast-paced book shares many inspirational stories that transformed the agriculturally oriented country of the 1950s and 60s into a high-tech nation today. The book covers various startup initiatives across multiple sectors, including groundbreaking afforestation techniques, the contribution of Intel's offshore research and development center to Intel's success over the years, and the novel idea of battery swapping in the early 2000s; these cases showcase the underlying entrepreneurship mindset among the population. In 2023, the country boasts world-class infrastructure and medical care systems, with a GDP per capita of \$52,642.4 at current prices.[a]

The book also discusses how Israel took inspiration from the US startup model and built close ties with the defense sector to fund startups in the technology sector. **DARPA (Defense Advanced Research Projects Agency)** is a key driver of innovation in the US, spearheading novel technologies across various industries, including the semiconductor sector. Its work features prominently in the book **Chip War by Chris Miller**, highlighting its significant contributions to technological advancements and national security. Startups drive continuous innovation as existing companies fail to consistently disrupt the market. For example, electric vehicle companies like Tesla and BYD have revolutionized the industry. At the same time, some major automakers have struggled to capitalize on the shift in consumer behavior toward greener options. Similarly, the emergence of generative artificial intelligence (AI) companies like **OpenAI (of ChatGPT fame), DeepSeek, Gemini** and **Claude AI** are some exemplary cases of disruptive technology companies. The impact of these AI-driven companies on productivity can only be measured over time. To understand productivity and the level of technology, it is imperative to look at the **Production Function** and the **Solow Model**.

Cobb Douglas Production Function

Cobb Douglas Production Function measures the effect of productivity on the economy. **Total Factor Productivity or Level of Technology is the driver of productivity in the long run.**

$A \times K^{\alpha} \times L^{(1-\alpha)}$. were

K: Structure, Equipment, Plant, Machinery etc.
L: Labor
A= Total Factor Productivity (TFP) or Level of Technology.

In this production function for the US, the share of labor and capital has remained constant over the year i.e., 70 percent labor participation and 30 percent capital participation.

Understanding the Solow Model

Dr. Robert Solow, the father of economic growth theory, made significant contributions to economic theory by creating the Solow-Swan growth model. This model explains long-run economic growth as a function of labor and capital, with the level of technology considered an exogenous factor. In the production function, the level of technology, also known as **Total Factor Productivity (TFP),** is exogenous, meaning it is not defined within the model. Trevor Swan independently made significant contributions to this model. Levers facilitating technological advancements include the Industrial Revolution and, more recently, the proliferation of the internet and artificial intelligence (AI). These inventions have raised employee productivity, increasing economic growth, assuming other factors remain constant. The Solow model attempts to explain the impact of technological progress on productivity growth through increases in capital per worker or the capital-labor ratio. The Solow Model outlines how labor, capital, and the savings rate, through the investment function and population growth, determine capital accumulation, leading to long-term economic growth. Advanced economies eventually reach a steady state when increases in the capital-labor ratio plateau. At the same time, emerging economies experience high growth due to rising capital-to-labor ratios, keeping the level of technology constant. The level of technology, however, is treated as constant and exogenous to the model. The discussion of the Solow Model primarily aims to introduce the concept of the steady state. Empirical studies examining the contribution of TFP growth to economic growth have generally found that technological progress is a significant contributor.

Total Factor Productivity at Constant Prices for the US and UK
(1st Jan 1954 to 1st Jan 2019)

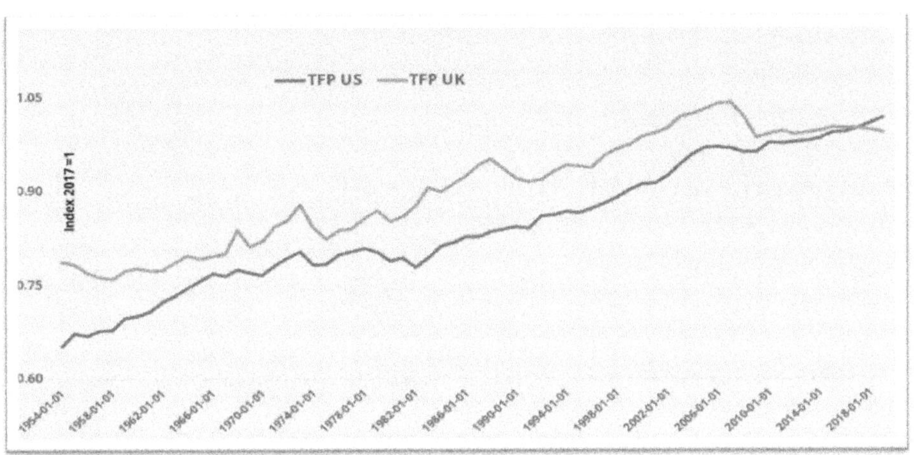

Data Source: University of Groningen and University of California, Davis, Total Factor Productivity at Constant National Prices for the United States [RTFPNAUSA632NRUG], retrieved from FRED, Federal Reserve Bank of St. Louis; https://fred.stlouisfed.org/series/RTFPNAUSA632NRUG, July 16, 2024. University of Groningen and University of California, Davis, Total Factor Productivity at Constant National Prices for the United Kingdom [RTFPNAGBA632NRUG], retrieved from FRED, Federal Reserve Bank of St. Louis; https://fred.stlouisfed.org/series/RTFPNAGBA632NRUG, July 16, 2024.

Reference: Feenstra, Robert C., Robert Inklaar and Marcel P. Timmer (2015), "The Next Generation of the Penn World Table," American Economic Review, 105(10), 3150-3182, available for download at *www.ggdc.net/pwt*.

Units: Index 2017=1, Not Seasonally Adjusted, **Frequency:** Annual; Chart; Author

$$National\ Income = Real\ Labor\ Income + Real\ Capital\ Income$$

National income is divided between payments to capital and labor. The size of payments depends on the marginal products of labor and capital. The share of labor and capital income remains the same regardless of the level of national income.

The Cobb-Douglas Production Function has the following characteristics:

The production function assumes constant returns to scale and has a diminishing marginal product of labor. The marginal product of labor (MPL) indicates how much output increases for each additional labor unit, holding other inputs constant.

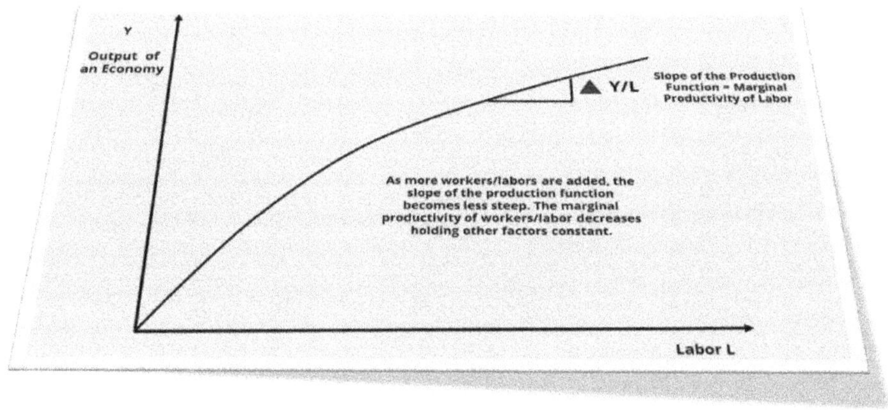

Image: Author

National Saving Investment Consumption Function

In the Solow Model, the capital-worker ratio (k) is defined as capital divided by labor, while output per worker is output divided by labor. All measurements are recorded per worker/labor. The output measured is output per worker. It is important to remember that in a closed economy, investment equals savings, and output is the sum of consumption and investment. Therefore, investment is a function of the savings ratio of output, depicted as the investment function $= sA_1K_t^{0.3}$, where K_t is the capital-labor or capital-worker ratio.

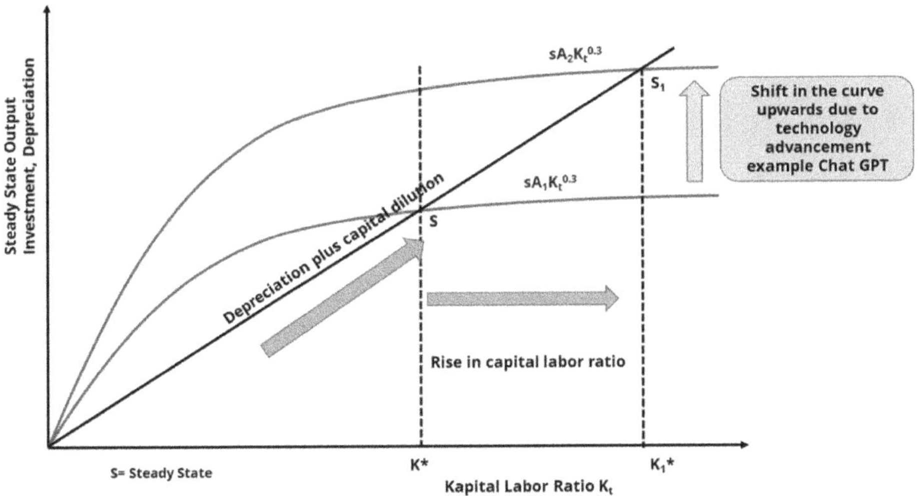

Image: Author

A is the level of technology measured as total factor productivity. A is an exogenous variable to the **Solow Model**, i.e. the unexplained part of the production function. **Output Y is investment plus consumption**. Because of population growth, capital dilution happens due to the increase in the labor force. $sA_1K_t^{0.3}$ is the investment function derived as the **capital-to-labor ratio** from the production function. At steady state S, investment per worker equals depreciation plus capital dilution since the *change in capital per worker is zero.*

Depreciation plus Capital Dilution (at K* and K_1*) = $sA_1K_t^{0.3}$

As shown in the image, the **capital-labor/worker** ratio increases in the initial years, which is measured through the slope of the investment function. When the economy approaches a steady state at K_1*, the change in the capital-worker ratio is zero because investment per worker equals the sum of depreciation and capital dilution. **Net investment** equals the *investment function, less depreciation and capital dilution.* According to the Solow Model, an increase in the labor force reduces the capital per worker. As the labor force increases due to higher fertility rates, leading to more workers in the economy, there is a need for increased capital infusion. Over time, the productivity of labor diminishes. However, the Romer Model views population growth positively. Dr. Paul Romer, a Nobel laureate and a professor at New York University (and formerly at the University of California, Berkeley), proposed the Endogenous Growth Model. This model explains the level of technology as an endogenous outcome of the economic system. Unlike neoclassical growth models, which treat technological advancement as an external factor, endogenous growth models incorporate technology and innovation as part of the system.

This means that an increase in the labor force can enhance productivity when effectively trained through various initiatives. Upskilling, quality education, and entrepreneurship are key enablers for boosting innovation and total factor productivity. Startups are nimble and can disrupt and scale businesses faster than established companies, many of them with high market share but low growth. BCG developed a four-category matrix to understand companies, using market share and growth as two variables for comparison. Startups have greater potential to become leaders in specific sectors by capturing market share through their uniqueness and value proposition. Startups within the technology sector have shown the best potential to disrupt the market. Many companies reinvented the wheel using innovative products that redefine the way of life. I covered one neoclassical growth model – The Solow model. Now, let's understand the Endogenous Growth Model. This is an important model as it explains productivity as an input. Unlike the Solow Model, where the level of technology is outside the model, hence constant, in the Endogenous Growth Model, the model can explain the level of technology.

Endogenous Growth Model & Entrepreneurship

While the **Solow Model** suggests that **high population growth** (higher labor force) lowers the capital-worker ratio, keeping capital constant and reducing output per worker, the **Endogenous Growth Model**, on the other hand, looks at an increase in population growth as an *enabler for total factor productivity* through well-thought policies, for example, fostering growth in human capital through quality education and entrepreneurship. These policies will amplify productivity through innovation, increasing the returns model. The **Endogenous Growth Model** is a significant economic long run model for policymakers to enable policies that promote technological advancement to increase productivity—for example, providing quality K12 and higher education, increasing research and development by the government, or promoting intellectual property rights through copyrights or patents to promote excludability of products and facilitate an increase in investments in technology. Many of the innovations globally are funded by the government or government-led initiatives or agencies, such as the U.S. Defense-funded **ARPANET,** which led to the invention of the internet or digitalization of payment services in selected countries. **The Origins of Endogenous Growth** by Paul Romer is an excellent paper tracing the assumptions behind the Endogenous Growth Model.

> Let me share an example of initiatives that drive economic growth, innovation, and productivity with a focus on sustainability," I said. They can be classified as steps used by policymakers who use **Endogenous Growth Model** as the central tenet.

The **European Union (EU)** is a global leader in structuring policies that advance green energy. The EU is driving innovation through its **Innovation Fund,** which provides capital to projects to solve climate change problems. The EU took a significant initiative toward zero carbon emissions by 2050. The European Commission, along with the assistance of the *European Climate, Infrastructure, and Environment Executive Agency (CINEA),* spearheads the Innovation Fund. The EU Green Deal, which plans to make the EU carbon neutral by 2050, is heralded as a major step in climate action, with initiatives like Sustainable Finance, the **EU Emissions Trading System (EU ETS),** and the **EU Climate Law.** *The EU Climate Law is the first of its kind to set targets for reducing and removing carbon emissions. The EU has set targets for 2030, aiming for a net 55 percent reduction in emissions compared to the 1990 level.* [b]

The key focus of the Innovation Fund is on renewable energy, energy storage, and energy-intensive industries. Funded through the innovative EU ETS mechanism, a groundbreaking carbon pricing trading system based on cap-and-trade, the Innovation Fund is making a significant impact. The Innovation Fund invests in startups and projects, with an expected corpus of *€40 billion (calculated using €75 per ton of CO_2 from the EU ETS system) from 2020 to 2030.* The EU ETS will be covered in detail under the carbon pricing chapter. The fund invests in small-scale and large-scale projects and has already awarded around €6.5 billion to over 100 innovative projects. The funding is based on five parameters, including the degree of innovation and cost efficiency. The fund partners with the **European Investment Bank (EIB),** one of the largest multilateral development banks, to provide technical and financial assistance through the **Project Development Assistance (PDA)** initiative. Although this activity focuses less on startups, it aims to drive productivity and innovation through entrepreneurial activities. By providing monetary and technical support, organizations can spend time solving complex problems within the sustainable sector that might not have been possible otherwise. These sustainable and scalable measures lead to sustainable business models that increase employability and productivity within economies.

"I took a moment to catch my breath. I had shared much information today, yet I am eager to explore one more example to further clarify my point. I will discuss generative AI as an example of technology enablers that drive long-term productivity improvements."

'Ah, yes, of course,' Solomon responded. 'Chatbots like ChatGPT are revolutionizing the way we work today. Makes sense.' I nodded and continued."

Large Language Models: Generative Artificial Intelligence (Gen AI)

Generative Artificial Intelligence (Gen AI) uses artificial intelligence to generate content such as articles, references, images, code, and videos. This technology is a game-changer in business, increasing productivity and enabling sectors like upskilling. These language-driven chatbots have emerged as conversation tools, adding a social aspect to technology. Chatbots like *ChatGPT, DeepSeek, and Claude* are advanced Gen AI based on Large Language Models that work on the neural network concept, mimicking the human brain's functioning. The AI industry was stuck before neural networks were used to train these generative AI models through enormous datasets, including images. Generative models are broader than descriptive models that are trained on specific functions.

ChatGPT defines itself as "an advanced AI language model developed by OpenAI, leveraging the power of a neural network system based on the GPT-4 (Generative Pre-trained Transformer 4) architecture. This cutting-edge technology allows ChatGPT to understand and generate human-like text, making it a versatile and powerful tool for a variety of applications."

A key factor is their ability to continuously innovate through disruptive technologies. This is where the startup ecosystem plays a pivotal role in rolling out disruptive technologies.

Understanding the startup lifecycle is crucial to gain a better perspective on the global startup ecosystem.

Let's begin by asking a few questions.

The Startup Lifecycle and the Valley of Death

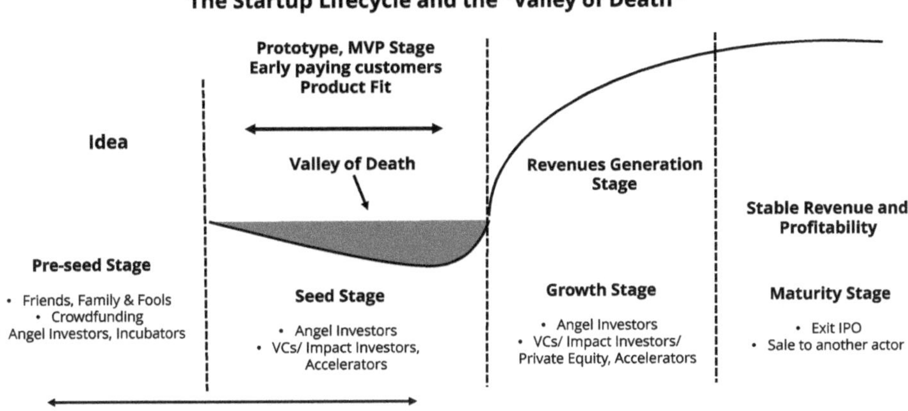

Image: Author

The Startup Journey Begins

The startup journey begins with idea inception. The key kick-start attribute is belief and passion in your idea. The idea must be implemented through a series of steps, which should be outcome-driven. There are a few questions every startup founder needs to ponder before embarking on the startup journey:

➤ What problem does your startup plan to address?

➤ How is your solution unique and disruptive compared to peers? Is your business scalable?

➤ What is your startup's target market segment? What is the Serviceable Obtainable Market?

➤ What go-to-market strategy would you use for your venture? Does your startup have network effects?

These pivotal questions will enhance your understanding of how your idea can succeed before you invest your time, capital, and energy into turning it into a full-fledged business. All these thoughts can be included in a document known as a Pitch Deck. A Pitch Deck and an exhaustive financial projection spreadsheet will be the most important documents for early-stage startups.

Guy Kawasaki, the famous Silicon Valley venture capitalist, shares some advice on what parameters to look for in a pitch deck. Solomon knew about this; I referred him to Guy Kawasaki's YouTube video on key points important for pitch decks. I shared a few pointers from my experience, looked at his startup's pitch deck, and shared mine. We exchanged some thoughts on ways to improve Solomon's startup pitch deck. Guy Kawasaki provides an excellent framework for determining which startups will most likely succeed. Startups that are unique in their offering and high in value are in the winner's corner. These startups have a clear differential in offering compared to peers while also winning in pricing their products. These startups often become disruptors, rapidly capturing market share. I suggested Solomon read Guy Kawasaki's *The Art of the Start 2.0*, an insightful book for entrepreneurs. I highly recommend Clayton Christensen's work to better understand disruptive innovation.

Pitch Deck Essentials

The pitch deck is among the most critical documents, including the problem and solution slides and a sound business and revenue model. Some key pointers are the **Serviceable Obtainable Market** or target market segment derived from the **Total Addressable and Serviceable Achievable Market**. This segmentation is key to understanding the clarity of thought required for building a brand through *brand management, go-to-market strategy, and other advertising and outreach strategies* needed over time. Understanding who your customers are is critical for structuring **key performance indicators (KPIs) or metrics** to measure your startup's milestones. These fluid metrics are essential for benchmarking your startup's progress. An initial KPI could be launching a **minimum viable product** with customers. Below are a few critical metrics for SaaS and PaaS-based startups.

> **Customer Acquisition Cost**: Marketing and sales costs to acquire a new customer.

- ➤ **Payback Period**: Customer Acquisition Cost (CAC) / Average Monthly Revenue per Customer.
- ➤ **Life Time Value:** Total amount you earn from your customers.
  - ○ Lifetime value is Average Revenue per customer × Average Lifespan of customer.
- ➤ **MRR:** Monthly Recurring Revenue.

One critical enabler for **PaaS (Product as a Service) startups** is to convert free users to paid customers if they have a free product version. PaaS leverages technology to build platforms where the audience can register for free and premium services. Examples could be **Edtech** and **Media** companies that sell products through a subscription-based model. **Netflix** is another example of PaaS. One of the KPIs most subscription-based online portals can consider is increasing **the lifetime value** of customers. Apart from retaining existing customers, startups could cross-sell other products to customers, such as different products or services. Qualities preferred in startups are scalability, healthy profit margin, repeat and cross-selling of goods and services, and a sustainable business model with a customer-centric focus.

Solomon said, "I would like to know more about the various actors in the startup ecosystem. I am keen to learn about the different initiatives within this sector." Solomon mentioned that he has incorporated some metrics for his startup's pitch. I started this topic with the three Fs.

The first funding comes from **FFFs – friends, family, and fools**. Crowdfunding is today another excellent avenue for raising capital from retail or institutional investors. This type of funding, in some cases, requires an equity stake in the business. Before investing, selected angel investors and venture capitalists look at sound pitch decks and financial projections. Usually, investors do require a working prototype. Nowadays, many incubators incubate companies, especially those building technology-oriented products. In India, **the Atal Innovation Mission,** the government's apex body governing innovation and entrepreneurship in India and abroad, has set up many incubators across India. Government-based incubators have become major powerhouses for building startups, especially those with long gestation periods and that need capital to build their products. Many of these incubators globally infuse capital at zero equity or charge subsidized prices for utilizing their services. Incubators enhance *knowledge* *capital, mentorship,* and *investor connections* for wannabe startups, a priceless enabler. Incubators build the research & development of startups and facilitate **Intellectual Property (IP)** registration, which is the bedrock of innovation and creativity. Many incubators prefer the deep tech sector or could be focused on themes such as fintech and biotechnology, while others are sector agnostic. **Incubators** are excellent powerhouses for startups to transform their ideas into functional prototypes and minimum viable products. They assist in refining business and revenue models, forging partnerships, and raising capital from investors. Some incubators take equity or charge a subsidized fee for using their premises, which include coworking space, mentoring, internet infrastructure, and other services.

Venture Capitalists (VCs) are institutional investors, compared to angel investors, who are usually high- or ultra-high-net-worth individuals who could be part of a larger network. VCs usually invest more capital than angel investors, are more active in guiding the company, and are more business-savvy.

We exchange a lot of knowledge on this.

Okay, what's the valley of death? I thought it was the Death Valley in California.

I smiled when I heard this.

Valley of Death

Death Valley conjures images of Death Valley in California, which is considered by many to be the hottest place on Earth. **Badwater Basin** is the lowest point in North America, at 282 ft (86 m) below sea level. The valley recorded a **high of 134°F (56.7°C) on July 10, 1913**.

Levers: The Framework for Building Repeatability into Your Business by Amos Schwartzfarb and Trevor Boehm is a highly recommended book for entrepreneurs. This book is excellent for understanding key economic enablers, benchmarking, and setting performance metrics that help build a robust financial model. It includes a chapter on financial modeling with a link to a spreadsheet and covers concepts such as calculating contribution margin and lifetime value. Levers is essential reading for startups operating on SaaS, PaaS, and similar models. The concepts are well explained, making it a must-read for entrepreneurs, particularly in technology.

Here, the valley of death is the seed stage in a startup's lifecycle, wherein the probability of startup failure is the highest. The seed stage is the most critical phase for startups, as this is when they are actively building their product. This stage is also known as the *"death valley"* because many startups fail during this period. Failure can occur for various reasons, such as the inability to build a working **minimum viable product**, poor product-market or founder-market fit, or lack of capital. Accelerators are an excellent option for startups seeking funding. Many global accelerator programs with regional chapters across various countries accept a limited number of startups into their cohorts. Some of these accelerators also select startups during the pre-seed phase. Notable accelerator programs include **Y Combinator** and **Techstars**. Techstars has many chapters focused on particular themes, such as its social impact accelerator program in Atlanta, US. Accelerators provide mentorship, refine business models, and help build startups from one stage to another.

Attending in-person accelerator programs to build your network with your cohort is essential. Accelerator programs typically span around three months, culminating in a demo day pitch to investors. These programs usually take an equity stake in their services, which they plan to sell their stake to other investors as the startup's valuation increases. **Slush**, based in Helsinki, Finland, is a unique global platform for startups to showcase their ventures to international investors. The event allows startups to attend and network with all actors within the startup ecosystem, including entrepreneurs, investors, accelerators, social change makers, policymakers, and business leaders. With a free flow of entrepreneurial milieu, Slush facilitates an international perspective, especially regarding technology companies.

Global accelerator programs and events like Slush are ideal for startups looking to expand to other locations, such as America and Europe. The startup ecosystem in some countries is rated among the best, offering abundant funding, talent, and enablers to propel your venture to new heights. To move to the growth stage, startups typically have a functioning product and a product-market fit. Solomon and his team had applied to Slush and felt their startup would get shortlisted to pitch live in front of the audience.

Growth Stage

During the growth stage, startups expand into new geographies or locations, recruit talent, and invest in equipment. Following the seed round, startups typically progress through **Series A, B, and C** funding rounds to raise additional funds for expansion. It's important to note that funding at each stage will dilute the holdings of founders and other investors, despite increasing the company's valuation.

Mistral.ai, a France-based startup, is an excellent example of the critical success of the European startup ecosystem.

Series A funding serves as a crucial barometer for measuring the vibrancy of a startup ecosystem.

Solomon interrupted me, mentioning how the EU had passed a regulation on artificial intelligence. He reconfirmed Gen AI poses ethical risks that have garnered the attention of regulators globally. **Geoffrey Hinton**, the father of artificial intelligence, who played a pivotal role in the emergence of Gen AI, quit Google's artificial intelligence unit, citing risks posed by artificial intelligence. Over the years, artificial intelligence has caught the imagination of science fiction writers and Hollywood. **"2001: A Space Odyssey"** is a high point of imagination, visionary thinking, and the reality of the artificial intelligence threat becoming real.

Keanu Reeves's blockbuster Matrix series epitomizes the rise of artificial intelligence and its potential takeover of humanity in the near future. This scenario seemed far-fetched a decade ago, but could become looks probable given the lightning speed at which artificial intelligence permeates our lives today.

The EU passed the first regulation governing artificial intelligence to safeguard people against its detrimental impacts. The EU is a thought leader globally, brainstorming novel policymaking within the ESG sector. The regulation of artificial intelligence addresses governance issues, establishing the EU as the de facto leader in judicious policy enablement worldwide.

The **European Union** passed the **Artificial Intelligence Act**, a landmark regulation to enforce a comprehensive legal framework on artificial intelligence. As Gen AI poses social risks, the regulation aims to ensure AI's safe, transparent, unbiased, and ethical use. The regulation categorizes AI systems based on risk levels and bans certain practices, such as social profiling based on racial or demographic profiles. Policy enablers enacted by the EU include setting up a governance board to ensure compliance with the Artificial Intelligence Act and establishing testing hubs to facilitate startups and medium enterprises in running AI models before release.

> Bonds are fixed-income securities that pay a recurring interest payment, also known as coupons, over the course of their tenure. These coupons are either quarterly, semi-annual, and/or annual. At maturity, the principal is returned along with the final coupon. However, there are special types of bonds, for example, zero-coupon bonds, that are issued at a discount to their issuing price with full value redeemed at maturity.

I heard him out. We both agreed that the EU is currently the best policymaking governing body in the world, especially in the ESG sector.

I continued with my narrative on startups.

As a startup's business expands, so does its revenue (top line) and, in many cases, its profitability. With economies of scale, the company gains more market power and the ability to negotiate better terms with supply chain partners, thereby enhancing the pricing power of its products. This stage typically involves a larger operational budget, recruitment of talent, and innovative customer insights to manage customer relationships better. During the growth stage, there is a rapid acceleration of revenues, usually above $1 million per annum, and depending on the annual revenues, private equity could also be investors.

Stable Revenues and Profitability

At this stage, many investors want to exit their holdings, ideally through initial public offerings. Investors may sell their stakes to other investors or venture capitalists. We chatted for a while before we left. I picked up the bill. I liked the young man; he and Ayana looked terrific together. I mentioned the upcoming get-together at my place and invited Solomon and Ayana. I promised to connect Ayana with an art gallerist and champion of the arts based in New York City. Solomon, delighted to hear this, shook my hand. It's always a pleasure helping him and Ayana. I would call him later to mention the day and time of the planned event. As I walked toward my electric vehicle, I felt glad to have met up with Solomon.

Chapter 4

Let's Order Sustainable Finance

After my evening run, I headed home. I had invited friends and prepared some delicacies. I especially loved the Pesto Cristo pasta and the unique coffee, a one-of-a-kind blend I had prepared. Caroline and I are food enthusiasts and use eco-friendly décor and art as central themes in our house. Caroline, Xu, Brad, and Krystal were already seated and chatting when I arrived. I greeted them warmly and joined the group. Krystal, a tall, striking lady, Caroline's friend, and a coffee aficionado, discussed the nuances of coffee-making, explaining various types of coffee beans from around the world and how they pair with different dishes. Krystal aspired to be a Hollywood actress and modeled for several global brands. A coffee-tasting session was underway, and we all sampled a variety of coffees. Our conversation soon drifted to other topics.

Krystal said, "Hey, Kish isn't sustainable finance big time now." I nodded.

Yes, that's true, Krystal. Considering **GSS+ (Green, Social, Sustainability, and Sustainability-Linked Bonds)** alone, it's more than $5 trillion.[a] If you include social and impact bonds, impact investing, and crowdfunding for sustainable purposes, the market size will be slightly larger. However, GSS+ still constitutes the majority of the sustainable finance sector.

> Bonds are fixed-income securities that pay a recurring interest payment, also known as coupons, over the course of their tenure. These coupons are either quarterly, semi-annual, and/or annual. At maturity, the principal is returned along with the final coupon. However, there are special types of bonds, for example, zero-coupon bonds, that are issued at a discount to their issuing price with full value redeemed at maturity.

Green bonds have the largest market share and are the most dominant among these GSS+ bonds.

Krystal asked, "Cool, what do you mean by bonds?" Since she had little experience in the financial sector, Caroline and I explained the capital markets while others contributed their thoughts.

During our discussion, Peter walked in with his son, Maverick. After exchanging greetings, I said, "Hello, Maverick, my boy!" and lovingly lifted him onto my shoulders. "My boy" is one of my favorite expressions—I often use it as a friendly greeting. In addition, I mentioned that social and development impact bonds are similar to pay-for-performance structures, where development actors are rewarded for achieving the results of interventions. Social Finance first implemented this type of structure.

Take the example of the Peterborough Social Impact Bond. Social Finance raised £5 million to target outcomes—in this case, reducing reoffending rates among prisoners with sentences of less than a year in Peterborough Prison. The key performance indicator here was the reduction in reoffending rates. Another critical point is the distinction between social and development impact bonds. In a social impact bond, like the one discussed above, the outcome payer is typically a government entity, and these bonds are generally implemented in advanced economies. On the other hand, development impact bonds are implemented in low- and middle-income countries and typically involve a third-party outcome payer, **_such as a donor organization_**. Xu, unconvinced, challenged me by saying that the payoffs of many impact bonds are not similar to those of derivatives. I agreed; that's why I mentioned they have a quasi-derivative payoff. Xu mentioned that he would explain how options work since that would be the most pertinent derivative to discuss here. Let me proceed with a simple, plain vanilla call and put options.

Options are derivative instruments whose value depends on an underlying asset. These assets can belong to various asset classes, including equities, bonds, or illiquid assets. I will discuss only two types of options here, as the topic is vast enough to warrant a separate book. The two key types are **call options** and **put options**. Options provide the **right, but not the obligation**, to execute a transaction involving the underlying asset within a specified period. For example, a call option gives the holder the right, but not the obligation, to buy an asset at a predetermined price during a specific time frame. Let's say I purchase a call option for a stock currently trading at $30. The option is valid for three months, and I pay a premium (a small upfront amount) to buy the option. Typically, an option contract will be large, for instance, 100 stocks per contract. I would exercise the call option only if the price of the underlying asset increases during the three months by more than the premium I paid. If the stock rises to $40, my profit would be **$40 - $30 – premium per share = $10 per share** (Ignore the premium here). For a 100-stock lot, this translates to a total profit of $1000. On the other hand, a put option gives the holder the right to sell the stock at a particular price, keeping all other information constant. For example, if I have a put option to sell the stock at $30 within three months, and the stock price falls to $20, I can sell it at $30 and then repurchase it at $20. This results in a profit of **$30 - $20 = $10 per share**, minus the premium I paid for the put option. In this case, the options are **American-style options**, meaning these options can be exercised at any time before the expiration date, unlike **European-style options**, which can be exercised only at maturity.

"I thanked Xu for explaining the concept so fluently. I used this example to explain how the payouts of some impact bonds can be categorized similarly to the payouts of plain vanilla options."

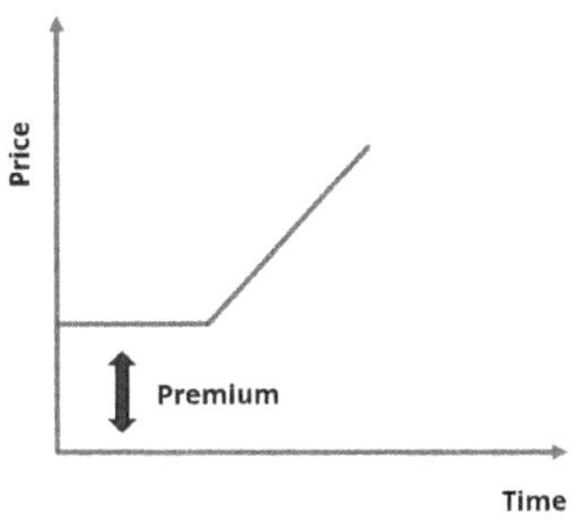

Krystal and Brad are very sharp and inquisitive. They immediately asked me about the key actors driving impact bonds globally. I replied that the main actors include investors, outcome payers, impact evaluators, technical assistance groups, intermediaries, and service providers. There are various social impact bonds, but I didn't understand the details initially. However, both of them wanted to know more. For example, they asked what I meant by an intervention and impact evaluator. To simplify, interventions refer to projects or policies designed to produce a series of causally interlinked outputs that achieve a long-term outcome. Impact evaluators measure these outcomes either qualitatively or quantitatively. These outcome-driven projects typically use a theory of change methodology.

Peter interjected and elaborated on the theory of change concept. He explained how outcome-driven projects are mapped backward through interventions or outputs to achieve the desired outcome.

For example, if the goal is to improve the effectiveness of K-12 education, one way would be to increase both the number and quality of teachers. Researchers could assess factors such as qualifications and previous experience to measure teacher quality. The project, when implemented, would be referred to as an intervention. The impact measurement could then be the improvement in student grades. Peter further illustrated with an example related to our café. If the goal (outcome) is to become one of the best cafes in town, the interventions could include hiring a top-quality chef, choosing the right location, ensuring an appealing ambiance, and providing excellent customer service. Key measures of evaluation would be high customer ratings, increased footfall, and overall customer satisfaction.

Caroline asked a quiz to make our discussion livelier: "Do you know who issued the first green bond?"

Peter chimed in: "I know this one. The **European Investment Bank** issued the world's first green bond, called a *Climate Awareness Bond (CAB)*, in 2007."

"Correct," Caroline replied.

Peter and Brad proposed starting with regulations, such as the **EU Sustainable Finance Framework**, before delving into the various types of sustainable bonds. I suggested we interconnect the discussion with key initiatives governing sustainable finance to provide a cohesive perspective. We all agreed. I prepared a snapshot of significant milestones in the sustainable finance sector from 2007 to 2023, highlighting key regulations that have reshaped the global landscape. I began with a quick overview.

Selected Key Milestones in Sustainable Finance

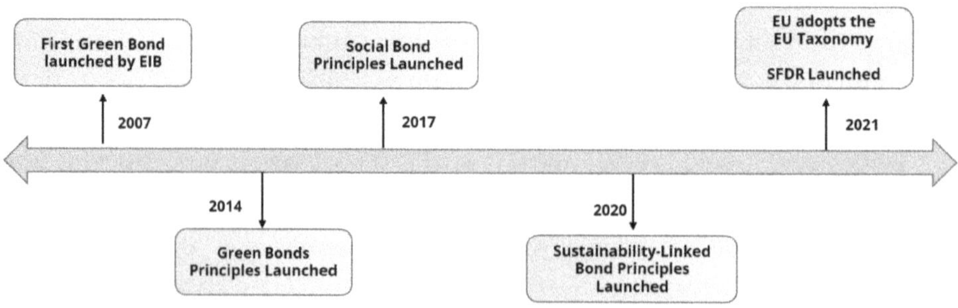

Above are selected key milestones in the emergence of sustainable finance. The launch of a green bond by the European Investment Bank and later by the World Bank set the tone for social financial innovation within the sustainable ecosystem. As the race to capital for social and environmental good began, the sustainable finance ecosystem expanded by launching **"The Principles"** for various types of sustainable bonds. In 2014, the **International Capital Market Association (ICMA)** introduced *the Green Bond Principles* (GBP), a set of voluntary guidelines that standardized the green bond market, improving transparency, integrity, and accountability. As we moved forward, I shared that we would delve deeper into these milestones. The launch of the EU Taxonomy enhanced the market for sustainable bonds.

Yet, this achievement pales compared to the size of the global debt market, which exceeds $100 trillion. As investors' appetite for ESG and ESG investment integration increases, the path toward ESG finance is progressing steadily. However, if trillions of dollars are required per year to reach the 2030 SDGs, especially in uncertain and tragic geopolitical conditions, the importance of sustainable finance is pivotal and utmost. Everyone appreciated the Global Sustainable Investing Assets snapshot, which sparked a discussion about various ESG investing strategies. ESG investing, also known as sustainable investing, continues to gain momentum. Before diving deeper, Caroline first pointed out the importance of understanding green bonds and sustainable finance. We all agreed, and our discussion turned to innovation. Although green energy initiatives began in the United States, China is leading in various advancements in this field. However, the European Union is the leader in implementing groundbreaking policies, particularly in the sustainable finance sector. One milestone is the **EU Sustainable Finance Framework**. The European Union has been a world leader in driving policies within the sustainable development sector, including sustainable finance. We must start with a brief overview of the **EU Sustainable Finance Framework**.

EU Sustainable Finance Framework

Based on the **Communication from the Commission to the European Parliament, The Council, The European Economic and Social Committee and the Committee of the regions Strategy for Financing the Transition to a Sustainable Economy report**, the EU will alone need EUR 350 billion per year this decade to achieve its ambitious 2030 emissions target within energy systems notwithstanding an additional EUR 130 billion per year to achieve other environmental goals. The work to improve on the existing EU taxonomy is laudatory in bringing in more themes example biodiversity, sustainable agriculture, natural gas, etc. Under the **Multiannual Financial Framework (2021 to 2027)** and **Next GenEU (NGEU)**, a total corpus of EUR 100 billion will be invested in biodiversity projects. **NGEU** plans to raise 30 percent of its EUR 750 billion capital through the issuance of green bonds showcases a huge focus towards the green label. The idea of various measures by the EU is to impact 23 million SMEs within the EU through enhanced access to sustainability advisory services. The report builds on enhancing and understanding the impact of digitalization services including *artificial intelligence, blockchain, big data, and the Internet of things* within the gamut of sustainable finance tools. **European Single Access Point (ESAP)** and the **Open Finance Framework**, will help to unleash sustainability-related information for a common good. An impetus within the climate adaption is given through increasing insurance coverage through a natural disaster board insurance dashboard **European Insurance** and **Occupational Pensions Authority (EIOPA)** fortifies companies against rising natural calamities due to climate change. An effort to strengthen corporate governance with green budgeting incorporation to better track and monitor climate and biodiversity spending under the 2021-2027 Multiannual Financial Framework and its alignment with the EU's ambition. Public-private partnership is a key mandate within the seventeen sustainable development goals, the EU EUR 1 trillion mobilization **Sustainable Europe Investment Plan** aims to attract capital in green label through public and private actors over the next decade.

Sustainable Finance Disclosure Regulation (SFDR)

One of the most critical aspects of the **EU Sustainable Finance Framework** is the **Sustainable Finance Disclosure Regulation (SFDR)**. One landmark regulation in the sustainable finance sector is the Sustainable Finance Disclosure Regulation (SFDR). The financial services industry plays a pivotal role in raising capital for sustainability-related causes, and the SFDR provides a framework for disclosing measures that enhance accountability, transparency, and the integration of adverse sustainability impacts in investment decisions. SFDR is a key step for the EU to move private capital toward net zero. According to the **Official Journal of the**

European Union, sustainability risk refers to an *environmental, social, or governance (ESG) event or condition* that could negatively affect the value of an investment. Asset managers and investors must understand how their investments or portfolios contribute to adverse ESG impacts. The SFDR identifies two key players within the financial services sector: financial market participants (such as asset managers, alternative investment fund managers, and manufacturers of pension products) and financial advisers. The broader objective of the disclosure framework is to drive more transparency and accountability within the system. This is done by requiring financial market participants (FMPs) and financial advisers to disclose the integration of sustainability risks and principal adverse impacts (PAIs) in decision-making at both entity and product levels. The aim is to create a uniform framework for integrating these risks at the investment level. Furthermore, these disclosures must be aligned with **(Markets in Financial Instruments Directive) MiFID** and **(Insurance Distribution Directive) IDD**. The SFDR is a crucial step toward resolving the principal-agent problem, wherein agents (e.g., financial advisers) may mis-sell investment products to clients. This regulation aims to ensure better alignment between investors' goals and the products financial advisers recommend. The SFDR ensures product disclosures align with their sustainability characteristics or objectives. **Article 6** focuses on disclosing sustainability risks, while **Article 8** provides information on how an investment product aligns with ESG characteristics. **Article 9** pertains to investment products with an investment objective within their mandates. Funds under Article 9 typically have a core ESG investment theme, whereas Article 8 funds may lack such a core theme.

I mentioned to Caroline to start the discussion on various sustainable finance bonds.

Before diving into the discussion on *Green, Social, Sustainability, and Sustainability-Linked Bonds,* I'd like to highlight a couple of key actors that play a pivotal role in shaping the sustainable finance sector," announced Caroline.

The International Capital Market Association (ICMA) is a champion of the global development sector. Formed as a nonprofit organization with headquarters in Zurich, Switzerland, ICMA has pioneered the development of global capital and securities markets. ICMA has been a leading collaborator in developing sustainable finance frameworks. These principles are voluntary sets of guidelines detailing the vision and mission of bonds in addressing environmental and social outcomes. These guidelines aim to standardize issuances across geographies, drive transparency, and enhance accountability within the global capital markets. These frameworks minimize greenwashing by various actors, especially corporations, that could use social financing mechanisms to improve their ESG ratings. For example, according to the **Climate Bonds Initiative**, corporations can receive a discount on coupons or "greenium" for the capital raised through sustainable bonds. $_c$ *"The Principles"* aid in improving the sustainable finance landscape and drive uniformity between different actors globally. The framework aids in documenting and quantifying the impact of the interventions funded. These core principles are designed for the issuers and investors to benchmark and understand their offerings based on the set of voluntary guidelines for their various classifications. ICMA is not the only sustainable finance guideline in the market. For example, the **Hong Kong Mortgage Corporation Limited Social, Green, and Sustainability Financing Framework** is a comprehensive guideline within the sustainable finance sector. The Climate Bonds Initiative has a strict set of guidelines for sustainable bonds. As mentioned, sustainable bonds began with green bonds when the **European Investment Bank** issued the first green bond in 2007. The European multilateral subsequently launched the **Sustainability Awareness Bonds** in 2018.

Okay, now I will begin our discussion on *Green, Social, Sustainability, and Sustainability-Linked Bonds using a top-down approach.* These bonds focus on environmental and social objectives. They are closely linked to the EU Taxonomy and UN SDGs, making them a credible framework for different actors to work within the sustainable development sector.

GSS+ (Green, Social, Sustainability, and Sustainability-Linked Bonds)

The GSS+ (Green, Social, Sustainability, and Sustainability-Linked Bonds) issuance stood at $5.7 trillion as of 31 December 2024. These figures are according to the Climate Bonds Initiative, another major champion within the sustainable development sector. The data pertains to bonds aligned with the Climate Bonds methodology. [a]

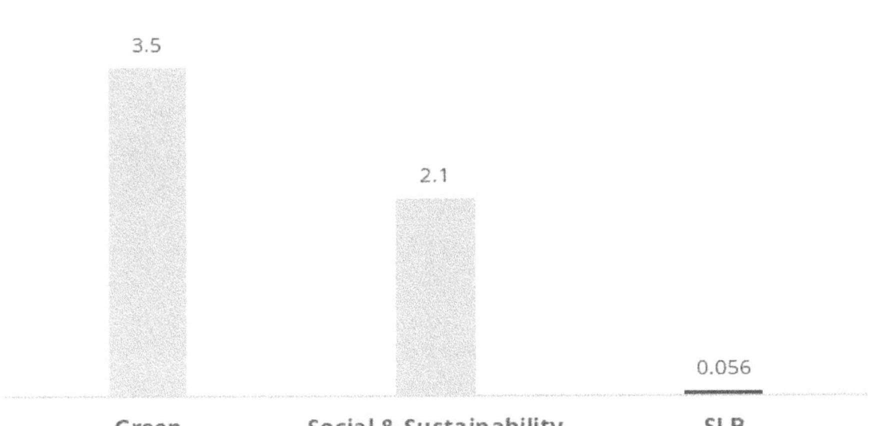

Data: *Climate Bonds Initiative*. *5 for 25: Delivering 5 trillion of climate investment annually by 2025. Retrieved from https://www.climatebonds.net/files/releases/cbi_5_for_25_01b.pdf.*

Chart: *Author. Figure in trillion USD.*

Above is an excellent overview of the issuance of various types of sustainable bonds, focusing on four key categories: Green, Social, Sustainability, and Sustainability-Linked bonds based on Climate Bonds Initiative data. Green bonds dominate the sustainable bond market, accounting for an average of approximately 54 per cent of total issuances from 2020 to 2024.

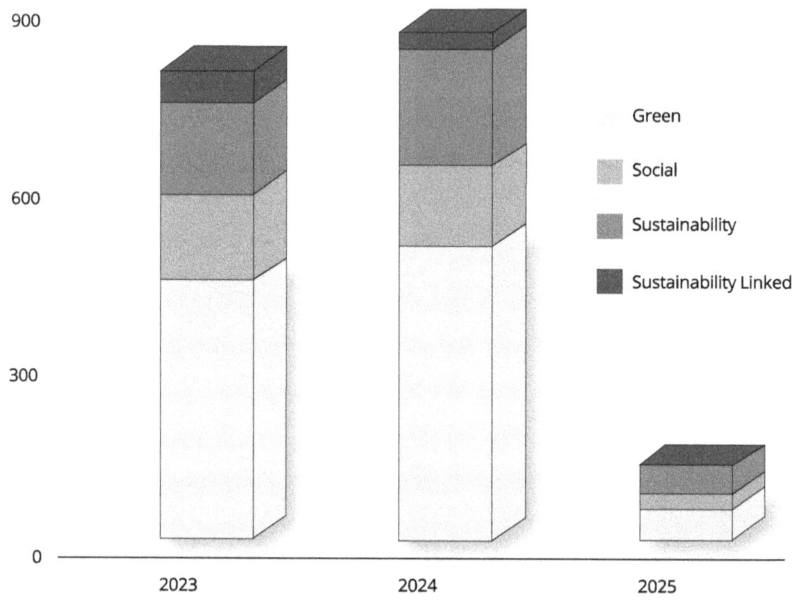

Data Source: ICMA; Luxembourg Stock Exchange (LuxSE); Chart Author; Link: *https://www.icmagroup. org/sustainable-finance/sustainable-bonds-database/*. Does not include matured bonds. Fig rounded off to one decimal.

Krystal asked whether Caroline had any insights on the region leading in sustainable bond issuance.

"Yes, it's Europe by a significant margin," Caroline mentioned. "From 2020 to 2024, Europe has consistently been the dominant issuer of sustainable bonds,"

It makes sense,"I thought out loud. Europe is one of the most innovative regions in the sustainable development sector, and these figures underscore its proactive approach to sustainable practices.

Snapshot of Global Sustainable Investing Assets, 2016-2022 (USD billions) including and excluding US data

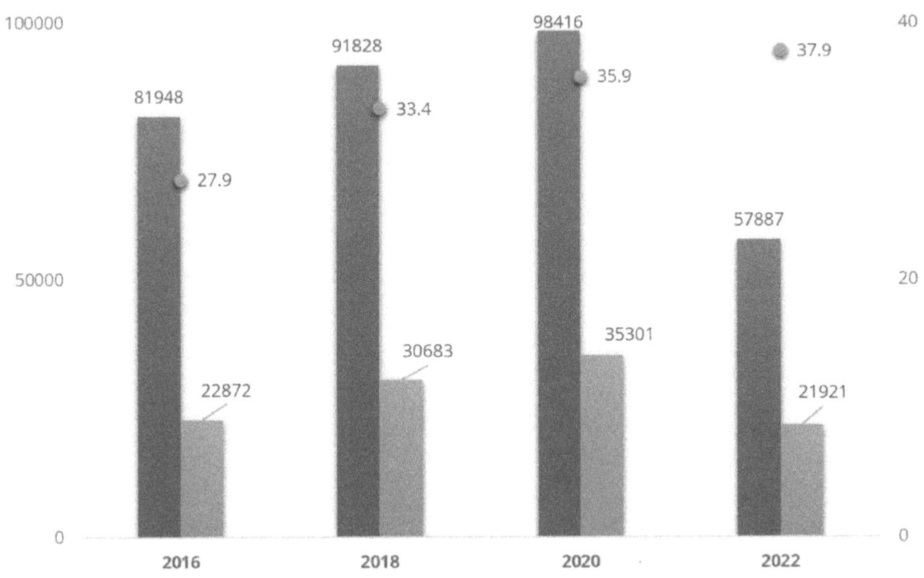

Data Source: GSIA; Chart Author

Everyone appreciated the Global Sustainable Investing Assets snapshot, which sparked a discussion about various ESG investing strategies. ESG investing, also known as sustainable investing, continues to gain momentum. Before diving deeper, Caroline pointed out the importance of understanding green bonds and sustainable finance first.

When we chat here, we refer specifically to the ICMA Bond Principles. While there are other taxonomies within the sustainable finance space— such as those developed by the Climate Bonds Initiative and various multilateral development banks—for the purposes of our discussion, we will focus on the ICMA guidelines. These are a voluntary set of principles, collectively referred to as "The Principles," which serve as the leading framework for sustainable finance instruments under the ICMA framework. "The Principles" include the Green Bond Principles (GBP), Social Bond Principles (SBP), Sustainability Bond Guidelines (SBG), and Sustainability-Linked Bond Principles (SLBP).

Green Bonds and Green Finance

Within the sustainable bonds category, which comprises Green Bonds, Social Bonds, Sustainability Bonds and Sustainability-Linked Bonds, green bonds are the largest category.

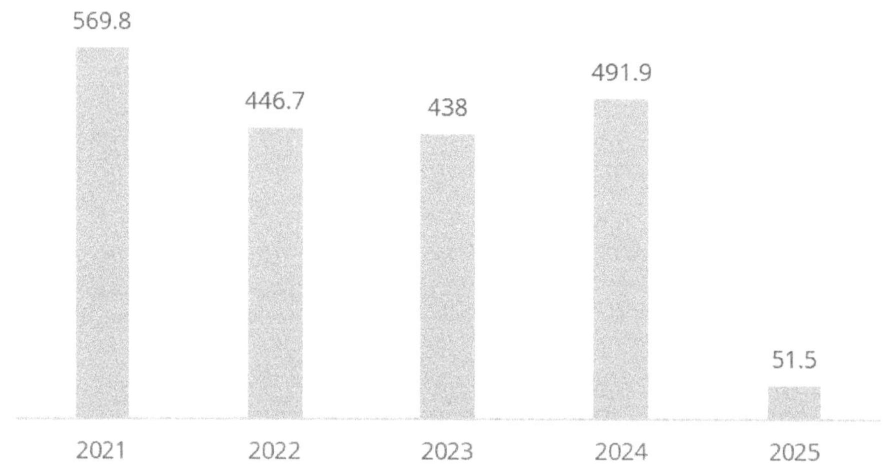

Data Source: ICMA; Luxembourg Stock Exchange (LuxSE); Chart Author; Link: *https://www.icmagroup. org/sustainable-finance/sustainable-bonds-database/*. Does not include matured bonds.

Green Bond Issuance in $ Billion

The launch of green bonds is a stellar moment in global development history that marked the inception of social innovation specifically targeting projects within the climate action segment. **Green Bonds and Green Finance** are types of debt instruments that target projects related to climate action in the following themes: **Climate Mitigation (Reduction of carbon footprints)** and **Climate Adaptation (How do we adapt to climatic changes)**. Governed by Green Bond Principles, a key measure is the use of proceeds of these bonds. Green bonds feature projects in climate mitigation that are involved in the reduction of carbon footprints and climate adaptation (increasing adoption of renewable energy) (SDG 7). Based on The Principles Guidance Handbook, eligible green projects include (not an exhaustive list) - renewable energy, energy efficiency, pollution prevention and control, environmentally sustainable management of living natural resources and land use, terrestrial and aquatic biodiversity conservation, clean transportation, sustainable water and wastewater management, climate change adaptation, circular economy and/or eco-efficient projects, and green buildings.[d]

The issuer can also target other environmental themes as long as they explain the underlying environmental impact these green projects intend to achieve. Before Caroline could continue, a few of us had questions. Brad, in particular, sought clarity on the distinction between *Climate Mitigation* and *Climate Adaptation*.

"Excellent question," I said. "Let me explain. Any intervention that reduces carbon footprints is an example of climate mitigation, while interventions designed to withstand the effects of climate change fall under climate adaptation. For instance, investments in clean technologies, such as solar or wind energy, and sustainable buildings are examples of climate mitigation. Climate Adaptation includes constructing resilient infrastructure to withstand climate change. Flood-Resistant Banks safeguard against high tides is an excellent example of climate adaptation."

Peter interjected, "What about afforestation?"

"Hmm. That's again an example of climate mitigation, as forests sequester greenhouse gases."

I nodded to Caroline to move ahead with "The Principles."

The green bonds are governed by **"Green Bond Principles"**, a key framework that governs these sustainable bonds. The four core components of **"The Principles"** are:

1. Use of proceeds,
2. Process for project evaluation and selection,
3. Management of proceeds and
4. Reporting (Allocation and Impact Reporting).

The green projects should align toward the **five stated environmental objectives** (*climate change mitigation, adaptation, natural resource conservation, biodiversity conservation, and pollution prevention and control*). Green loans have a separate set of standards known as **Green Loan Principles**. Green projects, including blue projects, can have social co-benefits and vice versa. However, like all sustainable bonds, the issuer decides the primary purpose of the bond based on the pay-by-type of use of proceeds bonds. **ReNew**, an Indian renewable energy company headquartered in Gurugram, Haryana, came out with the largest deal among non-financial corporates with a $7.8 billion green loan as of February 2025. In 2023, China was the largest source of green bond issuance, followed by Germany, the US, the UK, and supranational entities, according to the **Climate Bonds Initiative (CBI)**.

In 2023, the International Finance Corporation (IFC) made the largest commitments to the development sector with a capital of $43 billion. As a major champion within the development sector and part of the World Bank Group, IFC is the largest multilateral institution driving private capital and social innovation within the sustainable development sector. With a presence in over 100 countries, IFC tailors social financing instruments to target environmental and social outcomes interventions. Spearheading catalytic and blended finance in addition to innovative sustainable bonds, IFC leads the pack of other major multilateral organizations such as the *European Investment Bank, the Asian Development Bank, the African Development Bank,* and *the Inter-American Development Bank.* The multilateral organization updated its green bond framework to include more themes, such as new ocean, water, and biodiversity categories, increasing its reach across more sectors.

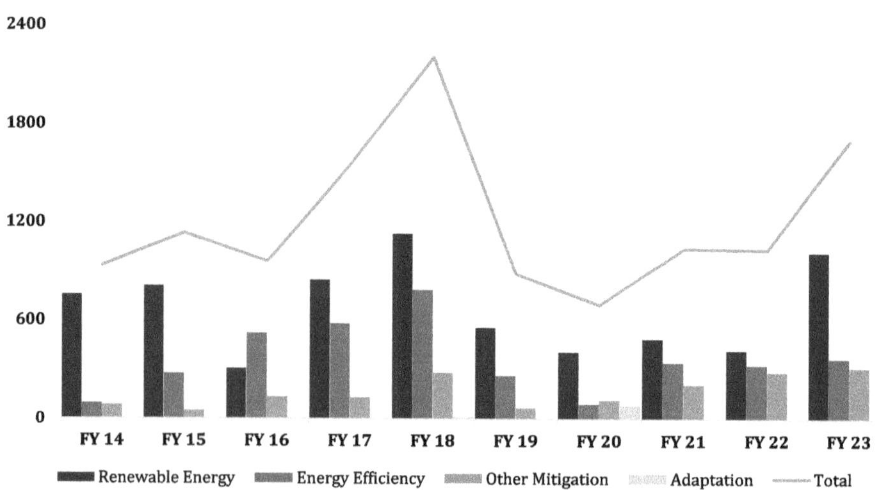

Some numbers in the above graph have been adjusted to reflect updated calculations; Data from IFC Green and Social Bond Impact Report; Chart Author - figure in USD million Link: https://www.ifc.org/en/insights-reports/2024/green-social-bond-impact-report-fy23

The importance of private capital cannot be understated. According to The World Bank, developing countries and emerging economies need $2.8 trillion of capital annually to transition toward a low-carbon economy by 2030. However, only $1.3 trillion of capital flows per year, creating a shortfall of $1.5 trillion.[b] With rising geopolitical risks and high debt among both advanced and emerging economies, the problem is further exacerbated. Sadly, the poorest countries, such as those in the Saharan region, are the worst affected.

Heat waves can devastate humanity, especially in the sub-Saharan areas, due to a lack of basic amenities, including electricity. The private sector will do the most work by attracting the majority of the capital for development through various actors, especially the multilateral. This can be achieved as the global capital markets have more than $200 trillion in capital. Herein, multilateral play a crucial role in driving sustainable change by raising capital through their coffers and the private sector.

Let's move on to another critical sustainable bond, which I consider an extension of green bonds.

Blue Bonds

These are a subcategory of green bonds, usually included within the green bond category. These bonds target outcomes within the sustainable ocean economy. In 2023, ICMA developed a framework to finance sustainable blue finance. This framework also draws inspiration from existing frameworks on the blue economy, namely the *IFC's Guidelines for Blue Finance, UNEP FI's Sustainable Blue Economy Finance Principles and associated Blue Finance Guidance, the UN Global Compact's Practical Guidance to Issue a Blue Bond and Sustainable Ocean Principles, the Asian Development Bank's Ocean Finance Framework and Green and Blue Bond Framework.*

Type of Use of Proceeds Bonds

Green bonds are the largest segment within sustainable bonds, with blue bonds, which can also be part of green bonds, constituting a smaller subset. According to **ICMA data**, transactions labeled as blue reached a value of $5 billion between 2018 and 2022. In 2018, the **Republic of Seychelles** launched the *world's first sovereign blue bond*, a $15 million bond from international investors. The proceeds of the bond support sustainable marine and fisheries projects. The World Bank assisted in developing the blue bond that primarily focuses on developing and nurturing the marine and blue economy of the nation.

Green Bonds that allocate 100 percent of their proceeds to the sustainable ocean sector can also be called Blue Bonds. Blue Bonds adhering to Green Bond Principles can similarly be labeled as green bonds. Similarly, Blue Bonds can also fall under the classification of Sustainability Bonds, provided they adhere to sustainability bond guidelines. This demonstrates how different types of bonds can be interchangeably labeled, provided they adhere to the respective bond principles. Ultimately, it's up to the issuer to designate the bond under which type of sustainable bonds it falls. The label can be extended to loans provided they follow the required framework. Blue Bonds covered themes include conservation and improvement of biodiversity, aquaculture, sustainable marine transport, marine population, marine renewable energy, etc. A few blue bonds also target freshwater outcomes, although most of them are designed for the sustainable ocean ecosystem. Like all sustainable bonds, blue bonds must follow the four pillars of 'The Principles' to qualify as blue bonds.

Social Bonds

Social Bonds Issuance in $ Billion

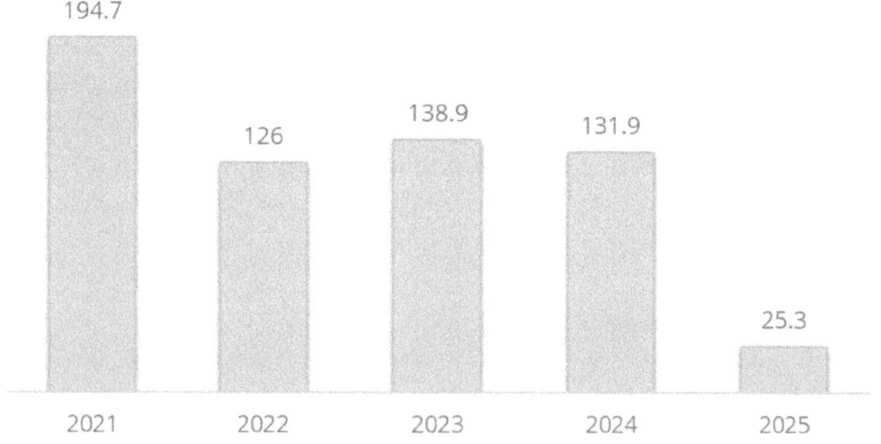

Data Source: ICMA; Luxembourg Stock Exchange (LuxSE); Chart Author; Link: *https://www.icmagroup. org/sustainable-finance/sustainable-bonds-database/*. Does not include matured bonds.

The emergence of social bonds remains one of the most critical enablers of social change and impact within the global development sector. According to the **Climate Bonds Initiative**, by the end of 2023, social bonds had the second-largest market share at 18.50 percent, just ahead of sustainability bonds. Europe has been the largest region in terms of volume since its inception. Among the actors, the **Korea Housing Finance Corporation (KHFC)** emerged as the largest issuer in the social bond market. KHFC issued $30.6 billion, accounting for about 20 percent of the social bond market volume, outshining CADES, the top issuer in 2022, with $23.9 billion issued in 2023 (CBI).

Xu requested a breakdown of the social bonds according to the actors. Caroline had the figures on her laptop.

Social Bonds enable the development and implementation of new and existing projects with positive social outcomes. This is the only type of sustainable bond that exclusively targets interventions within the social sector. Other bonds target exclusive environmental outcomes, such as **Green and Blue Bonds**, while **Sustainability** and **Sustainability-Linked Bonds** target either a combination of environmental and social outcomes or one of the two. Sustainability-Linked Bonds have another as a third criterion.

Quiz 1: A company based in emerging markets issues sustainable bonds to finance projects to build highly affordable housing for the elderly and homeless. The project costs $30 million, and to partially fund it, the company raises $10 million from the capital markets. What type of bonds does the company issue?

a. Social Bonds
b. Green bonds
c. Transition Bonds

Social bonds enable the development and implementation of new and existing projects with positive social outcomes for targeted populations. Social Bonds also help promote the concept of a **'Just Transition'**, a key element in fostering an equitable environment as we progress toward achieving the United Nations Sustainable Development Goals. The advent of artificial intelligence, automation, and digitalization will lead to job losses, and reskilling will be an important step toward a more profound transition. Social Bonds are structured to include these themes and fund the capital gap for achieving the Sustainable Development Goals. Social Bonds follow the ICMA Social Bond Principles. These bonds have a detailed set of classification of projects. For example, some of the themes include affordable basic infrastructure (e.g. clean drinking water, sewers, sanitation, transport, energy, etc.), access to basic services (e.g. health, education and vocational training, healthcare, financing and financial services, etc.), affordable housing, job creation including through the potential effect of small and medium-sized enterprises financing and microfinance, socio-economic advancement and empowerment. The intention is to encourage social good; these interventions target underserved, marginalized people, people living below the poverty line, undereducated, people with disabilities, migrants, etc.

While researching for work, both Caroline and I dug deep to find the various maturities of social bonds. This would lead to an excellent understanding of how the proceeds of these bonds were used for various interventions.

If you want to know more about innovation within green energy, learn more about the innovation fund.

Years to Maturity Analysis of the Social Bonds

Years to maturity analysis of the social bonds. The maximum maturity is within the 1 to 5-year maturity followed by the maturity at the shortest end of the curve, with more than 50 percent of social bonds between 0 and 5 years.

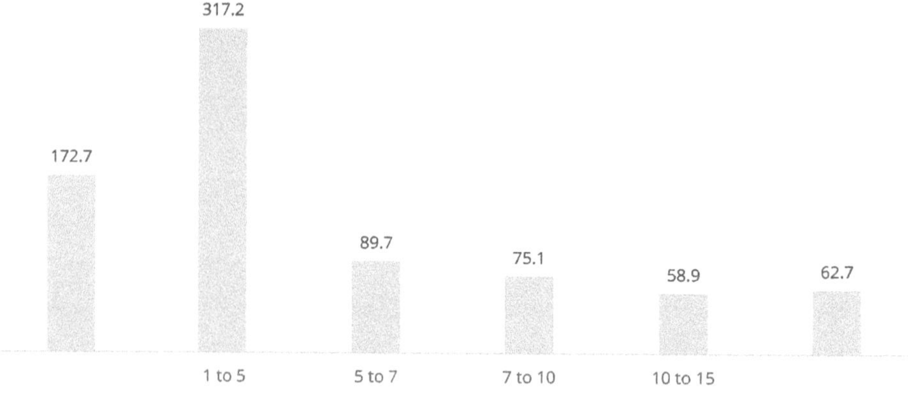

Data Source: ICMA; Luxembourg Stock Exchange (LuxSE); Chart Author; Link: *https://www.icmagroup.org/sustainable-finance/sustainable-bonds-database/*

Social bonds are driven by establishing the principles of social bonds, a global framework for issuing these bonds supported by ICMA. Notably, the first social bond, **"Banking on Women,"** was introduced by IFC, followed by "Inclusive Business," although neither strictly adhered to the Social Bond Principles (Social Bonds, Impact Invest Lab). While Social Bonds align with socially responsible investing principles, it is essential to acknowledge that the most prominent investors are still primarily driven by financial gain.

Quiz 2: A company is closing its construction business to focus on its rapidly expanding sustainable infrastructure business. Instead of laying off employees in the construction division, the company decides to train and reskill them for roles in the new business. This is an example of which of the following?
a.   Just Transition
b.   Red Label
c.   No Transition

As Caroline concluded, I shared a case of social bonds.

IFC Electrifies Côte d'Ivoire through Social Bond

IFC has introduced an innovative social financing tool to help low-income households access subsidized electricity in Côte d'Ivoire. The country has made significant strides in electrification compared to its peers in the West African Economic and Monetary Union (WAEMU). Notably, Côte d'Ivoire's commendable achievement lies in generating a third of its power from hydro sources, with no reliance on coal—a remarkable feat. The country's implementation of the "Electricity for All" program, which aims to subsidize electricity to ensure universal access, particularly for marginalized communities, is pivotal given the escalating impacts of climate change. Marginalized communities in sub-Saharan Africa bear a disproportionate burden of extreme weather events, such as droughts and heatwaves, leading to significant human suffering, including deaths and migration.

Securitization, in essence:
This financing tool creates a special purpose vehicle to pool illiquid assets, which are then converted into tradable securities. These special purpose

vehicles aim to transfer risk from the balance sheets of organizations, typically banks and asset managers, to separate entities. Securitization often involves the creation of tradable tranches with varied risks, including senior, mezzanine, and subordinated tranches. Indeed, the riskier the tranche, such as the subordinated tranche, the higher the potential interest rate charged and the return it offers.

The Social Bond:

The structure functions as a pay-as-you-go tool to fund perimeter connections for households unable to afford meters connecting to the national power grid. This social bond is being implemented in Côte d'Ivoire, a country that has made remarkable progress in promoting affordable energy. As part of the ongoing 10-year Electricity for All program, subsidizing electricity has made significant progress in urban areas. However, rural areas still face challenges due to high meter costs. Côte d'Ivoire and IFC have issued a $97 million social bond to address this.

People wanted to know more about securitization. However, now is not the time to dive into the complexities of this structure, so I decided to take an in-depth look at it later.

Sustainability/ Sustainable Development Bonds
Sustainability Bond Issuance in $ Billion

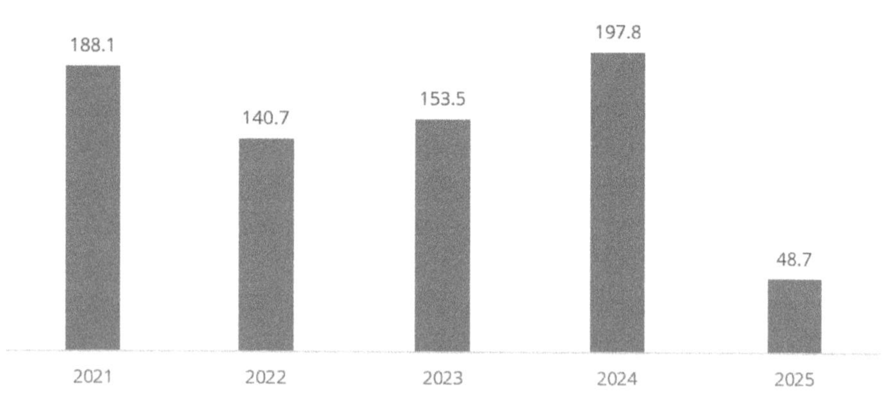

Data Source: ICMA; Luxembourg Stock Exchange (LuxSE); Chart Author; Link: *https://www.icmagroup.org/sustainable-finance/sustainable-bonds-database/*. Does not include matured bonds.

Sustainability Bonds follow the Sustainability Bond Guidelines, coordinated by the **International Capital Market Association**. All GSS bonds adhere to the four core pillars within the principles: 1. Use of proceeds, 2. Process for evaluation and selection of eligible operations, 3. Management of proceeds, and 4. Reporting. In this case, the bonds would be aligned with the **<u>Sustainability Bond Guidelines framework</u>**. The World Bank's Sustainable Development Bonds are issued under their own framework, supporting projects in countries financed by the International Bank for Reconstruction and Development (IBRD).

Improved healthcare, affordable healthcare, and equitable education are some of the social projects listed within the framework, while clean technology and conservation of biodiversity would be some of the themes within the environmental sphere. The World Bank has a triple credit rating, showcasing the strength of its balance sheet and its member countries. The **Sustainable Development Bonds** issued by the World Bank are bought by various actors, including governments and asset managers like pension and insurance companies, as well as individuals. The environmental and social framework sets a long-term strategic outlook for the multilateral and the standards and regulations that the bank needs to adhere to while financing through **Program-for-Results (PforR)** and **Development Policy Financing (DPF)**. The programs have their own standards that are aligned with those of the environmental and social framework.

Sustainability-Linked Bonds

Sustainability-linked bonds (SLBs) are among the most recent additions to the GSS+ (Green, Social, Sustainability, and Sustainability-Linked) bond market. Sustainability-linked bonds have the lowest share at approximately 1 percent of the GSS+ issuance.[a] Various global business and social ecosystem actors increasingly use sustainability-linked themes within these bonds to address socio-economic issues and/or the environment and/or social and/or governance (ESG) criteria within a predetermined period. The core components of these bonds must align with **Sustainability-Linked Bond Principles (SLBP)** and include a selection of **Key Performance Indicators (KPIs)**, calibration of Sustainability Performance Targets (SPTs), bond characteristics, reporting, and verification. These bonds follow proceeds for general purposes, although they can also employ the use of proceeds approach, i.e. financing eligible projects. In that case, these bonds must follow Sustainability-Linked Bond Principles and green, social, or sustainability-linked bond principles, depending on the use of proceeds. These bonds employ financial or structural adjustments like variable coupon, maturity, repayment amount, etc., as part of bond issuance. (ICMA Guidance Handbook & Q/A). SLBs have gained popularity among corporates, allowing issuers to tailor bond offerings based on specific selected sustainability factors known as KPIs and SPTs. One way would be to vary the bonds' coupons depending on their achievement level of Sustainability Performance Targets. If the performance exceeds the predetermined performance targets, the coupon reduces (interest paid out to bondholders on the principal amount), and if they miss these targets, the coupon increases. For example, **Enel,** a European multinational, is a pioneer in issuing sustainability-linked bonds.

Sustainability-Linked Bond by KPI Theme

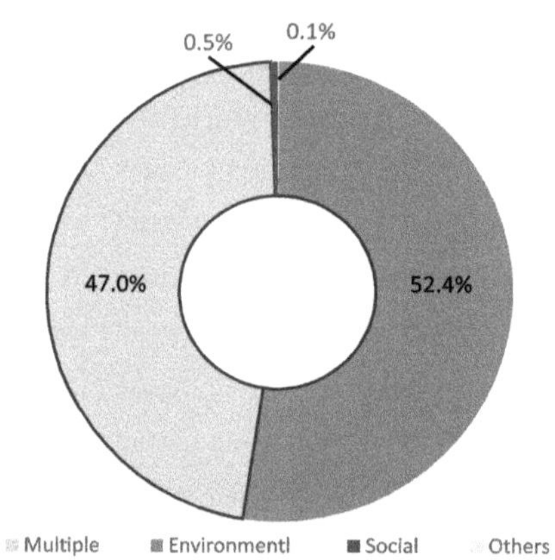

Data Source: ICMA; Luxembourg Stock Exchange (LuxSE); Chart Author; Link: *https://www.icmagroup. org/sustainable-finance/sustainable-bonds-database/*

Sustainability-Linked Bond Principles employ customized KPIs aligned with sustainability performance targets to track the accountability and impact of these bonds. These KPIs are linked to environmental, social, governance, or multiple themes. Some of them target socio-economic issues, such as gender equity.

Here, "other" means KPIs are different from environmental, social, governance, or multiple.

Case Study: <u>**Consider a hypothetical case of a company that raises capital**</u> through international capital markets through a two-year sustainability-linked bond. This bond pays a variable coupon linked to the company's sustainability performance targets. The company sets key sustainability benchmarks, such as increasing the use of alternative energy in its operations and improving operational efficiency annually. The company establishes **key performance indicators (KPIs) for Year 1 and Year 2** to propel sustainability improvements. If the company achieves the target in year 1, it will pay a reduced coupon rate of 10 bps points and a reduced coupon rate of 15 bps in year 2. However, if the company **fails** to meet its target in Year 1, it will pay a **coupon of 3%** and pay an **additional 5 bps increase** in Year 2 if it fails to achieve the benchmark target again. Below is an indicative pathway for coupon payouts over two years. This case illustrates a **step-up and step-down bond structure**, where the coupon rate is variable coupled with the company's sustainability performance relative to its predefined benchmarks. The coupon is paid on the outstanding principal amount.

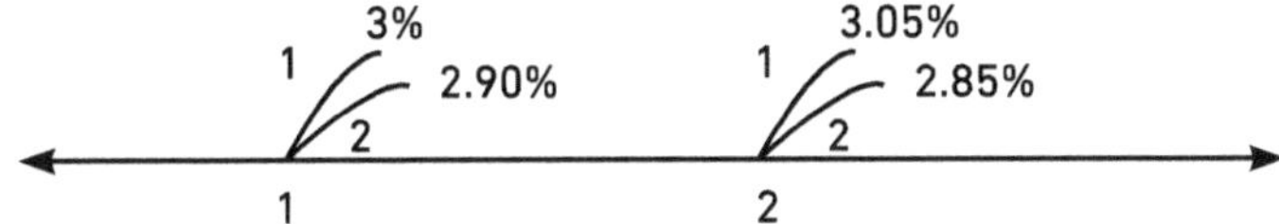

Coupon payment pathway over two years. There are two scenarios 1 and 2.

Year	Coupon Rate Targets are not met (1)	Coupon Rate Targets are met (2)
1	3%	2.90%
2	3.05%	2.85%

Quiz: A renewable energy company is committed to achieving sustainability outcomes and has set a long-term mission to drive sustainable change. It is planning to improve waste management and conserve energy, with a focus on reducing Scope 1 and Scope 2 emissions. To support its mission and values, the company is issuing sustainable bonds linked to specific target outcomes. If the targets are met, the company will pay lower coupon payments on the face value of the bonds; otherwise, the coupon payments will increase, depending on the tax slab. What type of bonds are these?

a. Green bonds

b. Sustainability-Linked Bonds

c. Sustainability Bonds

After the riveting discussion on sustainable bonds, we all decided it was enough for the day. The conversation about the bonds turned out to be very comprehensive. It was around 9:30 pm, and I needed to work with Caroline on a presentation about Smart Beta strategies and their impact on the ESG investing sector. We all bid farewell to each other. Myself, Xu, Peter, and Solomon had plans to meet for lunch, so we finalized the details—day, time, and venue—before departing for our respective places.

Chapter 5

Workout Day

I sped to the gym in my Tesla with Caroline for our weekly workout session. Both of us are regular gym-goers and passionate fitness enthusiasts. We also frequently went camping and hiking across the U.S. *Seattle, known for its scenic hiking trails*, is a global melting pot for outdoor aficionados. We trained at a world-class gym—spectacular in every aspect, with a spacious layout and state-of-the-art equipment. The gym offered a variety of complementary workouts, from functional training sessions and martial arts to yoga, spinning, and other community-building activities. It quickly became a popular hub for my friends, where we exercised and socialized together. Weekends are unique because most of our group meets to work out together. Caroline volunteers for a weekly yoga class at the gym, and I make it a point to attend her sessions whenever I'm in town. I practice yoga with Caroline almost daily, working for about 30 minutes whenever possible, preferably in the morning. We meditate and practice mindfulness early in the morning after stretching and mobility exercises. This would be our key togetherness time as we would start our focus on breathing before delving into self-awareness and various forms of mindful techniques. While I enjoy yoga, I primarily focus on compound movements for strength training. These exercises simultaneously engage multiple muscle groups and joints, making them efficient and highly effective. CrossFit is an excellent example of a workout program that emphasizes power exercises. Compound movements, like squats, bench presses, deadlifts, military presses, and snatches, help build muscle mass and strength. Combined with high-intensity cardio exercises like sprints, swimming, or HIIT (high-intensity interval training), they significantly enhance endurance and overall fitness. HIIT is particularly effective at improving strength and endurance in a short period. **Mat Fraser**, widely regarded as one of the Fittest Men on Earth, won five consecutive

CrossFit Games titles (2016–2020), demonstrating the power of these types of exercises.

Another major fitness trend is martial arts, with boxing and MMA gaining popularity among the masses in recent years. Martial arts like *MMA, Wushu, Krav Maga, Wing Chun, Karate, Tai Chi, Judo, and Taekwondo*, to name a few, are gaining popularity globally. I am proficient in Wing Chun, though Xu is a true art master. On the other hand, Peter has experience in various martial arts, but his forte is boxing. He coached me in boxing, and I quickly gained a solid level of expertise under his guidance. Xu, Yun Tang, and I regularly practice Tai Chi, making measurable progress in Tai Chi. Élise, who grew up in France, learned Judo as a child, a discipline she has since mastered. Adriana and Caroline have developed expertise in Pilates, regularly practicing this form of repetitive exercise. We usually started with a brief warm-up followed by strength exercises when our group met. Élise typically led the women's group.

HIIT is a common thread among most of our group, and we usually try to attend a group class once per week. I often trained Caroline in strength exercises and frequently went to the gym together. *Joshua, Robert, and Jennifer* are exceptional trainers preparing for the CrossFit championship. Joshua grew up in Texas and became a professional CrossFit and fitness trainer. Robert and Jennifer are a couple. Robert grew up in New York, and Jennifer, a native of Philadelphia, traveled around the US for education and work. They are regulars at the gym, and I have fostered a close relationship with all of them. They regularly come over to our house and gel well with my network of friends. I made it a practice to work out in the gym with Joshua, Robert, and Jennifer to gain key insights into their training methods and dietary habits.

Today, all of my gang is meeting at the gym. As I walked in, I saw Peter and Xu waiting, so I joined them, and we headed to the locker room. Caroline and the other women walked toward their changing room, and we split into two groups. I had planned an intense workout routine for the day, incorporating cardio and strength exercises. I'm preparing for the Boston half-marathon, so I focus on building strength and endurance.

Xu said, "Hey bro, what will we do today?"

I replied, "I'm planning to do intense cardio for 30 minutes, with a key focus on legs, including some power exercises. For legs, I think front and back squats, lunges, leg extensions, and the glute work. But before that, I'll start with bench presses and clean and jerk exercises."

Peter and Xu remarked, "That's a powerful routine."

"Yes," I replied. Today, I have a super workout planned. We all gave each other a high five, as I mentioned: I am a power guy.

We regrouped afterward for some mobility drills before a few of us headed to the treadmill. I then asked Xu if he was free to practice Wing Chun. He agreed, so I fit in Wing Chun practice before starting my weight training exercises. Peter had his routine planned, focusing on the chest and shoulders today, while Solomon would join me later for a leg workout. After a brief chit-chat, we all started on our respective fitness programs. The Wing Chun session had energized me, and Solomon joined in, focusing on grappling techniques.

Krav Maga is designed to emphasize real-world scenarios, and comparing it with Wing Chun allows me to take the best elements from both martial arts. Mixed *martial arts (MMA)* has recently gained popularity due to its practical application in real-world situations, including self-defense. I grew up admiring Chinese martial arts, and with Xu's guidance, I've been working on improving my technique and developing skills in Jeet Kune Do.

This form of martial art, credited to the legendary Bruce Lee, moves away from the structured approach of Wing Chun toward a philosophy of adaptability. The technique is grounded in practicality, taking a more nuanced approach to combat, making it better suited for real-life situations. Jeet Kune Do is highly combative, enhances focus, and aids in personal development. Heavily influenced by various martial arts, including Wing Chun, boxing, and fencing, Jeet Kune Do is often credited with paving the way for the emergence of mixed martial arts as we know them today. Bruce Lee was also a student of Ip Man, whose name is synonymous with Wing Chun, immortalized in movies. I am a huge fan of Jet Li, one of the greatest proponents of Wushu, popularly known as Kung Fu. I credit Jet Li as one of the key influencers of my interest in Chinese martial arts. 武術*(Wushu), where* 武*(Wu) means martial, military, or combat, and* 術*(Shu) means art, method, technique, or skill,* represents a broader category of Chinese martial arts. Wushu was developed as part of a Chinese government initiative to standardize and promote martial arts as an integral part of Chinese culture and tradition. While it incorporates elements from traditional martial arts like Wing Chun and Tai Chi, modern Wushu has evolved into two distinct branches: contemporary Wushu, which focuses on performance and competition, and traditional Wushu, which retains its combat applications. Wing Chun, a specific conventional martial art, stands apart with its focus on close-quarter combat and self-defense. Unlike the performance-driven aspects of contemporary Wushu, Wing Chun emphasizes efficiency and practicality in actual combat situations, featuring techniques designed for close-range effectiveness. After an intense martial arts session, I transitioned to strength training with Solomon, shifting my focus to squats and other power training exercises. I thanked Xu and, along with Solomon, moved toward the weight training section in the gym. Xu went ahead with his martial arts routine, deeply engrossed in the art.

As the day progressed, we found that working out together strengthened our bond of friendship. Exercising with partners is always a great experience – it increases motivation for staying fit and reduces the risk of injury. Working out with your better half fosters a sense of togetherness and companionship. I regularly met with Caroline to check on her strength and conditioning workouts. I designed a bespoke routine for her and monitored her form. After our rigorous workout, we all gathered for a few stretches before joining Caroline for the yoga class.

Yoga is incredibly beneficial after strenuous weight training; while resistance training compresses the muscles, yoga stretches them, promoting relaxation and recovery. Yoga further aids in increasing focus and mindfulness, making it part of my well-being regimen. Swimming is another excellent post-workout exercise that aids in recovery. With her melodious and heartwarming voice, Caroline guided us through various Hatha yoga poses with grace and precision. Her affable personality resonated with everyone, making her a crowd favorite. After a refreshing shower, we made plans to visit a vegan restaurant renowned for its delicious buffet. *Joshua, Robert, and Jennifer* joined our group, making the lunch even more special. Some of us planned tennis sessions the following day after the fun-filled meal.

In the interim, I called an upscale lounge bar in Bellevue to make reservations for the evening. We bade farewell and headed to our respective destinations. Although I felt elated, I was exhausted from the day's activities. I sped home with Caroline, eager to make plans to move to our new home in *Queen Anne*. We have been deeply involved in designing our new abode because we are excited about this new chapter. The house on a hill offers stunning views of the Seattle skyline. The home features a barbecue area on the lawn, a music recording studio in the attic, and a spacious garden. Designed with minimalism and simplicity in mind, the house perfectly suits our vision. Final touches are happening, and I hope to take possession of the place in mid-December.

Chapter 6

Carbon Pricing

Approached by a leading business and policy school to deliver a guest lecture on how taxation and other mechanisms are being implemented globally to stem greenhouse gas emissions, I started reading on this topic in detail. This would be an excellent opportunity to create an online course for my edtech. I begin with carbon pricing. I recently read **"The Quest" by Daniel Yergin,** one of the foremost thought leaders in the energy sector. It is a must-read for anyone who wants to know the history of energy, including the emergence of clean fuel. The book is very comprehensive, tracing the history of the transition and adaptation to renewable energy. It begins with the breakup of the Soviet Union and articulates the presence of fossil fuels in our lives. **Carbon Emissions** are negative externalities in many industries that cannot be quickly addressed or accounted for. Since greenhouse gas emissions contribute to adverse conditions for humanity, it is essential to tax these externalities. As a rule of thumb, negative externalities should be taxed because the social cost is higher than the social benefit. Various forms of carbon pricing are implemented globally to curtail carbon emissions due to the social cost associated with these emissions. This taxation aims to discourage or reduce product or service use. Similarly, positive externalities require subsidization because the <u>**social benefit exceeds the private cost**</u>. Subsidizing these services or products would encourage more people to use them. For instance, air travel produces carbon emissions that must be addressed through various mechanisms to improve our lives. The most well-known form of carbon pricing is the **Emissions Trading System (ETS),** while others include **Carbon Tax** and **Carbon Crediting Mechanisms.** These are known as direct forms of carbon pricing. The genesis of carbon pricing rests on Europe, the quintessential region that innovated various facets of carbon pricing. **Carbon Pricing** has come a long way since it was first implemented in the EU through the ***Emissions Trading System (EU ETS)*** in 2005. According to the report titled **"State and Trends of Carbon Pricing International carbon markets 2024 by World Bank Group"**, carbon taxes and emissions trading systems today have a global coverage of 24 percent of carbon emissions. As of 31 April 2024, 75 carbon taxes and emissions trading schemes are in operation worldwide.[1] Both of these measures serve as one of the most effective ways of decarbonization by advanced and some emerging markets. It's not easy to put a social cost on carbon emissions. *The social cost of carbon can be defined as the economic damage to the environment due to adding one metric ton of carbon dioxide, also known as the marginal social cost of adding greenhouse gas emissions. Termed as pay as you pollute, carbon pricing in economic parlance is known as the social cost of carbon and is measured as* **metric ton of CO_2 equivalence (tCO_2e).**

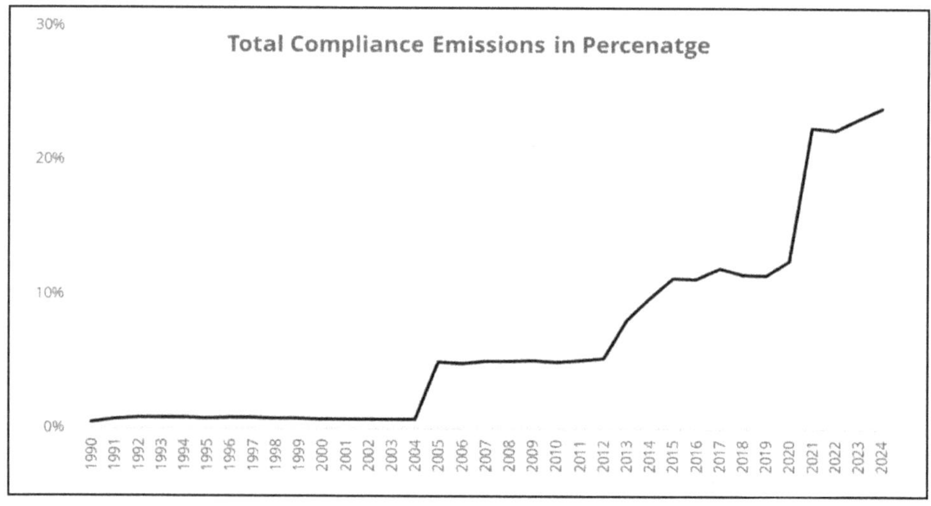

Data Source: World Bank. (2024). Carbon Pricing Dashboard. Retrieved from *https://carbonpricingdashboard.worldbank.org/*. The figure is converted into a percentage and rounded off to two digits. Last update: 1 April 2024. **Chart:** Author

According to the estimates of the High-Level Commission on Carbon Prices, the carbon prices needed to be \$40-80/ton of carbon dioxide equivalent (tCO_2e) in 2020 and increase to \$50-100/tCO_2e by 2030 to be on track to limit temperature rises to well below 2°C.[2] In 2023, global carbon pricing initiatives generated the most significant amount of revenues at \$104 billion, with the European Union Emissions

Trading System (EU ETS) contributing the lion's share. [3] ETS is the most effective carbon pricing tool for governments, with revenues from ETS accounting for 70 percent of the carbon pricing revenues from government interventions—however, the revenues raised through direct carbon taxation pale compared to the fuel subsidies generated globally. High fuel subsidies negate the revenues and productive work gained through various carbon pricing mechanisms. According to the Institute for Climate Economics (I4CE), in 2022, over half of the carbon revenues raised in selected jurisdictions were allocated to climate and nature-based projects. [4] This move has recently significantly advanced the cleantech sector with a jump in cleantech startups. The proceeds are also given back to households that are adversely impacted by climate change. Despite a surge in carbon pricing markets in new countries such as **Brazil, India, and Türkiye**, the global coverage of carbon emissions is not expected to go beyond forty percent anytime soon. The **Carbon Border Adjustment Mechanism (CBAM)** is operational and aims to limit carbon leakage by taxing imported goods and services based on their carbon footprint. As carbon taxes could shift industries to locations that do not have carbon taxation, CBAM nullifies this effect for imported goods and services into the EU. As this policy becomes a standard norm among all the advanced countries, it will also nudge emerging markets to adopt similar direct taxation policies.

Understanding Externalities

Carbon Emissions are negative externalities in many industries that cannot be quickly addressed or accounted for. Since greenhouse gas emissions contribute to adverse conditions for humanity, it is essential to tax these externalities. As a rule of thumb, negative externalities are taxed because the social cost is higher than the social benefit. Policymakers have used these kinds of direct taxation to improve humanity through various policies. Cigarettes across many advanced countries are taxed due to their detrimental impact on both active and passive smokers. *Arthur Cecil Pigou*, a brilliant English economist at the University of Cambridge, known for his work in welfare economics, is the first to suggest taxation to curtail negative externalities. An excellent example of taxing negative externalities is an excise tax on packs of cigarettes, a policy used to reduce the consumption of smoking due to well-being and costs related to both active and passive smoking. Excise tax affects the supply curve, with a fraction of the taxes being passed on to the customer. Various forms of carbon pricing are implemented globally to curtail carbon emissions due to the social cost associated with these emissions. Taxation aims to discourage or reduce product or service use. Similarly, positive externalities require subsidization because the *social benefit exceeds the private cost*. Subsidizing these services or products would encourage more people to use them. For instance, air travel results in carbon emissions, and various mechanisms need to be implemented to lessen these carbon emissions. The most well-known form of carbon pricing is the **Emissions Trading System (ETS)**, while others include **Carbon Tax and Carbon Crediting Mechanisms**. These are known as <u>**direct forms of carbon pricing**</u>.

> **Market failures arise due to imperfections in markets, including lack of perfect competition, externalities, and other inefficiencies.**
>
> Externalities can be considered market failures, as their presence does not reflect the true cost of goods produced. Negative externalities arise when social costs exceed private costs, while positive externalities result when social benefits (benefits to society) exceed private benefits. Carbon emissions from various sources are an excellent example of a negative externality. These emissions lead to adverse health effects, causing higher healthcare costs and personal trauma. Policy makers can measure social costs by calculating the incremental health costs of diseases between two time periods. For example, using 2010 as a base year, calculating the average healthcare expenditure per household between two time periods leads to an economic estimate. A critical assumption is that increased pollution is one of the causes of rising healthcare costs, keeping other factors constant. However, it's next to impossible to measure factors such as mental anguish. Policy makers address these externalities through various approaches. Taxing negative externalities is one common way of offsetting the increase in social costs, aiming to dissuade proliferation of carbon emission sources. Cap and Trade already discussed in detail is another example of addressing negative externalities. Additionally, encouraging the use of clean technologies through subsidies serves as a driver of positive externalities.

The genesis of carbon pricing rests in Europe, the quintessential region that innovated various facets of carbon pricing.

Carbon pricing instruments around the world, 2023

Map shows jurisdictions that have implemented Direct Carbon Pricing Instruments - Compliance instruments (Emissions Trading Systems (ETS) and Carbon taxes) and/or domestic carbon crediting mechanisms, subject to any filters applied. The year can be adjusted using the slider below the map.

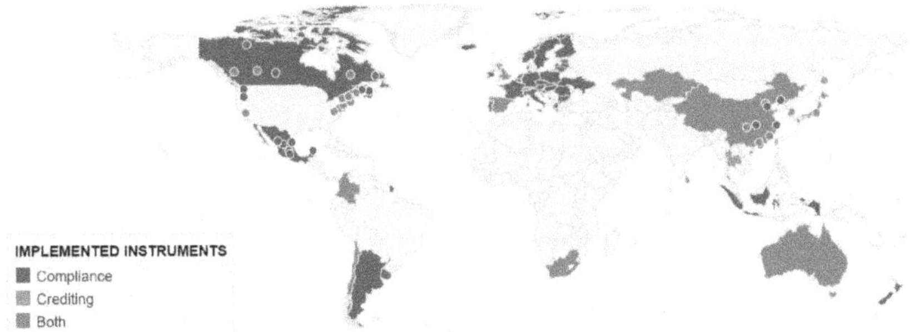

Chart & Data Source: World Bank. (2024). *Carbon pricing instruments around the world, 2024* [Map]. Carbon Pricing Dashboard. Retrieved from *https://carbonpricingdashboard.worldbank.org/*. Compliance instruments are considered "Implemented" once they have been formally adopted through legislation and compliance obligations are in force and enforced. Crediting mechanisms are considered implemented if they have issued credits (or have frameworks in place to allow credits to be used domestically, such as in South Africa).

The impetus for carbon pricing began with the **Kyoto Protocol,** which laid down the foundation for international cross-markets for carbon pricing, although the concept of carbon pricing predates the Kyoto Protocol. The Kyoto Protocol's aim was to reduce greenhouse gas emissions, and various carbon pricing mechanisms facilitate this reduction.

Carbon Tax

Governments can directly tax entities that generate greenhouse emissions to reduce these carbon emissions. There are *two significant types of carbon markets – Voluntary carbon markets and Compliance Markets*, with the latter related to **Article 6 of the Paris Agreement. The Kyoto Protocol** introduced the concept of carbon trading mechanisms through international emissions trading and project-driven mechanisms. Under **Article 6** of the Paris Agreement, carbon credits can be traded internationally to help countries meet their **Nationally Determined Contributions (NDCs).**[5] These goals have a more strategic long-term focus.

Compliance markets focus on domestic obligations set by countries requiring companies to meet emissions requirements. **Voluntary carbon markets** are typically more flexible and have a more recent focus on achieving climate finance with companies and other actors participating to fulfill their voluntary environmental goals and corporate social responsibility commitments.

Carbon Crediting Mechanism

CORSIA is an excellent example of a carbon crediting mechanism. (Carbon Offsetting and Reduction Scheme for International Aviation) is a global initiative specific to the aviation industry that aims to limit the net emissions of CO_2 to 2020 levels. It seeks to stabilize net CO_2 emissions from international aviation at 2020 levels through carbon offsetting and reduction efforts. Airlines are required to purchase and surrender carbon offset credits to compensate for their emissions above the 2020 baseline. The offsetting requirements will increase gradually over time. CORSIA is a

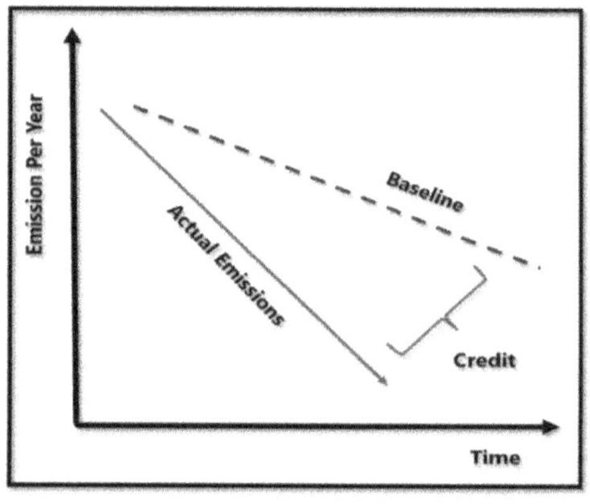

form of carbon crediting mechanism, a mandatory policy where airlines can purchase carbon credits from emission reduction projects to offset their emissions above the baseline. Carbon crediting works as a voluntary emissions reduction exercise, generating revenue by selling these credits. It can also be used in compliance markets.

Various ways of climate mitigation, such as clean technology, afforestation, or biodiversity conservation, can lead to a reduction in greenhouse emissions. Referring to the chart, any reduction in carbon emissions below the baseline would generate credits that can be traded with other actors via the market-driven emissions trading mechanism. Under the EU ETS cap, entities are assigned a specific emission allowance for greenhouse gases. Any decrease in these emissions results in credits that the entity or actor can then sell to other entities through the ETS mechanism.

Emissions Trading System (ETS)

An **Emissions Trading System (ETS),** on the other hand, is a market-based approach to reducing greenhouse gas emissions. In an ETS, **a cap is set on the total amount of emissions allowed,** and **companies can trade**

emission allowances among themselves. For example, in the EU ETS, allowances were either free or allocated through auction, although free allowances are no longer valid in many sectors. Those who can reduce emissions at a lower cost may sell their excess allowances to others who find it more expensive to reduce emissions. This creates a financial incentive for companies to invest in cleaner technologies and reduce their emissions.

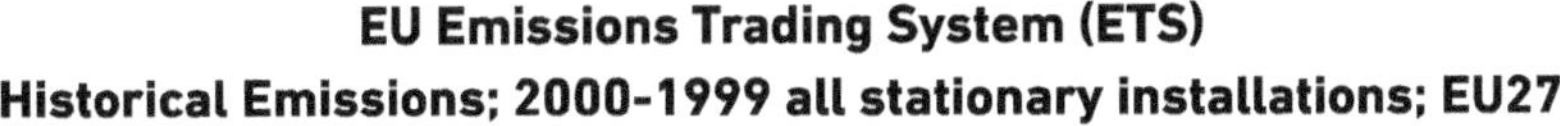

EU Emissions Trading System (ETS)
Historical Emissions; 2000-1999 all stationary installations; EU27

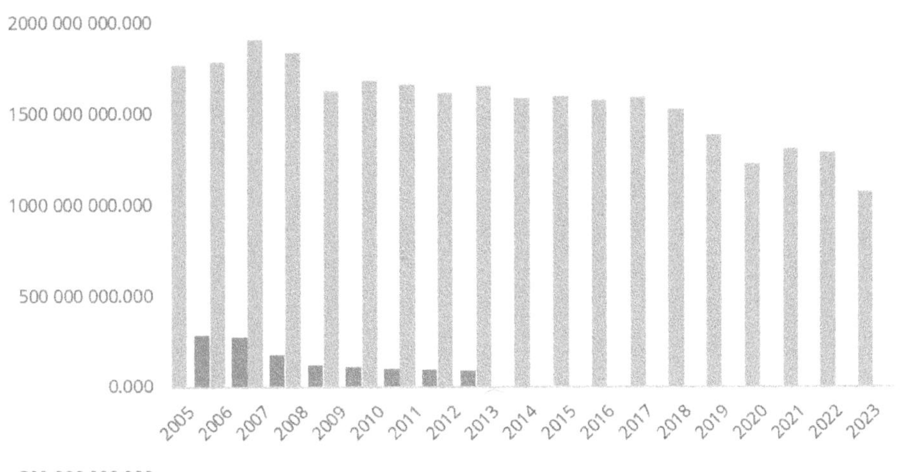

Data: European Environment Agency. "EU Emissions Trading System (ETS) Data Viewer." 2024,*https:// www.eea.europa.eu/en/analysis/maps-and-charts/emissions-trading-viewer-1-dashboards*
Emissions unit – tCO_2 eq Chart Author

As of today, the **European Union (EU) Emissions Trading System (ETS)** is the second-largest emissions trading market, with China overtaking the EU. First pioneered and popularized by the European Union (EU), the Emissions Trading System (ETS) operates as a market-driven mechanism under a **cap-and-trade framework**. The EU emissions market includes 27 member states with 11,000 power stations and manufacturing units. The *EU ETS covers about 38 percent of the total* EU GHG emissions. Started in 2005, the EU ETS is a colossal step in building a global emissions trading market. In this novel concept, European actors are allocated free allowances with caps on the carbon emissions that industries and companies can emit. This predetermined limit on carbon emissions is known as the "cap" in the "cap-and-trade" system. *Each allowance gives the holder the right to emit one ton of CO_2 or other equivalent greenhouse gases, such as nitrous oxide and perfluorocarbons.* Actors could trade, i.e., buy or sell, these allowances or carbon credits. Carbon permits are allocated to actors within the business ecosystem, with a predetermined cap on permissible pollution levels. Regulatory authorities assign a set number of emission units per actor, with penalties imposed for exceeding these limits. Actors can trade their carbon allowances to manage emissions within the specified threshold. The ETS operates by establishing a limit on the total greenhouse gas emissions permitted by participating entities, progressively reducing this cap over time to drive overall emission reductions. Since 2013, emission allowances have been automatically allocated through auctioning. As mentioned, there are two types of allowance allocation: **free and through auction**. As the carbon emissions are capped yearly, these allowances can be traded through the secondary market. This can be through trading in allowances along with a derivatives market. Analogous to stock market trading, wherein investors buy and sell securities, the ETS facilitates trading among institutional or business entities, although focusing on carbon allowances. Over the years, there has been a lot of criticism of free allowances, especially during the previous phase, and slowly, free allowances are being phased out from certain sectors. Paid allowances bought through auctions lead to a price defined for spreading pollution, leading to a carbon tax per se on carbon emissions. These revenues are notable for funding clean technology investments for the EU and member nations through the **Innovation and Modernization Funds**. Additionally, they can procure limited international credits from emission reduction projects worldwide. These allowances are a catalyst for actors to be more energy-efficient.

Is Efficiency the Fifth Wonder?

The importance of efficiency is so significant that **Daniel Yergin**, in his seminal book on energy, **'The Quest'**, defines it as the fifth fuel. The cap-and-trade feature is an excellent framework to provide checks and balances to curtail emissions and promote clean energy. This policy is beneficial for both carbon mitigation and clean energy adoption, and it is more tuned toward carbon mitigation. These regulatory actions lead to innovation, especially within clean technology, and lay down an ecosystem for collective action within climate change. **The EU Emissions Trading System: Method and Effects of Free Allowance Allocation** by Policy Department for Budgetary Affairs Directorate-General for Internal Policies PE 755.098 - October 2023 is a noteworthy analysis of the allocation of free allowances in ETS. One insightful coverage has been the use and methodology of benchmarks by the European Commission from Phase 3 (2013–2020) and the first part of Phase 4 (2021-25). Product benchmarks are defined as greenhouse emission intensity (tons of GHG emitted per ton of product produced) compared to the top 10 percent of the most efficient installations covering a specific product.

The amount of free allowances an installation will receive is simplified in the equation below:

Free allocation = Benchmark × Production Data × Discount Factors

For the first part of Phase 4, production data is based on each installation's average historical production for 2014-18, e.g., tonnes of output. This is multiplied by the relevant product benchmark. Two discount factors are applied where necessary: a downward adjustment is applied to sectors not at high risk of carbon leakage, and a correction factor is applied to different sectors to ensure that the total free allocation will not exceed the cap of the free allocated allowances. Refer to The EU Emissions Trading System: Method and Effects of Free Allowance Allocation by Policy Department for Budgetary Affairs Directorate-General for Internal Policies PE 755.098 - October 2023 for a detailed analysis.

The impetus given by China to green energy will have a significant impact on its Emissions Trading System (ETS). China is committed to achieving carbon neutrality by 2060. Recently, the ETS market in China overtook the European Union in terms of volume coverage; however, the European Union is more sophisticated in terms of the implementation of pricing and regulations. Considering the EU had the first-mover advantage, the ETS in the EU is more mature than any other market. For ETS to achieve global dominance, the United States must play a much larger role than it currently does. Various forms of direct carbon taxation are steps in the right direction and will become increasingly important as we move forward.

Chapter 7

Are your investments Smart Beta?

Caroline's work recently expanded to focus on integrating ESG principles, such as Smart Beta strategies, into investment frameworks. These strategies utilize factors like growth, value, and volatility. Since I had been researching this area, I decided to sit down with Caroline to help structure her presentation for her guest lecture at a leading business school in the U.S. The rise of passive trading has been exceptional recently. According to the efficient market hypothesis, active fund management often fails to deliver alpha over the long run. This perspective has contributed to the proliferation of passive *exchange-traded funds (ETFs)*, a positive development. Caroline and I are enthusiastic about Smart Beta investments, representing a middle ground between active and passive strategies. Smart Beta is more flexible, following a rules-based approach linked to specific investment parameters that I mentioned earlier.

Caroline: I want to discuss the standard capital asset pricing model before diving into the Smart Beta model. This helps students understand the nuances between active and passive investments.

Me: I agree. To ensure the narrative flows smoothly, we should also use graphs to illustrate the rise of ETFs globally.

Caroline: I agree. Can we validate the use of the ESG theme and Smart Beta with a research paper?

Me: That's a fantastic idea! It makes sense to incorporate research findings into your presentation.

"Excellent!" Caroline cried out. "Okay, this is how I am planning the presentation. I will begin with a brief overview of ESG investing, discussing global market share, followed by an overview of exchange-traded products, including a global overview of ETFs and then ESG ETFs."

Kish, how do you map risk using probabilities scenario? Generally, risk-adjusted return ratios like the *Sharpe Ratio, Treynor Ratio, Sortino Ratio, Jensen's Alpha*, etc., are used. For example, excess return (over risk-free rate) is divided by standard deviation for the Sharpe ratio, while for the Treynor Ratio, excess return is divided by Beta. Sortino Ratio is similar to the Sharpe ratio except that it captures the standard deviation of only the downside observations, unlike the Sharpe Ratio, which captures standard deviation at both sides of the curve. Ratios like *Sortino Ratio, VaR (Value at Risk), and Expected Shortfall (ES)* are used to understand downside risk.

For a unit of risk, analysts can cover various portfolios' performance. Since these ratios aid in standardizing risk, investors can compare different portfolios or asset managers' risk-adjusted performances.

A Peek at Statistics – Standard Normal

Standard deviation as a measure of risk in a portfolio can be an excellent gauge. Investors use various other measures, but it is better to define returns in terms of risk-adjusted return. The distribution of return of listed equity and debt investments is usually considered normal, i.e., observations are normally distributed like a bell-shaped curve. Normal distributions have a mean and a standard deviation that is symmetrical and unimodal. Normal distribution follows a bell curve distribution, with zero skewness, having symmetry about the mean, *kurtosis of 3 (excess kurtosis of zero)*, where **Mean = Median = Mode**. Kurtosis measures the heaviness of tails or outliers. An excess kurtosis (i.e., a measure greater than 3) indicates a non-normal return with more data points further from the mean. Investors are more concerned with the tails; fatter tails mean more outlier observations on either side of the curve, ignoring other parameters that can impact extreme values like error, etc. Alternative investments tend to have more observations or data points on either side of the mean. Alternatives or alternative investments are one of the categories of asset classes; these types of investments include hedge funds, private equity, venture capital, or leverage or derivatives as part of the investment style. For example, hedge funds or derivatives use the long-short style of investing in equities. Historical returns are not suitable for analyzing future trends for investments. For example, in options pricing, implied volatility means the market implies the future volatility of a stock based on changes in options pricing. This example is enunciated to discern the difference between historical and implied volatility. The return distribution of alternatives doesn't have a normal distribution, is less transparent, and has different measures to understand risk. These asset classes are suitable for diversifying risk from a portfolio as they are less correlated with traditional assets but have shown a higher correlation with conventional assets during the financial crisis. However, alternatives have an inherent risk of liquidity, and some investment managers may not allocate a sizable portion of their holdings to alternative investments. Alternative Investments have concepts like hurdle rate, clawback, and waterfall structure that need to be covered separately from traditional investments. Many alternative investments have a higher tail risk than traditional investments, with some not linked to market prices.

Yes, but during the time of a financial crisis, all asset classes have shown to be highly correlated, deviating from the normal distribution curve and generating negative returns," Caroline interjected. "That's why investors are highly focused on the heaviness of the tails.

I nodded True.

You can also use Z-Score for calculating probabilities of observations. This is extremely valid for normal distributions. T-distributions are used for smaller sample sizes and generally have fatter tails. As the sample size of T-distributions increases, the distribution is more akin to a normal distribution. Non-parametric tests are used for non-normal distributions.

"From this normal distribution of returns, one can convert it into a standard normal," I continued.

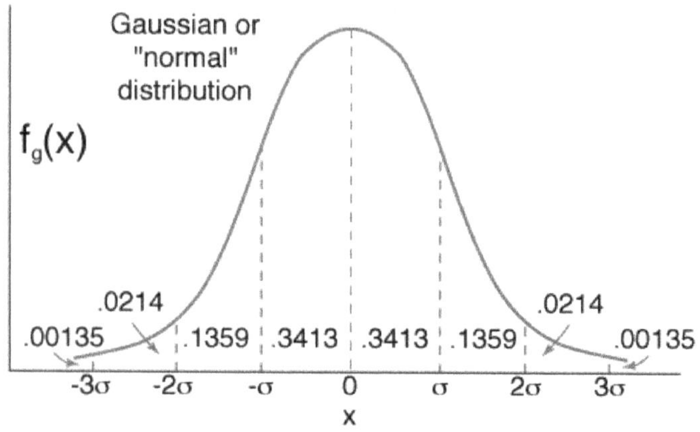

Above the Standard Normal Curve

Price-to-Book (P/B) Ratio

Investors seeking to assess a company's balance sheet strength relative to its stock price should consider examining the **price-to-book (P/B) ratio**. Many individuals are unaware that the P/B ratio is appropriate for this purpose. **Book Value** is determined by subtracting a company's total liabilities from its total assets, resulting in shareholder equity. The P/B ratio compares the current share price to this underlying book value, which can be calculated from the balance sheet financial statement. Among the three financial statements — *balance sheet, income statement, and cash flow statement* — the P/B value and other valuation metrics are among the most critical ratios for evaluating a stock's valuation. A low P/B may indicate potential undervaluation, while a high ratio could suggest overvaluation or expectations of high future growth. Tracking P/B trends over time is also beneficial. The renowned investor **Benjamin Graham**, whose book **'The Intelligent Investor'** remains highly recommended despite being first published in 1949, emphasized the importance of the price-to-book value as a key measure for understanding stock valuation. Graham considered a stock trading at a book value of less than 1.5 to be undervalued. The rationale behind paying a 50 percent premium over book value, representing shareholder equity, is an adequate benchmark for assessing valuation while keeping other factors constant. Although this rule has been widely followed, in today's high-growth industries, investors are willing to purchase companies at much higher price-to-book values, especially in sectors like technology, healthcare, or renewable energy. This is because the earnings growth trajectories justify paying higher premiums. With the right management and technology leadership mix in a dominant market position, investors may invest in companies with elevated price-to-book ratios.

This helps understand variability around the mean, crucial for measuring outliers regarding abnormal returns. The standard normal distribution is a unique normal distribution with a mean of zero and a standard deviation of one. Approximately **68 percent** of the distribution lies within **one** standard deviation, **95 percent** within **two** standard deviations, and **99.7 percent** within **three** standard deviations. This understanding is essential for assessing the probability of outliers, especially in investment management. It is generally preferable to have a large pool of observations, typically greater than 25, that are **independent and identically distributed (IID).** The **Z-score** is one way of capturing the probability of observations. The **Z-score of an observation** is defined as the number of standard deviations it falls above or below the mean. Z-scores are used to calculate probabilities using the standard normal distribution. By using various methods, the value of a Z-score provides the probability associated with a given observation.

Since the total area under the standard normal curve is **1**, one can subtract the probability value associated with a Z-score from **1** to determine the probability of an observation being in the right-hand tail of the distribution. For example, suppose you need to calculate the probability of an index return exceeding **50 percent**, given that the **mean historical return is 25 percent.**

First, compute the Z-score and find the corresponding **p-value** using a Z-table or Excel formulas, etc.. Then, subtract this p-value from **1** to determine the probability of returns greater than **50 percent**. I have simplified this explanation; for a more detailed analysis, refer to a **statistical textbook**. Additionally, many more statistical concepts, such as **hypothesis testing**, are employed in research.

> Caroline confirmed. She, along with the head of research, is presently researching the impact of better ESG ratings on the financial performance of stocks. Let's take this discussion on another day. I asked Caroline how she is evaluating different asset managers based on performance.

Risk Analysis and Performance Attribution: Brinson Attribution

Risk analysis in portfolio management is often based on measures like Beta, Sharpe Ratio, and Jensen's Alpha, which provide insight into risk-adjusted returns. However, these metrics are inadequate in capturing performance attribution analysis when comparing the performance of various fund managers. This is where performance attribution analysis, particularly Brinson Attribution, became popular among asset managers to evaluate fund managers' performances.

Brinson Attribution divides the total portfolio return into three key effects:

1. **Allocation Effect** – Evaluates the impact of asset allocation decisions across different asset classes, such as equities, debt, alternatives, and cash. The selection of the weightages across these asset classes is important, highlighting tactical allocation due to market momentum.

2. **Selection Effect** – Measures the impact of selecting specific securities within an asset class. For instance, a manager might overweight technology stocks or renewable or clean energy sectors, leading to outperformance or underperformance. This is one way portfolios can be more aligned with the theme of ESG. They can include companies that have strong ESG ratings. This concerns not only equities but also other asset classes. For example, asset managers could invest in bonds aligned with Green, Social, and other sustainable development-linked goals. For example, sovereign green bonds.

3. **Interaction Effect**: This aspect captures the interplay between allocation and selection. If you overweight an asset class and outperform through security selection within that asset class, the interaction effect is positive. However, if you overweight an asset class but underperform in stock selection within that overweighted asset class, the interaction effect becomes negative.

Interaction reflects how well-aligned and coherent your allocation and selection decisions are in contributing to positive risk-adjusted alpha generation.

Fund managers use a top-down approach to allocate assets across broad categories before selecting individual securities. For example, based on market conditions, pension funds may shift allocations between equities, bonds, and cash or cash equivalents. Superior performance can stem from either asset class momentum (e.g., overweighting equities or debt) or skilled security selection (e.g., overweighting specific sector stocks, for example, technology or the clean tech sector) that might lead to superior investment performance. Interaction is the third variable that captures the value added that is not attributable solely to the asset allocation or selection of securities.

Let's put the CAPM model to practical use. I asked Caroline to write the equation in the presentation – Start with a proxy for the market portfolio.

Proxy for Market Portfolio

The best estimate for market portfolios can be observed through proxies. **S&P 500**, widely regarded as the best single gauge of large-cap U.S. equities, can be considered a market portfolio. **MSCI World Index**, a highly liquid index with a portfolio of global securities, can be regarded as a proxy for the Global Index. In a perfect world, this benchmark index will be the market portfolio. However, in the real-world, proxies are used for the market portfolio. It's tough to calculate betas of interventions or projects in emerging markets; hence, approximation would be the best way to calculate them.

Look at the *Capital Asset Pricing Model* below.

$$E(R_i) = R_f + \beta_i \ (R_M - R_f)$$

> **CAPM** = Risk-free rate + Beta (Market Risk Premium)
> R_f = Risk-free rate. The risk-free asset has zero variance and zero correlation with risky assets.

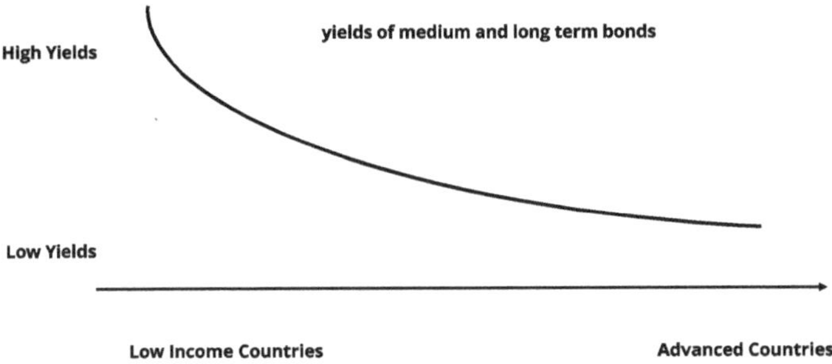

The risk-free rate is country-specific and closely resonates with the advancement of nations. The yields of medium to long-term bonds vary based on the economic advancement of countries. Bonds from advanced countries typically have lower yields than those from emerging markets and low-income countries. This difference in yields reflects several factors:

the capital markets' sophistication, the economy's inflation, and the socio-economic parameters. This is a general assumption; there are exceptions to this rule.

The risk-free rate is usually the yields of short-term bonds, for example, T-bills in the US. However, leading valuation subject market expert (Aswath Damodaran) proposes matching the duration of a project or intervention with the maturity of the government bond used as the risk-free rate.

Risk-free rate in local currency = Government or Sovereign Bond Rate – Default Spread

I suggested to Caroline that she close her teaching with the research paper and allow sufficient time for questions and answers. **"I love inquisitive students; this helps me understand their thought processes and critical thinking skills."**

Caroline agreed, and we both began writing a brief about the presentation. The draft turned out well.

Finally, we wrapped up our discussion on various models. Over the years, multifactor models have evolved within the investment management sector. These models incorporate various macroeconomic variables as factor loadings.

For example, I can develop a model that includes the advancement of economic development within a country—such as GDP per capita—or the strength of capital markets—such as the size of the equity and debt markets—as key determinants of the model's output. The International CAPM (Capital Asset Pricing Model) extends the traditional CAPM by incorporating a global perspective on asset allocation, with currency exchange rates as a key factor. One of the most well-known multifactor models is the **Arbitrage Pricing Theory (APT)**, which is based on the law of one price.

Eugene Fama and Kenneth French also introduced the three-factor model, which was later expanded into a five-factor model. The original three-factor model incorporates key variables: **market risk** (excess return of the market), **size** (SMB - Small Minus Big, which captures the size effect), and **value** (HML - High Minus Low, which accounts for the book-to-market effect). Fama and French later modified the model to include two additional factors, resulting in the five-factor model. However, discussing these advanced models is perhaps best left for another day.

To begin with, we both agreed that ESG investing is becoming a key enabler globally, with an exponential rise in both active and passive investment styles. According to GSIA, assets under management of total sustainable investments stood at $30.321 trillion. This is across a few countries or regions; the assets were reduced over 2020 due to a change in the methodology applied in the US.[1] **Exchange-traded funds (ETFs)** have become increasingly popular, especially in advanced countries. These passive investments are primarily ETFs or index funds linked to various indices across asset classes. Another strategy that blends both active and passive modes of investment is **Smart Beta**.

Smart Beta or Strategic Beta

Smart Beta, also known as Strategic Beta, is a systematic active investment that uses various strategies that focus on specific factors such as *value, quality, momentum, size, dividend, growth, or low volatility*. These factor types are in the form of indexes derived from a broader set of market cap-weighted indexes. The increasing popularity of ETFs can be attributed to their lower costs, transparency, liquidity, and diversification benefits. Unlike index funds, ETFs are traded as stocks and can be redeemed in real time; ETFs have a lower tracking error and better liquidity than index funds. According to data shared by the Board of Governors of the Federal Reserve System (US), Exchange-Traded Funds (ETFs) total financial assets are more than $9 trillion as of July 1, 2024. The combination of ESG investing and Smart Beta strategies has led to the emergence of ESG Smart Beta Exchange-Traded Products, aka ETPs.

These funds incorporate ESG factors into their Smart Beta strategies, allowing investors to focus on responsible investing within their portfolio management. The growth of ESG Smart Beta ETPs is expected to continue, looking at the global trend as investors increasingly prioritize *sustainability and responsible investing*. According to data shared by the Board of Governors of the Federal Reserve System (US), *exchange-traded funds (ETFs)* had total financial assets of $9.97 trillion as of July 1, 2024. To put this into perspective, this represents an increase of 26,990 percent between January 1, 2000, and July 1, 2024, or 271 times the value on January 1, 2000. An increase in ETFs also suggests an increase in Strategic Beta ETFs. This showcases the rise in passive investment among investors. Smart Beta, also known as Strategic Beta ETPs (exchange-traded products), has also gained traction as investors seek to enhance returns or reduce risks compared to traditional market cap-weighted indices.

Understanding Exchange-Traded Products

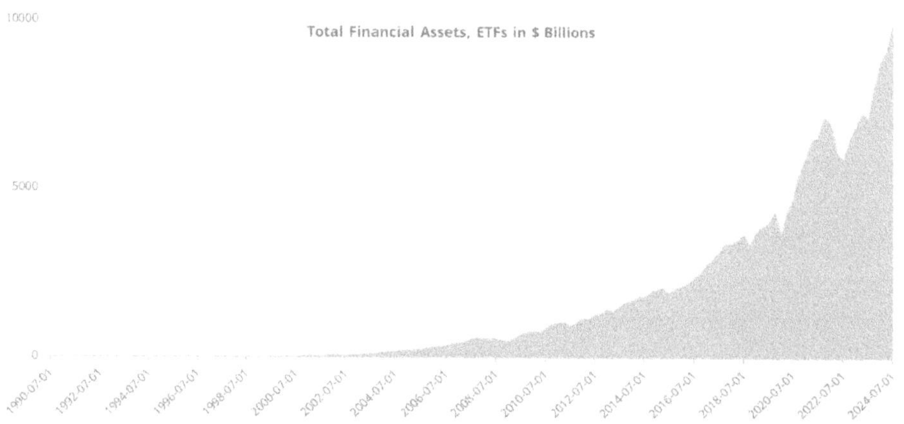

Data: Board of Governors of the Federal Reserve System (US), Exchange-Traded Funds; Total Financial Assets, Level

[BOGZ1FL564090005Q], retrieved from FRED, Federal Reserve Bank of St. Louis; *https://fred.stlouisfed.org/series/BOGZ1FL564090005Q,*

January 15, 2025. Billions of Dollars, Quarterly, Not Seasonally Adjusted; **Chart:** Author

Looking at Research – The Impact of ESG in Smart Beta Strategy

With the rise in sustainable investments, ESG strategies today within the investment sector are highly valued. The research paper titled **"Integrating ESG Analysis into Smart Beta strategies"** by *Federica Lelasi, Pietro Zito and Paolo Ceccherini* explores the rise of Smart Beta strategies within the ESG sector. The paper found that **Smart Beta** is better suited for integrating ESG strategies. Smart Beta Strategy relies more on rules-based instead of fundamental financial analysis. Smart Beta strategies select stocks based on factors such as value, volatility, quality, and size. The emergence of Smart Beta strategy in recent years has led to a factor-based investment style that blends passive with active investment strategy. Smart Beta ETFs are fast rising within the global asset management sector as this style of investment marries the best from both styles of investing. Smart Beta can be used to generate superior returns by keeping ESG ratings as one of the factors while designing investment portfolios. Research has shown that increased sustainability does not reduce the risk-adjusted performance of most Smart Beta strategies.

We both reviewed the final material and were delighted with the outcome. Caroline hugged me in gratitude for helping her out, and we shared a passionate kiss. Feeling deeply satisfied, I looked forward to her taking an excellent class with her students, confident that her knowledge and charm would captivate everyone. As it turned out, I was correct. Caroline received resounding applause from the students.

Chapter 8

Blended Finance

Blended Finance has become an important tool for financing projects within the global development sector. While it has been a part of mainstream finance, only recently has it emerged as a mainstream tool for financing development projects, notably due to multilateral banks, especially the *International Finance Corporation (IFC)*.

The OECD defines blended finance as the strategic use of development finance to mobilize additional finance toward sustainable development in developing countries.

IFC & blended finance

The **International Finance Corporation (IFC)** defines blended finance as the use of relatively small amounts of concessional donor funds to mitigate specific investment risks and rebalance the risk-reward profiles of pioneering investments that cannot proceed on strictly commercial terms. Blended finance is structured as co-investments with private capital to fund sustainable development projects while delivering financial returns. **Blended Finance** often addresses market failures within the economy, particularly in emerging and frontier markets where certain development interventions are not economically viable. To circumvent, blended finance forges public-private partnerships, a structure built into every blended finance transaction. By mobilizing additional capital to implement the **Sustainable Development Goals (SDGs),** blended finance fosters *partnerships among governments, foundations, development finance institutions, and private actors.*

These partnerships leverage *concessional resources (e.g., soft loans with lower interest rates and longer repayment periods)* or *non-concessional funds,* offering a transformative policy perspective. A key objective of blended finance is to catalyze the global implementation of sustainable development goals. By leveraging innovative financing instruments—such as *equity, debt, risk-sharing mechanisms, and guaranteed/insurance products like first-loss guarantees, structured finance, and performance-driven grants—* blended finance drives public-private partnerships. To achieve this, blended finance provides private investors with credit enhancement tools, such as first-loss guarantees, to cushion potential losses. Initial losses are typically borne by donors, multilateral development banks, development finance institutions, and impact investors to attract private capital. One standard method is senior subordination, using a waterfall structure to prioritize private investors' returns.

In first-loss guarantees, donor capital absorbs the initial layer of losses, de-risking investments for private partners. This represents a fundamental shift in the role of blended finance. Originally viewed as a collection of financial structuring instruments, blended finance is a noteworthy strategic tool for addressing social inequities.

Addis Ababa Action Agenda & blended finance

The pivotal moment in attracting blended finance is the **Addis Ababa Action Agenda**. This meeting marked a critical turning point in mobilizing all sources of finance and leveraging public finance for social good. The Addis Ababa meeting clearly defined a global framework that aims to make blended finance a mainstream tool, highlighting the increasing complexities of social financing structures within broader financial systems.

Blended finance gained further momentum in October 2017 when leaders from various **Multilateral Development Banks (MDBs)**, including the World Bank Group, African Development Bank, Asian Development Bank, European Bank for Reconstruction and Development, Inter-American Development Bank, Islamic Development Bank, and European Investment Bank, along with **European Development Finance Institutions (DFIs)** such as CDC Group, Proparco, DEG, FMO, IFU, and Swedfund, endorsed the DFI Enhanced Principles. These principles built on the 2013 DFI Guidance for Using Investment Concessional Finance in Private Sector Operations.[2]

These principles are tabulated from one to five: "*Anchor blended finance use to a development rationale, design blended finance to increase the mobilization of commercial finance, tailor blended finance to the local context, focus on effective*

The **DFI Working Group on Blended Concessional Finance for Private Sector Projects Joint Report, March 2023** update covers blended concessional finance in detail for 2021. Based on the report, lower-middle-income countries dominated the blended concessional funds, particularly in the sub-Saharan region. The trend in 2021 was similar to previous years; lower-middle-income countries have regularly attracted maximum concessional funding and funding from DFIs. If new commitments by concessional finance providers and DFIs are to be considered, the finance/banking sector led the figures, followed by infrastructure and other sectors. However, if private investments are included, infrastructure is the sector that attracts the most investments. In recent years, there has been an increase in the use of performance grants in the finance and banking sectors. The sub-Saharan African region, which received the largest concessional amount, received the largest amount in all sectors mentioned above. Although there are issues with categorizing themes due to overlapping categorization challenges, climate finance remains the key thematic area attracting blended concessional financing by DFIs. The only category to have seen a constant increase in DFI Private Sector Blended Concessional Finance Project Commitments from 2017 to 2021 is concessional finance.

partnering for blended finance, and monitor blended finance for transparency and results".[1]

The updated principles refined the guidelines for concessional blended finance, promoting the crowding-in of private capital through best business practices and setting high standards for its application. Blended finance now operates as a strategic public-private partnership tool, mobilizing additional funding for sustainable development, particularly in developing countries. Its evolution from a financial innovation instrument to a tool for addressing social inequity marks a significant shift in its strategic use.

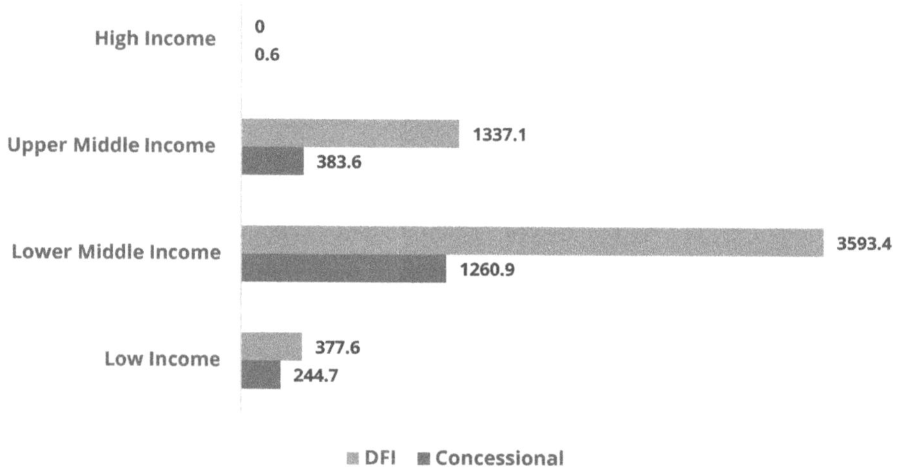

Concessional and DFI New Commitments by Country Income Level, 2021 ($Millions)

Data from DFI Working Group on Blended Concessional Finance for Private Sector Projects Joint Report, March 2023 Update; Chart Author

A perfect example of a public-private partnership as expounded by the **United Nations' seventeenth Sustainable Development Goal (SDG)**; blended finance incorporates various actors for sourcing funding using *the risk-return* hypothesis. The riskier an asset, the higher the return premium desired by investors. This is precisely why commercial investors would not fund many projects in the development sector due to the lack of market-linked returns. Given the high risk involved in financing projects or interventions that impact less privileged sections of society and the paucity of capital, especially in frontier markets like the sub-Saharan region, blended finance is a game-changer, providing the bazooka to nudge private players to participate in interventions within these markets. Unsurprisingly, the sub-Saharan region dominates the use of blended finance by region.[1] Social financing innovation facilitates balanced portfolios to attract commercial capital to complement public capital.

One of the key blended finance principles is to use balanced risk allocation in investment structures that minimize development finance while enhancing commercial finance to address socio-environmental outcomes.[1]

Convergence is a global thought leader for blended finance that shares a comprehensive overview of insights and trends in blended finance. Its members are *private investors, public agencies, and philanthropic foundations* that fund development interventions and businesses looking for investments. *According to Convergence*, blended finance has mobilized in excess of $240 billion in developing countries for sustainable development. The top private investors are impact investors like *Ceniarth LLC, Calvert Impact Capital, responsAbility Investments, and banks such as Standard Chartered Bank, Societe Generale, Sumitomo Mitsui Banking Corporation, BNP Paribas, DWS, HSBC, and GLS Bank*. Deal size ranges from $110,000 to $8 billion. The median deal size between 2010 and 2018 is $64 million. Funds dominated the vehicles used for financing – **equity, debt, and fund of funds**. **Blended Finance** uses the theory of risk and returns while blending various funding sources through public-private partnerships.

According to Convergence, concessional finance is in the form of *equity, first-loss debt or equity, investment-stage grants, and debt or equity* that bears risk at below-market financial returns to mobilize private sector investment.

Blending Archetype Funding

Commercial Capital is market interest rate-linked loans while developmental capital can be grants, various kinds of guarantees, and loans usually at concessional rates. Concessional capital is the leading archetype of funding.

Tranche Structure

The mobilization of concessional capital is a key enabler in this type of financing mechanism. Guarantees, either in part or in full, have been utilized by entities to attract private capital. The use of insurance is discussed in detail later. Performance-based grants, also known as outcome-based or results-based financing, are increasingly gaining popularity as they condition funding on achieving specific outcomes. Impact bonds, commonly called "pay-for-success" instruments, are a prominent example of this concept. Structured finance usually uses securitization; there is a case discussed ahead. Concessional blended finance addresses market failures by financing projects that are not viable through private funding alone. To remain sustainable, such projects require credit enhancement structures, like *first-loss guarantees or subordination structures (e.g., senior, mezzanine, or subordinated debt)*. In a first-loss guarantee, Development Finance

Institutions (DFIs) use their capital or investments from impact investors or philanthropic entities to safeguard private capital by absorbing initial losses. Note: Private investors might also participate in other tranches including mezzanine and subordinated debt depending on their risk appetite, return expectations etc. However, private investors will most likely participate in the senior tranche.

The waterfall structure illustrates the hierarchy of claims to cash flows for various tranches, ranked by seniority—starting with the senior tranche, then the mezzanine tranche, and finally the junior tranche.

In this setup, public investors can invest in **either the equity tranche alone or in both the equity and mezzanine tranches**. The equity tranche will absorb the first-loss, as the junior tranche is not always an equity tranche. The next loss will be absorbed by the junior tranche (if different from equity), followed by the mezzanine tranche, and finally the senior tranche. Senior debt, mezzanine, subordinated debt, and equity represent the order of cash flow rights for investors. Senior debt supersedes other financial instruments like mezzanine and subordinated debt. Subordinated (or junior) debt is the riskiest portion of the debt structure, absorbing losses first. To compensate for this higher risk, subordinated debt offers the highest interest payments compared to mezzanine and senior debt. Senior debt, being the least risky, offers the lowest interest rates.

Below is a snapshot of the total DFI concessional finance project costs by region in 2021.

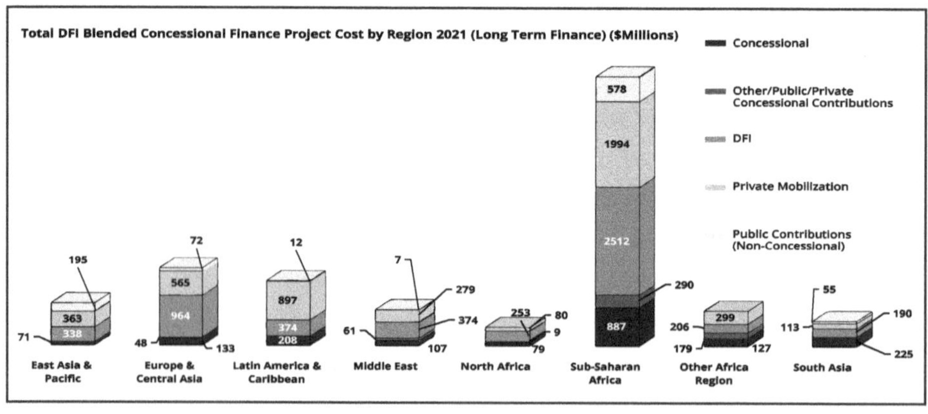

Data from DFI Working Group on Blended Concessional Finance for Private Sector Projects Joint Report, March 2023 Update; Chart Author

Concessional Commitment Volume by Blended Concessional Finance Instrument, 2021 (Percentage)

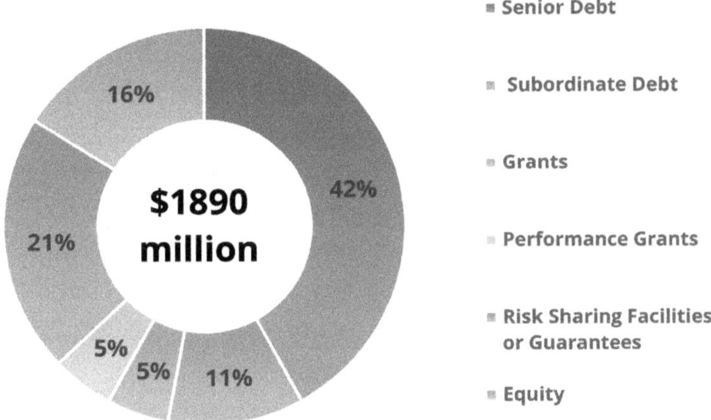

Senior Debt proved to be the most used financial instrument used by actors for **Blended Concessional Finance** followed by risk-sharing facilities or guarantees. Grants, once the ubiquitous mode of financing projects in the development sector, came in third. The report does not cover crowdfunding, another technological innovation, for raising concessional capital.

Data from DFI Working Group on Blended Concessional Finance for Private Sector Projects Joint Report, March 2023 Update; Chart Author

Crowdfunding can be used for blended concessional financing, attracting retail investors and high-net-worth individuals for private capital.

Growth of Annual blended finance Activities

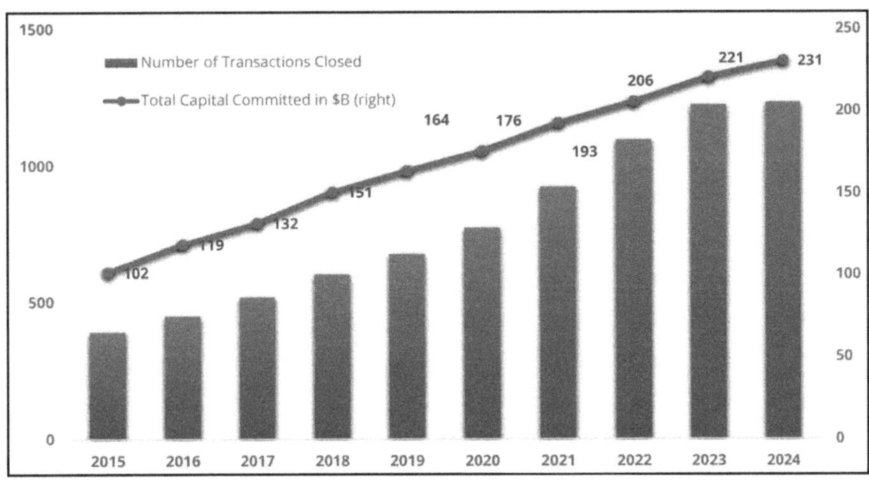

Growth of Annual blended finance Activities | Data Source for both charts: Convergence; Chart Author
Link: *https://www.convergence.finance/blended-finance*

The left axis: Number of transactions closed.

The top public investors are multilateral and DFIs, with **IFC** as the global champion, followed by **the Netherlands Development Finance Corporation, US International Development Finance Corporation, European Investment Bank,** and **IDB Invest**, respectively, as the top five public donors. The **Shell Foundation, Bill & Melinda Gates Foundation,** and **Omidyar Network** dominate the top three philanthropic investors.

To better understand various investment structures using blended finance or other financial tools, it's essential to grasp fundamental financial concepts. The ***Capital Asset Pricing Model***, *Value at Risk (VaR), and Expected Loss* are financial concepts widely used in developing structured financing. These form the backbone of various bonds used within the international development sector. VaR, also known as value at risk, is used predominantly within the financial markets to quantify the maximum possible loss over a specific period. Third-party agencies calculate default rates and are accessible for calculating risk-free rates in local currencies. Multilaterals, DFIs, and other actors are issuing bonds in local currency to circumvent exchange rate risks. These include sustainable bonds using blended finance to target socio-environmental themes through interventions. Third-party agencies calculate default rates and are available for calculating risk-free rates in local currencies. Multilaterals, DFIs, and other actors are issuing bonds in local currency to circumvent exchange rate risks. These include sustainable bonds using blended finance to target socio-environmental themes through interventions.

Expected Loss: EL

EL = PD * LGD * EAD = PD * (1-RR) * EAD

PD = Probability of Default, LGD = Loss Given Default, EAD = Exposure at Default; RR = Recovery Rate

Various methods are available for measuring and monitoring these financing instruments. More details can be found in the OECD Working Paper by Habbel, V., et al. (2021). The theory of change model is widely used to provide a comprehensive framework for blended finance, benefiting all stakeholders. Additionally, **IRIS+ metrics**, developed by the **Global Impact Investing Network (GIIN),** are frequently used by impact investors to measure and manage social and environmental impact across various sectors.

Chapter 9

Results-Based Climate Finance RBCF

Scaling Climate Action by Lowering Emissions (SCALE)

I walked with alacrity to meet **Élise** at her office. I had taken on a consulting assignment in the social impact sector, which involved researching complex social financing structures within the global development sector. The sustainable finance sector now features many innovative, complex structures. The advent of blended finance has sparked the creation of many innovative financial structures involving multiple actors through public-private partnerships. Complex structured products are deployed regularly, and today, my primary focus is on results-based climate finance. Élise holds a master's degree in applied economics and the social impact sector, with prior experience with multilateral development banks. Our discussion focused entirely on **Results-Based Climate Finance**. At the outset, Élise was deeply impressed by my understanding of global financial markets and products. She quickly began discussing recent initiatives and innovations, highlighting the Scaling Climate Action by Lowering Emissions (SCALE) program as a key example.

Élise said, "Kish, let's begin with SCALE. This is one of the foremost initiatives for reducing carbon emissions."

Sure. I said, "Go ahead. I had briefly read about the initiative."

Working as a catalyst, it raises and provides guidance for social financial innovation that facilitates projects that reduce carbon emissions, improve public health and well-being, stimulate economic growth through job creation and upskilling, enhance biodiversity, and much more. Countries can use their carbon credits as part of their Nationally Determined Contribution (NDC) commitments.

I interrupted Élise, "Good that you mentioned NDCs. The idea became a hallmark of the Paris Agreement where NDCs were introduced as part of a voluntary framework."

Élise replied, "True. But sadly, it's non-binding, making it difficult to explore its potential fully."

I continued, "Élise, I'm keen to discuss results-based climate finance—something akin to pay-for-success models, such as social and development impact bonds. However, these are structured as bonds, so they differ in several ways."

Élise said, "Ah, I love this new kind of development financing. Where were we? Jeeves says—" and laughed. Jeeves, of course, is a central character in many of P.G. Wodehouse's books. We both grew up loving Wodehouse's works, a shared favorite from our childhoods. And with that, our discussion began. Unlike other forms of funding, results-based climate finance provides funding ***after results or milestones are achieved.*** The results of this type of social financing are linked to *emission reduction or verified carbon credits*. This type of novel financial innovation is an impact bond but structured in a different pay-for-success manner. An excellent example of results-based climate finance is the World Bank's IBRD 5-year $50 million principal-protected emission reduction-linked note implemented in Vietnam. The bank has earmarked three key areas to focus on for **RBCF** – natural climate solutions, sustainable infrastructure, and fiscal and financial solutions like carbon taxes.

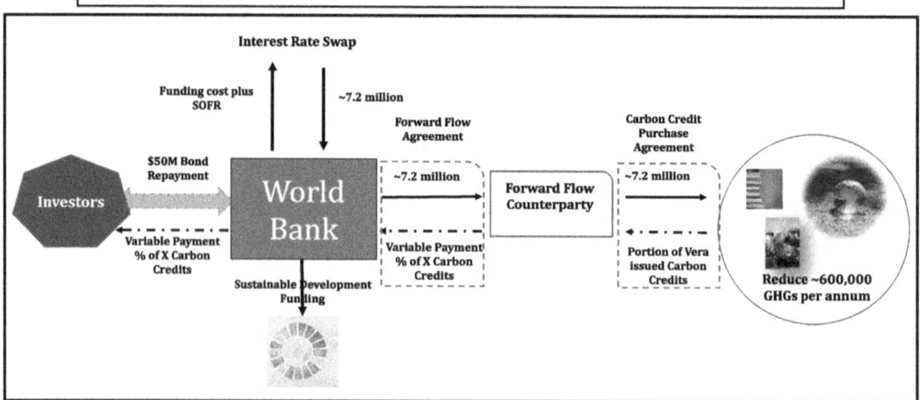

Source: The World Bank; Case Study Vietnam Emission Reduction-Linked Bond; Image Author

One of the most innovative climate financing solutions is the World Bank's IBRD 5-year $50 million **principal-protected emission reduction-linked**

note. A first of its kind, the financing instrument focuses on carbon pricing with a variable interest linked to carbon credits. The bond works as a zero-coupon bond, issued at a discount to the par value, but also includes a variable coupon rate. This feature makes the bond especially attractive as you have a guaranteed principal with a low fixed coupon rate.

However, investors have the scope to earn an expected total return of approximately 4.84 percent on the bond with a minimum return of 0.52 percent. Issued at a discount to face value with an issue price of 97.38 percent, investors receive the principal at maturity and a variable payment linked to the number of **Verified Carbon Units (VCUs)** issued by Verra for the water purifier project, paid semi-annually, subject to a cap. "VCUs" are units issued into the Verra Registry, each VCU representing a reduction or removal of one ton of carbon dioxide equivalent (CO_2e) from the atmosphere. Verra is a nonprofit standard-setting body that certifies carbon reduction projects and issues VCUs through its Verified Carbon Standard (VCS). Structured to deliver 300,000 water purifiers to 8,000 schools in Vietnam, the bond is unique within the climate finance sector, targeting K-12, higher education, and community schools. Furthermore, the bond aims to reduce greenhouse gas emissions by 600,000 tons annually for the next 10 years. The triple-A-rated note is listed on the Luxembourg Stock Exchange.[a]

"Ok," I interjected. Let me clarify the returns. Zero-coupon bonds, like Élise mentioned, are issued at a discount to their face value. For example, if a bond's face value is $100, and you purchase it for $97, the redemption price upon maturity after two years is $100. This feature gives you a $3 return over two years, translating to a simple annualized return of 1.5 percent."

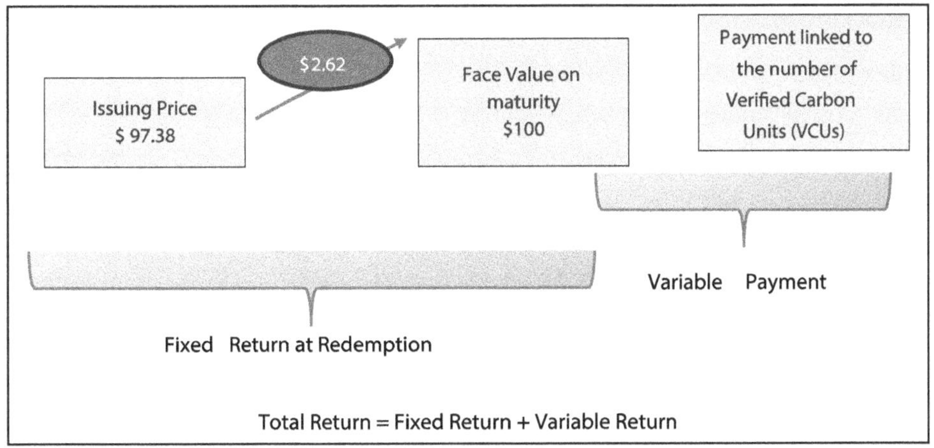

Élise continued.

The project developer is the Vietnamese company **The Sustainability Investment Promotion and Development Joint Stock Company (SIPCO)**, with Citi as the lead manager. **The Vietnam Ministry of Education and Training** is the public institution responsible for selecting educational institutes and distributing water purifiers. All purifiers are made in Vietnam and are free for all educational institutes. The investor forgoes regular coupons to fund the purification project through an inflow of $7.2 million in capital invested by an interest payment linked to SOFR. The $7.2 million interest amount is not paid to the investor but funds the project in Vietnam. The instrument is a financially innovative instrument, structured as an interest rate swap with a fixed upfront payment on one side and a variable payment on the other. Let's begin with a significant borrowing rate that has replaced LIBOR: SOFR. SOFR is crucial as a benchmark for variable rate instruments, such as floating rate bonds, interest rate swaps, and derivatives. The interest rate swap is one of the most common plain vanilla swaps. In an interest rate swap, two parties exchange cash flows: one based on a fixed rate and the other on a variable rate over a notional amount. At the swap initiation, the present value of the two cash flow streams is typically equal. The variable rate in interest rate swaps is often linked to benchmarks like SOFR.

What is Secured Overnight Financing Rate (SOFR)?

According to the Federal Reserve Bank of New York, the **Secured Overnight Financing Rate (SOFR)** is a broad measure of the cost of borrowing cash overnight collateralized by Treasury securities. After the LIBOR controversy and scandal, the world needed a new benchmark to reference the cost of borrowing. SOFR is very important as trillions of dollars of loans are now linked to this rate. SOFR replaced LIBOR (London Interbank Offered Rate) as the global quintessential benchmark rate for borrowing.

Secured Overnight Financing Rate Data

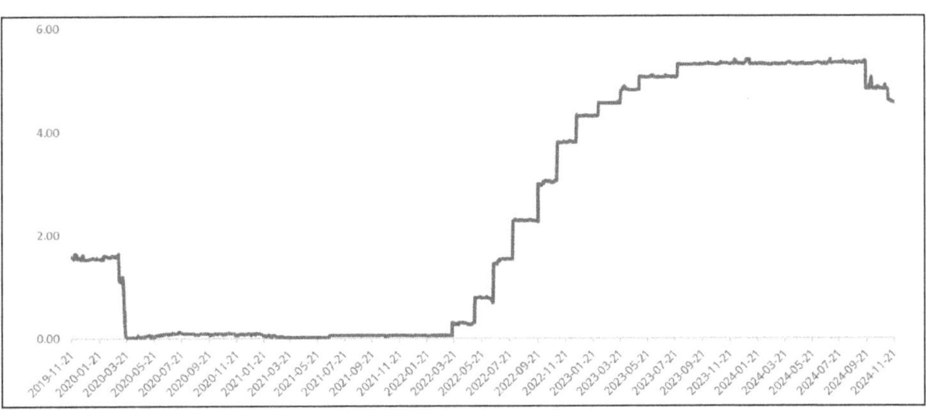

Federal Reserve Bank of New York, Secured Overnight Financing Rate [SOFR], retrieved from FRED, Federal Reserve Bank of St. Louis; https://fred.stlouisfed.org/series/SOFR, November 25, 2024. Percent, Not Seasonally Adjusted. Chart; Author.

In 2014, the U.S. established the **Alternative Reference Rates Committee (ARRC)** to transition to a new benchmark reference rate following the LIBOR scandal. **SOFR (Secured Overnight Financing Rate)** was introduced in April 2018, calculated by the New York Federal Reserve, and is published daily on the New York Fed's website. Unlike LIBOR, SOFR is a backward-looking reference rate derived from overnight repurchase agreements (repos). The SOFR is a secured rate because U.S. Treasury securities collateralize it. It involves multiple actors within the financial service sector, including non-banks, making the overnight rate a more robust and transparent benchmark. *SOFR has a daily trading volume of $2.24 trillion as of November 26, 2024*, although the notional amounts are much higher. The New York Fed calculates the rate as a volume-weighted median of daily transactions.

Secured Overnight Financing Daily Volume

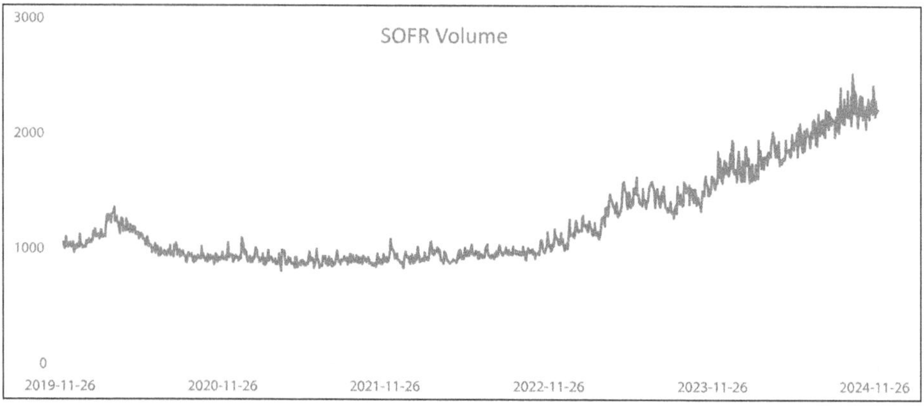

Federal Reserve Bank of New York, Secured Overnight Financing Volume [SOFRVOL], retrieved from FRED, Federal Reserve Bank of St. Louis; https://fred.stlouisfed.org/series/SOFRVOL, 27 November 2024. Billions of U.S. Dollars, Not Seasonally Adjusted. DGS5: Market Yield on U.S. Treasury Securities at 5-Year Constant Maturity, quoted on an Investment Basis, Percent, Daily, Not Seasonally Adjusted; DGS10 Market Yield on U.S. Treasury Securities at 10-Year Constant Maturity, Quoted on an Investment Basis, Percent, Daily, Not Seasonally Adjusted

It's good to understand more about interest rate swaps.

Interest Rate Swaps

Swaps are off-market transactions that are not traded on exchanges and function as over-the-counter derivative instruments. Swaps come in various forms, including interest rate swaps, currency swaps, constant maturity swaps (CMS), constant maturity treasury swaps (CMT), equity swaps, and more. For this discussion, these types will be reviewed. Among these, interest rate swaps are the most widely used and hold significant importance in the derivatives market. In a plain vanilla interest rate swap, two parties exchange cash flows tied to a notional principal amount. One leg of the swap has a fixed interest rate, while the other is linked to a floating rate. The fixed rate, often called the **swap rate**, is predetermined, while the floating rate is typically linked to a reference rate like **SOFR** (Secured Overnight Financing Rate). These swaps are structured to ensure that the fixed interest payments over the life of the swap approximately match the variable interest payments. This is achieved by aligning the **net**

present value (NPV) of the fixed and floating cash flows to zero at the swap's inception.

The **swap rate** represents the fixed rate paid to the receiver throughout the swap's term. Interest rate swaps carry two primary risks:

1. **Interest rate risk**: For the party paying a floating rate, rising interest rates increase payments, while falling rates lower them.
2. **Credit risk**: The possibility of one party defaulting on its payment obligations over the swap's life.

The **swap curve**, which is derived from forward rates, is often based on SOFR and reflects macroeconomic factors such as the state of the economy, inflation expectations, central bank policies, and issuers' creditworthiness.

Let's look at an example of a three-year interest rate swap with a fixed rate of 3.70 percent and a notional amount of $100. Assume that the cash flows, i.e., coupon payments, are made semi-annually. The receiver of the fixed payments holds a long swap position, while the payer of the fixed payments holds a short swap position. In the figure below, consider hypothetical SOFR forward rates. The three-year period is divided into six intervals, with the first net long swap position calculated for June 30, 2025 (time period 1). Notably, the net cash flows for the long swap position are zero at this point.

A helpful way to conceptualize a swap is to think of it as being long a 3.70% fixed rate bond while simultaneously short a floating rate note linked to SOFR. At the swap's inception, the net present value (NPV) of cash flows is zero, although actual cash flows over the life of the swap may vary depending on interest rate movements.

Élise agreed, "That's an excellent way to explain a swap note. Swaps are an effective tool for hedging interest rate risk."

"Yes, they're also vital for matching duration and managing asset-liability alignment," she added. Pension funds and other asset managers commonly use swaps for these purposes.

Start Date	End Date	Rates	Notional Amount $100	
31-12-2024	30-06-2025	3.50%	Notional Amount	**100**
30-06-2025	31-12-2025	3.91%	Swap Rate	3.70%
31-12-2025	30-06-2026	3.72%		
30-06-2026	31-12-2026	3.75%		
31-12-2026	30-06-2027	3.73%		
30-06-2027	31-12-2027	3.60%		

A look at the calculations below. The fixed receiver receives cash flows semi-annually at the rate of 3.7 per cent. The fixed rate payer receives cash flows linked to SOFR calculated from the SOFR forward rates. The receiver of the fixed payment is in a long swap position; the payer of the fixed payment is in a short swap position. The net cash flows to the long swap position are zero at the end of the swap tenure.

Time Period	30-06-2025	31-12-2025	30-06-2026	31-12-2026	30-06-2027	31-12-2027
Cash Flows to Long Swap Position (1)	1.85	1.85	1.85	1.85	1.85	1.85
Cash Flows to Short Swap Position (2)	1.75	1.96	1.86	1.88	1.86	1.80
Net Cash Flows to Long Swap Position (1-2)	0.10	-0.11	-0.01	-0.03	-0.01	0.05

Forward Curve: SOFR – Projected interest rate in percent

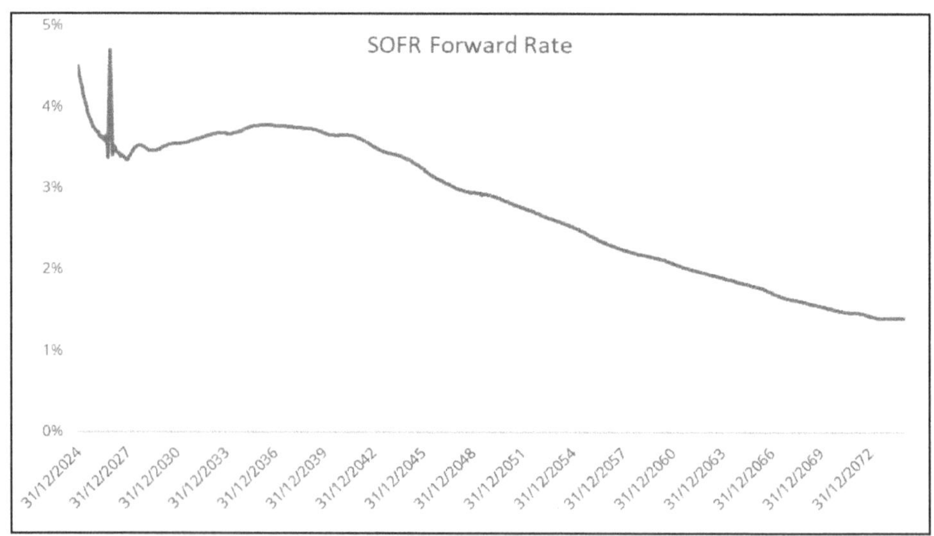

Data: Blue Gamma; SOFR Forward Rate; **Chart:** Author Link:. Link: https://app.bluegamma.io/interest-rate-curves/usd

Date: 7 December 2024. Refer to the disclaimer in the annexure.

10Y Swap Rate: Forward-starting – Expected Swap Rate in percent

Data: *Blue Gamma; Expected 10Y Swap Rate USD forward-starting;* **Chart:** *Author Link: https://app. bluegamma.io/interest-rate-curves/usd.*

This graph displays the 10-year forward-starting swap rate trajectory derived from the forward curve, based on current market expectations. Semi-Annual vs 6M Compounded SOFR. Date: 7 December 2024. Refer to the disclaimer in the annexure

While this discussion does not delve deeply into interest rate swaps, it touches upon **constant maturity swaps (CMS)** due to their importance in today's financial markets.

Constant Maturity Swap (CMS)

A Constant Maturity Swap is a specialized interest rate swap where the floating leg is linked to a constant maturity point on the swap curve instead of short-term rates like SOFR. The term of these swap contracts can vary from a few months to several years, while the constant maturity reference point remains fixed at a specified tenor throughout the life of the swap.In a CMS, one leg typically references a fixed rate or SOFR, while the floating rate is tied to a swap rate of a specified maturity, such as 5 or 10 years. In a constant maturity treasury (CMT) swap, the floating rate is mapped to the yield of a treasury bond of a specific maturity. The swap yield curve used in these agreements is derived from U.S. Treasury securities with various maturities.

According to the Federal Reserve, yields for nominal Treasury securities are interpolated from daily yield curves, incorporating data from both non-inflation-indexed and inflation-indexed securities at constant maturities. CMS-based swaps are more complex to price due to convexity adjustments, which account for the non-linear relationship between the CMS rate and the underlying yield curve. Pricing these instruments requires advanced mathematical techniques and detailed modeling, which are beyond the scope of this discussion.

Market Yield on U.S. Treasury Securities at 5-Year and 10-Year Constant Maturity

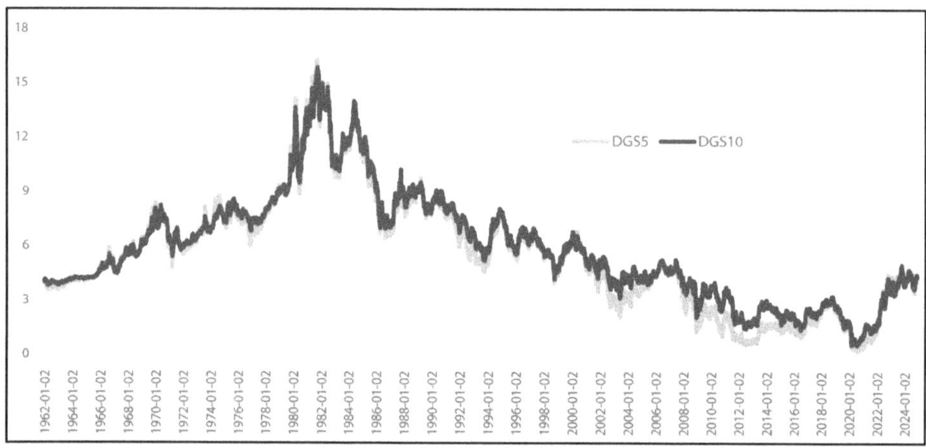

Chart: Board of Governors of the Federal Reserve System (US), Market Yield on U.S. Treasury Securities at 5-Year Constant Maturity, Quoted on an Investment Basis [DGS5], retrieved from FRED, Federal Reserve Bank of St. Louis; https://fred.stlouisfed.org/series/DGS5, November 25, 2024. Board of Governors of the Federal Reserve System (US), Market Yield on U.S. Treasury Securities at 10-Year Constant Maturity, Quoted on an Investment Basis [DGS10], retrieved from FRED, Federal Reserve Bank of St. Louis; https://fred.stlouisfed.org/series/DGS10, November 27, 2024. DGS5 - Market Yield on U.S. Treasury Securities at 5-Year Constant Maturity; DGS10 - Market Yield on U.S. Treasury Securities at 5-Year Constant Maturity; Chart Author

Forward Flow Agreement

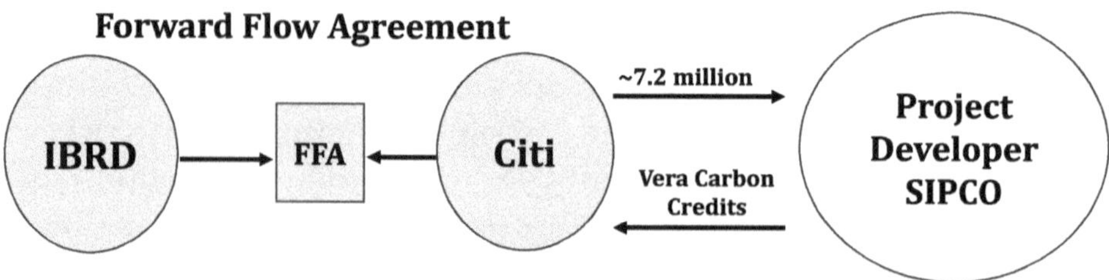

IBRD enters into a forward flow agreement with Citi wherein the International Bank for Reconstruction and Development (IBRD) pays an upfront amount to Citi for project development. Investors forgo coupon payments to front-load the project expenses with investors' return linked to the future carbon credit sales revenue from the project. Citi pays VCU-linked interest rates to IBRD in this bond. This is the variable part of the payment in the bond. Citi pays an upfront amount to the project developer to buy 300,000 water purifiers for 8,000 schools and maintain the project. This removes any relationship between IBRD and the project developer. Citi works as an intermediary where Citi pays and receives carbon credits from the project developer. Citi would, in turn, pay back a VCU-linked interest amount depending on the number of VCUs the project generates. These Verra carbon credits, the first 1.8 million tons of carbon credits sold, are earmarked for bondholders. If the number of VCUs is less than the projected demand, the forward flow agreement between the two parties dissolves, and Citi does not pay back the required amount. The investors are unable to have the maximum total return as the variable coupon diminishes. Although investors *do not face carbon credit price risk*, they are exposed to reinvestment, interest rate risk, and other bond risks. In case the forward agreement becomes void due to a certain reason or Citi is not able to pay the VCU-linked interest amount, the investors get their principal back along with the minimum return. This is an excellent example of a principal guarantee along with a variable payment. The bond follows IBRD's Sustainable Development Bond Framework.

Social Impact

The project aims to improve public health and well-being by eliminating the need to burn fossil fuels for water purification. In the process, harmful greenhouse gas emissions are avoided due to water purifiers, which lower pollution. The project drives easy access to clean drinking water for children and youth in educational centers. Additional costs associated with fuel are removed. The Vietnam projects have many other benefits, including enhanced economic opportunities by creating jobs and improving gender equality. The project supplies clean drinking water to 2 million children.

"This is an excellent example," I said, thanking Élise. We went on to discuss various other instruments and examples. Before parting ways, we agreed to meet again. Both of us were attending a global green energy event in Hong Kong and made plans to catch up during the two-day conference. Élise is one of the speakers, and I look forward to hearing her insights. We departed on a positive note.

Chapter 10

Understanding Complex Investment Products within the Global Development Sector

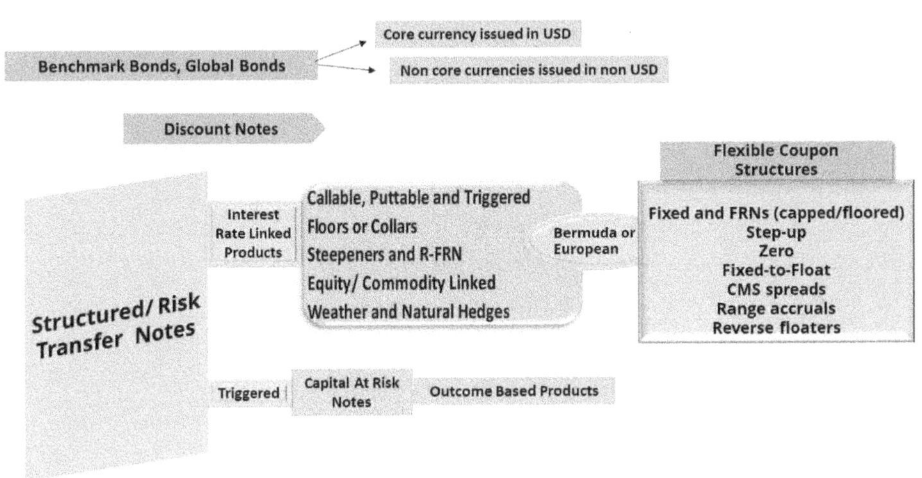

Image: Author

The Unending Crisis

The past few years have not been good, with turmoil unfolding unabated. From the onset of the pandemic to conflicts, high inflation, and widespread supply chain and lifestyle disruptions, the global crisis is unending. The world is experiencing unprecedented human and economic upheaval. One key economic variable that acts as a universal disruptor is inflation. Supply chain disruptions drive food prices, constituting a significant financial burden for poorer economies. Moreover, high inflation typically precedes higher interest rates, and higher interest costs lead to high borrowing costs. This exacerbates the fragile economic systems of low-income and emerging economies, as rising interest payments create a compounding effect, further straining their financial stability and keeping other factors constant. Meanwhile, inflation has eased due to aggressive policymaking, but global debt continues to soar. According to World Bank estimates, interest costs for the poorest countries have quadrupled over the past decade, reaching $34.6 billion in 2023. Without accelerated efforts, eradicating extreme poverty could take decades. The *World Bank Group's International Debt Report 2024* highlights that in 2023, developing countries allocated 4 percent of their GDP—approximately $1.4 trillion—toward debt servicing. Additionally, the external debt of low- and middle-income countries reached $8.8 trillion.[a]

Amid these challenges, the World Bank and other multilateral institutions have been exceptional in disbursing more capital to developing countries than they received in interest payments. High borrowing costs make capital scarce, with less budget allocation toward social welfare initiatives. This is particularly true of low-income countries where currency depreciation is another significant risk. Unsurprisingly, nearly 700 million people worldwide still live in extreme poverty, earning less than $2.15 per day, according to the World Bank.[b] This underscores the need for specialized structured finance solutions to support low-income and emerging markets navigating unprecedented humanitarian distress, political uncertainty, and high interest rates. Mechanisms such as floating rate notes, dual currency notes, and other innovative financial instruments can be crucial in achieving this goal. Major multilaterals have used various financing mechanisms to reduce financing costs and increase loan amount and duration, including extending grace periods for repaying loans. These loans could have amortizing features. In this case, the principal and interest are repaid over the bond's life with a periodic repayment schedule. These types of bonds are usually used in mortgage and asset-backed securities. We look at a few products with an introduction to structured products.

Structured Products

Structured products are a significant component of structured finance and have gained widespread acceptance in global financial markets. These bespoke financial instruments are commonly used by institutional investors, family offices, high-net-worth, and retail individuals as tools for various financial objectives. Many structured products are primarily used for risk mitigation by preserving capital while others aid in *enhancing yield*, *hedging*, and *portfolio diversification*. These financial instruments can be used to increase customer returns by leveraging, hedging their positions on the underlying securities, and taking positions in assets whose returns are less correlated with other asset classes. These innovative financial instruments facilitate tailoring investment products around an underlying asset based on the customer's needs without the need to take exposure to the underlying asset directly. For example, structured products like structured notes can be linked to equity, commodities, interest rates, foreign exchange, etc. Structured products linked to equity indices are popular among conservative investors who want to preserve capital and be part of the upside linked to the equity markets. A popular index can be the well-diversified S&P 500 index, wherein the structured product preserves capital at the end of the product's tenure with a percentage of upside participation.

Multilaterals are increasingly deploying these products within the development sector with measurable impact. Usually, plain vanilla structured products have zero-coupon bonds and embedded options. For example, consider a three-year structured product note with a capital guarantee on redemption at the end of three years and a 30 percent upside of the S&P 500 index. Most of the proceeds are invested in a zero-coupon bond, with the rest in call options linked to the S&P 500 Index. If the equity markets are higher, the investor gets principal plus 30 percent in the upside participation of the index. However, the investor receives the principal back if the equity markets go down. This is because the zero-coupon bond is bought at a discount to the face value and matures to the face value in three years.

If the S&P 500 trades at 30 percent higher at maturity compared to the initial benchmark, the investor receives the principal plus 9 percent of the upside (30 percent participation in the 30 percent index gain).

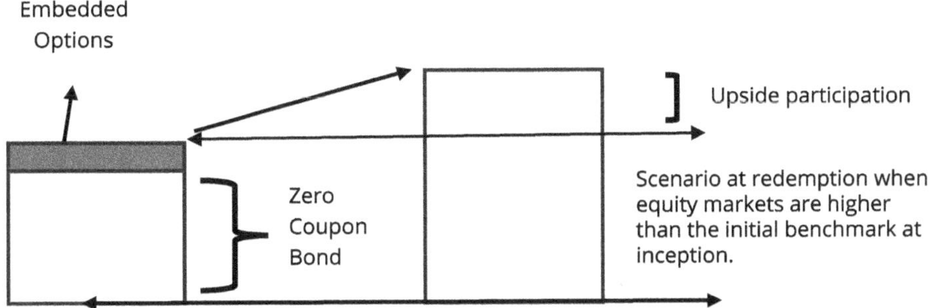

Payoff of an equity linked plain vanilla structured product on maturity when equity markets outperform at maturity.

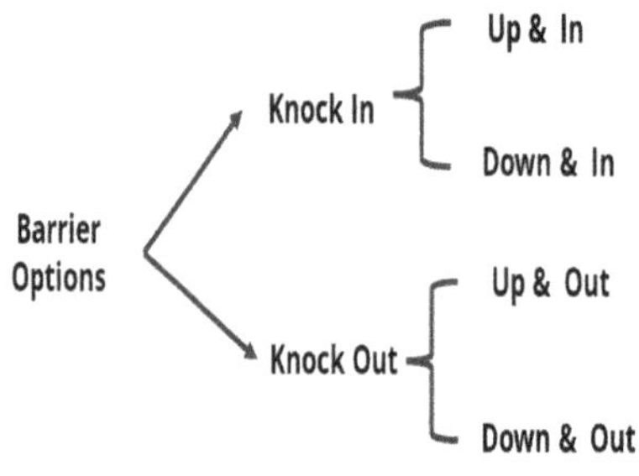

Similarly, structured products can be linked to commodity indexes, interest rates, or other indices. These products are not without risk. They have counterparty or credit risk, market risk, illiquidity risk, and call or prepayment risk. Many products are callable, i.e., they can be retired before maturity, leading to reinvestment for the investor. However, many structured products are more complicated than the ones discussed above. Options have been discussed before. American options can be exercised anytime during their tenure, while European options can only be exercised at the end of their maturity. Bermuda options are a special type of option that can be exercised during specific periods or dates within their tenure. Understanding barrier options is essential as some products released by the multilateral use the barrier concept. Barrier options are divided into two types:

1. **Knockin Options**: These are triggered when a specific barrier (i.e., a predetermined price or event) is breached.
2. **Knock-Out Options**: These are the opposite, becoming worthless if the barrier is crossed.

These are various kinds of barrier options. Up & In is activated when the upper level is crossed, Down & In when the lower barrier or predetermined level is breached. Up & Out becomes valueless when the upper barrier is crossed, or Down & Out when the lower barrier falls below the predetermined level.

Interest Rate-Linked Structured Products

Range accruals notes are another popular product among investors. These are digital based option products wherein investors receive a coupon if the underlying index for example SOFR lies within a range of interest rates over a time period.

This is the case of a range accrual note linked to a single index. Take, for example, a structure with an annual coupon of 5.5 percent for the 180-day period. The investor receives an annualized return depending on how many days SOFR lies within the predetermined range. This is an excellent product for investors who want a better return than other investment products and have a favorable view of how the underlying will perform over the period. The investor faces an enhanced yield but could receive no coupon if the underlying index, herein SOFR, does not lie within the range over the period. *Over the past decade*, multilateral organizations have increasingly utilized structured products as part of their financial strategies, often to manage risks of sovereigns and act as intermediaries for transferring risk to the capital markets.

> **Curve Accrual Notes** take a call on the underlying interest rate curves. For example, CMS Curve (30CMS-10CMS) or Constant Maturity Treasury (10CMT-2CMT). These notes give above average return until they are called by the issuer. **Steepeners** are type of structured products that take a view on yield curve. Check the section on term structure of bonds. These types of structured products are not widely used within the development sector.

Usually, plain vanilla structured products have zero-coupon bonds and embedded options. Major multilaterals like The World Bank are market leaders in innovating unique social financing structures that mitigate risk for sovereigns, subnationals, and municipalities. Market-based products transfer risk to financial institutions and capital markets, resulting in better risk management for investors. Key multilateral works as an intermediary by transferring risk to actors within the capital markets. Take the example of **market-based CAT bonds**, a moniker for catastrophic bonds that are part of various products taken out by The World Bank to address contingent risk due to natural disasters.

> Step-up and step-down coupons feature variable interest rates that either increase or decrease over the bond's tenure based on a predetermined schedule.

Floating rate notes with Caps, Floors, or Collars

Interest Rate Caps, Floors and Collars

The issuer can call callable notes before the notes mature. The issuer calls these notes when the circumstances are favorable to the issuer. Autocallable notes are similar to callable bonds except that they have a predetermined level, i.e., the auto-call level. If the Autocallable level is triggered, then the note is called back. Take the example of a structured market-linked note to the DAX index. If the autocallable level rises above the 80 percent of the value of the index that serves as the benchmark i.e. initial trading value (during the observation dates over its maturity) the note will be called back. These types of products are not used within the development sector. Usually, the investor gets a higher return over a short period, as the note is called during the earlier observation dates.

Multilateral Institutions often use financial instruments like caps, floors, or collars with floating rate notes to manage interest rate risk. For example, the IBRD offers bespoke interest rate caps and collars to borrowers, enabling them to cap their floating rate payments or establish both an upper and lower limit using an interest rate collar. Since many projects are undertaken in developing countries where loans are typically issued as floating rate loans, an increase in interest rates can strain national budgets. This may force countries to adopt measures such as spending cuts, tax increases, or other fiscal adjustments. *(The World Bank – Taking the Risk out of Interest Rate Risk).* To understand more about interest rate caps and collars, we look at their payoff structure to know more about how they function.

Floating rate notes can include caps and floors that are interest rate agreements where the reference rate is set at different strike prices. Interest rate floors set a minimum payout if the reference rate for example SOFR falls below a pre-determined level. On the other hand, interest rate caps payout when the upper level is breached. For example, an investment product of three years will payout whenever the SOFR goes above 4 percent over the next three years.

Interest Rate Cap is a risk management strategy that limits debt payment on a floating rate loan, such as a loan linked to SOFR. An Interest Rate Cap sets an upper limit on the amount of interest to be paid, ensuring that borrowers are protected from rates rising above a predetermined level. A cap option is a risk management tool that limits debt payments when interest rates exceed a predetermined level. Such borrowing is typically for long durations, where interest rate volatility poses significant risks. An Interest Rate Floor is activated when interest rates fall below a predetermined level, offering protection to lenders by ensuring a minimum interest income. An Interest Rate Collar is a combination of a cap and a floor that limits the payoff to within a specific range of interest rates. It combines both an interest rate floor and an interest rate cap. Below is an explanation of how a collar strategy can be implemented with SOFR (Secured Overnight Financing Rate). This strategy can also be applied to other asset classes, including equities. However, the payoff structure will differ if you own the underlying asset.

Example of a 3%-5% Collar

Let's consider a hypothetical collar with a lower bound (floor) of 3 percent and an upper bound (cap) of 5 percent.

Cap Structure

Caps provide a payoff when interest rates rise above 5 percent. If a borrower linked to a floating rate, for example, SOFR, wants to limit its debt payment, the borrower can purchase call options on SOFR with a strike price above 5 percent. For instance, an entity with **variable rate debt** (e.g., SOFR + a spread, assuming the spread is minimal for simplicity) may face higher borrowing costs if interest rates rise. To mitigate this risk, the entity can buy call options on SOFR at a strike price of 5 percent. If SOFR exceeds 5 percent, the seller of the call option compensates the buyer for the difference in the amount due to the increase in the interest rates. Above, the premium is paid for buying the call option. Suppose the entity has $100 of debt.

If SOFR rises to 6 percent, the seller compensates the buyer for the difference:

$$\text{Compensation} = \frac{100 * (6\% - 5\%) * \text{days}}{360}$$

This ensures the buyer is shielded from rates exceeding 5 percent. However, the buyer must pay an upfront premium for this protection.

Floor Structure

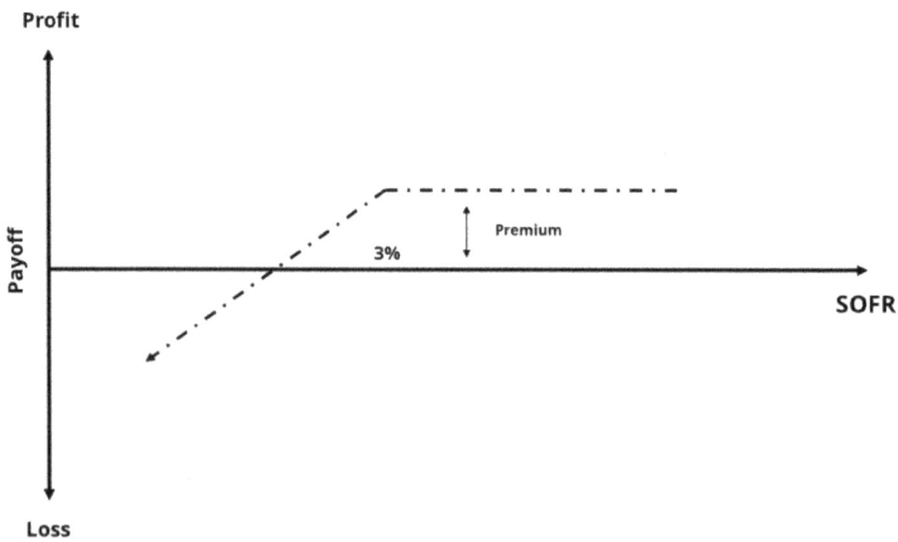

If you anticipate interest rates will remain between 3 percent and 5 percent, you can sell put options at the 3 percent floor. If rates drop below 3 percent, the seller incurs a loss and compensates the buyer for the difference between 3 percent and the actual rate over the relevant period. The selling put option of SOFR is to earn a premium, so you can reduce the costs associated with buying the call option. This strategy is good if the interest rates remain within the range desired. In the side figure, the premium is earned for writing or selling the put option. However, if interest rates fall below 3 percent, the seller of the put option has to pay the buyer the option of debt payment of the difference between 3 percent and the interest level during the period. This strategy works well when the seller is confident rates will remain within the 3 percent and 5 percent range. The seller gains the premium from selling the put option. One purpose of the collar is to limit your premium payment for the call option by writing puts. This strategy assumes a stable rate environment and is suitable when the view is that the interest rate will remain high in the medium to long-term.

Payoff 3%-5% Collar

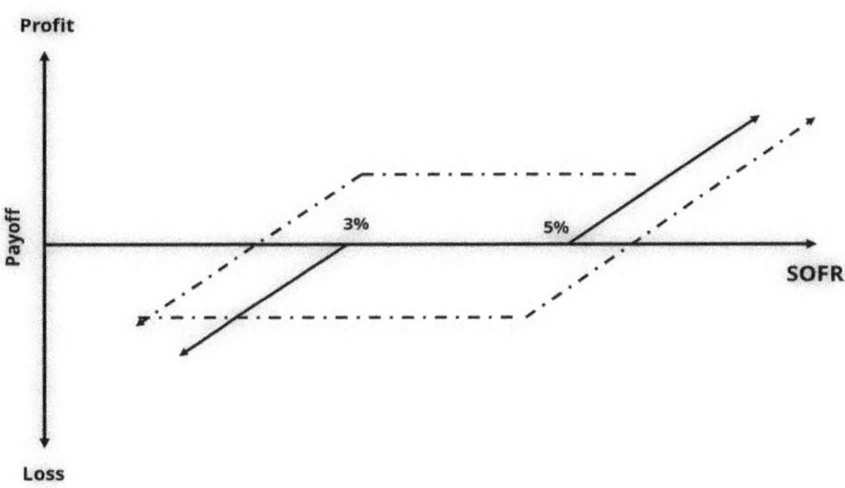

Outcome-Driven Bonds

Catastrophe (CAT) Bonds

Catastrophe (CAT) Bonds with parametric triggers are an innovative way of addressing the impact of natural disasters that need instant relief. Multilaterals also have many options to address nature-related disasters, but CAT bonds have proven immensely practical. Catastrophe (CAT) Bonds are financial instruments designed to transfer risk to a third-party when an event strikes, such as an earthquake, tsunami, or wildfire. Chile, being prone to natural calamities, has opted for insurance against these events. The *World Bank has created Catastrophe (CAT) Bonds specifically for Chile*, serving as insurance against the events above. The $630 million financial structure comprises a $350 million CAT bond and a $280 million CAT swap. CAT bonds provide Chile with three years of insurance protection. Under this arrangement, Chile pays an annual insurance premium to the World Bank, ensuring a predetermined payout based on the severity of damage caused by earthquakes. Listed on the Hong Kong Stock Exchange, the World Bank successfully raised the amount from various investors, including ILS funds, asset managers, pension funds, and reinsurers. Through this structured financial mechanism, Chile can minimize the economic impact of damages by paying a relatively small premium compared to the potential payout, which depends on the extent of the damage caused by earthquakes. The World Bank, one of the largest multilateral banks globally, holds significant market power in structuring and raising capital through its network of investors and leveraging its global network for outreach activities. Swaps are off-market transactions not traded on exchanges and function as over-the-counter derivative instruments. CAT swaps are akin to credit derivatives (CAT bonds are event-based unlike credit derivatives that are credit-based) wherein one party pays a premium to the other party for insuring against an event, such as earthquakes and tsunamis. Catastrophe (CAT) Bonds and related ILS (insurance-linked securities) are not new financial innovations. Their genesis started after Hurricane Andrew, the costliest natural disaster in US history. Since its inception in the late 1990s, the market for these types of bonds has increased and is now increasingly being deployed within the development sector.

Eurekahedge ILS Advisers Index

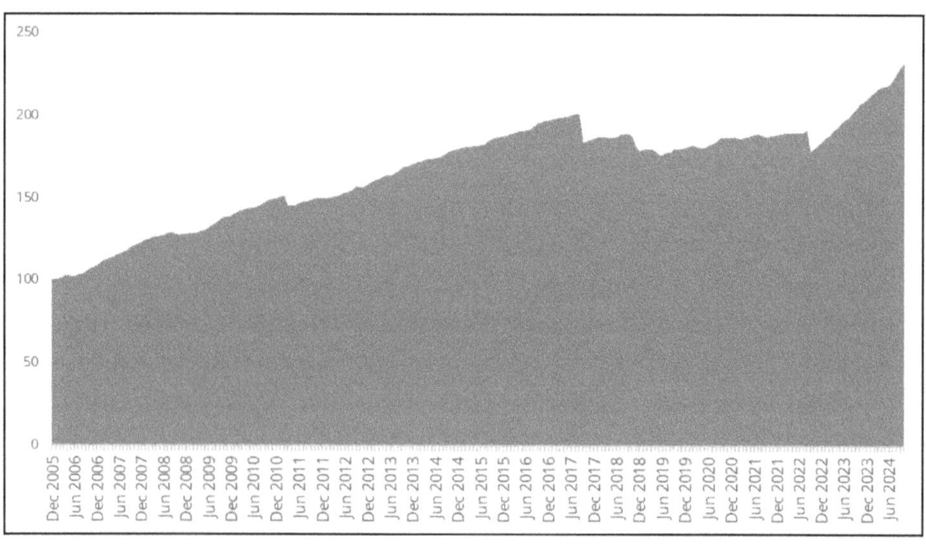

The Eurekahedge ILS Advisers Index is ILS Advisers and Eurekahedge's collaborative equally weighted index of 26 constituent funds. The index is designed to provide a broad measure of the performance of underlying hedge fund managers who explicitly allocate to insurance-linked investments and have at least 70% of their portfolio invested in non-life risk. The index is base weighted at 100 as of December 2005, does not contain duplicate funds, and is denominated in local currencies. For more information about ILS Advisers, please visit *http://www.ilsadvisers.com*. Link to the **data:** *https://www. eurekahedge.com/Indices/IndexView/Special/635/Eurekahedge-ILS-Advisers-Index*; **Chart:** Author

Index-based and parametric CAT bonds comprise over 50 percent of the market, allowing for more customizable and diversified risk transfer than traditional indemnity bonds. The onset of ILS leads to a high growth alternative asset class for investors, especially institutions, as it has a low correlation to stocks and bonds. A highly liquid capital market allocates more capital for public and private sectors to diversify across insurance risk and hedge risk against natural disasters. This product is designed to limit human trauma from natural disasters.

Understanding Credit Default Spreads

Credit Default Swaps remain the most common type of credit derivatives. *Credit Default Swaps (CDS)* are essentially credit protection by an entity in case of a fallout due to unforeseen circumstances, such as credit events, that can lead an entity to default on its obligations. A protection buyer takes insurance against a referenced entity or asset from a protection seller in these financial instruments. During this contract, the protection buyer would pay a premium, usually quarterly, to the protection seller on a predetermined notional amount against the default by the referenced entity over a period of time. If during this time, the referenced entity defaults, the protection seller needs to pay the difference between the face value and the recovery value. For example, suppose the notional amount is $10 million, and the protection buyer needs to pay $5000 per quarter to the protection seller for insuring the credit risk. In that case, this amounts to $20,000 per annum. If the recovery value is 35 cents to the dollar, the protection buyer must be paid $10 million minus 0.35 * $10 million = $6.5 million in case of default by the referenced entity. CDS can be an excellent tool to mitigate risk; however, they can cause global havoc, as seen during the credit crisis. The reason is that protection sellers further sell protection to other protection sellers to diversify their risk. So, when a number of major financial institutions go down, it produces a cascading effect, like a domino effect, that takes down several protection sellers, leaving them bankrupt due to the numerous notional values involved. An excellent example is the 2008 financial crisis, where Bear Stearns and AIG, for instance, brought down major protection sellers. CDS thus enables both hedging of and speculation on credit risks. When improperly used for excess speculation (e.g., the subprime mortgage crisis), they can facilitate leverage that causes severe systemic vulnerabilities in the financial system over time and crash severities worse than the underlying defaults alone warrant.

Chapter 11

Structured Finance

Structured Finance is pivotal in mobilizing private capital within the development sector. It is widely used in project finance, securitization, and Collateralised Debt Obligations (CDOs) to customize various features that meet the needs of both investors and issuers. Structured Finance typically involves the pooling of assets, which are often backed by cash flows from *asset-backed securities (ABS) or mortgage-backed securities (MBS).* These assets can be both existing assets or future flow structures. *In future flow transactions, cash flows will originate from the sale of assets in the future in exchange for the purchase of securities by investors.* These assets typically undergo a process of securitization to delink the credit risk of the originators from the new entity formed as a special purpose vehicle (SPV).

Credit enhancements are commonly employed by multilateral institutions, such as the International Finance Corporation (IFC), to mitigate risk, attract new investors, open international markets, and reduce borrowing costs. Credit enhancements can be both internal and external. Third-party guarantees such as guarantees given by the IFC or Asian Development Bank to cite examples are external credit enhancements. Techniques such as partial credit guarantees or risk-sharing mechanisms are frequently used by various multilaterals. Internal Credit enhancements include the distribution of cash flows into tranches based on the risk-return matrix, overcollateralization, subordination, excess spread, etc.

The assets are offloaded into the SPV, which separates the balance sheet of the assets from the originator's financials, establishing it as a separate legal entity. This structure helps create special purpose vehicles as independent entities. Cash flows from these assets can then be segmented into separate tranches representing varying degrees of risk and return. Senior, mezzanine, and junior debt tranches are sold to investors. However, there are instances where SPVs and tranches are not required, such as pass-through securities, where the cash flows associated with the underlying assets are directly passed on to investors. Structured Finance is increasingly deployed in the international development sector to reduce risk, increase participation (especially through public-private partnerships), and facilitate cross-border transactions. It allows issuers to extend loan tenors and access domestic and international financing at lower interest rates. Many entities, particularly in emerging and low-income countries, face significant challenges accessing cross-border funding. Structured Finance addresses these challenges through various credit enhancement techniques.

Securitization

Structured Finance is typically segmented into *senior, mezzanine, junior, or equity tranches*. These tranches are sold to various investors depending on the risk profile of investors. The waterfall structure is designed to showcase the seniority of cash flow to investors that flow from the senior tranche to the mezzanine to the junior or equity tranche. The senior tranche receives the first cash flows and is the least risky of all the tranches. The mezzanine

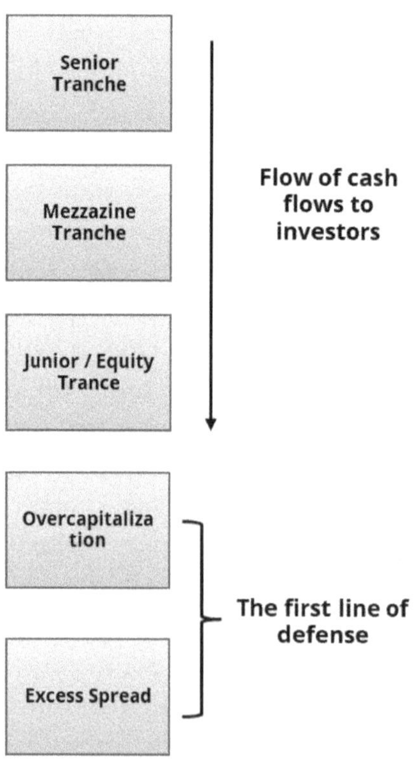

is riskier than the senior tranche but less risky than the junior or equity tranche. Risk-averse investors will always invest in senior tranches. This is where various financial institutions can aid in credit enhancement by guaranteeing or sponsoring the first-loss tranche i.e. the junior tranche or mezzanine tranche. **Credit Enhancements are commonly employed by multilateral** banks, such as the **International Finance Corporation (IFC)**, to mitigate risk, attract new investors, open international markets, and reduce borrowing costs.

Subordination, widely used in securitization, these enhancements serve as financial buffers that absorb losses, typically in the junior tranches, thereby encouraging investment in loans or bonds that might otherwise be deemed too risky. This approach is particularly useful for securities backed by underlying mortgage or asset based securities. Within the realm of securitization, credit enhancements act as vital financial tools. For example, development institutions often sponsor junior or mezzanine tranches to mitigate risks associated with underlying assets turning into non-performing assets. For instance, multilaterals may offer *partial credit guarantees, letters of credit, cash collateral, overcollateralization, subordination, excess spread, risk-sharing arrangements, or first-loss provisions*. Since investors do not have recourse to any collateral due to securitization, credit enhancements make structured finance more conducive for investments. By stepping in with various guarantee mechanisms, multilaterals reduce the likelihood of default and improve recovery rates through structured interventions. Under Partial Credit Guarantees, the guarantor will be guaranteed to pay principal and/or interest up to a predetermined level. (Refer to Structured and Securitized Products – IFC). When institutions like the IFC provide support, the associated issuances often achieve top-tier AAA credit ratings, better borrowing costs, lower probability of defaults, make the issuance in local or foreign currency, etc.

Overcollateralization and Excess Spread

Two crucial first line of defense features are **Overcollateralization** and **Excess Spread**. Overcollateralization administers the first cushion by mobilizing assets greater than liabilities, helps filter bad assets, and lays the foundation for absorbing mortgage losses. The excess collateral serves as an additional buffer that protects bondholders, especially senior tranche investors, after the junior or equity tranche absorbs initial losses. **Excess Spread** or excess interest is the gap between the interest earned on assets and interest disbursed on liabilities. This feature is another attribute for assigning provisions internally in case the pool of mortgages experiences losses.

Chapter 12

New Year Wrap Up

We had all gathered for a house party on New Year's Eve at my place. I had recently moved into our Seattle neighborhood house at **Queen Anne** and chose the New Year as the perfect occasion for a housewarming party. The house is perched on a hill and has a stunning view of Seattle's skyline. I had set up a stage for a rock show, open barbecues, and bars serving beer, wine, and soft drinks. I planned to surprise my guests with a spectacular fireworks celebration at midnight for the finale. As the night progressed, it was time to wrap up the festivities, but I had also planned something special—our first rock group performance. I had envisioned a small gathering of about 50 people with a few close friends, relatives, and acquaintances. Over the past few weeks, I rehearsed vocals for selected songs from the rock and metal genre. **Peter** and **Yun Tang, Adriana, Xu, and Élise** all arrived within a few minutes of each other. Yun Tang looked ravishing, dressed like a true rock star. I knew her graceful dance moves would steal the spotlight. Xu came dressed as John Travolta – an iconic look complemented by Élise, who was stunning in a Catwoman costume. They promised a surprise, and their dashing appearance a hit with everyone. Adriana looked as gorgeous as ever. Caroline graciously took gifts from everyone, which included champagne and a box of Cuban cigars. I had explicitly requested Peter to bring a pack of Cuban cigars for the group—a little something special for the occasion. Caroline looked angelic and gorgeous in the Valentino dress I had gifted her. The gown, made of silk, exuded elegance and sophistication. Caroline looked like a top-notch Hollywood actress dressed to kill. As the host, I entertained the guests with one-liners and jokes throughout the evening. I also prepared a special menu of delicious vegetarian and non-vegetarian dishes. The atmosphere was alive with laughter when Solomon arrived with Ayana. Both looked splendid, and their presence added to the charm of the evening.

Brad walked in with his friends, looking happy. He's likely to join an impact investment firm this coming summer. Peter had helped him network with impact investors in America, and he'll probably be moving to Washington, D.C., soon. I had an animated discussion with his friends before networking with other guests. I invited a few friends who shared insights on rising geopolitical risks. As the evening went on, people naturally grouped up, enjoying the cool breeze and each other's company. Wanting to speak with my gang, I paused entertaining guests. Most of the guests arrived, mingling and making the atmosphere lively. I called out to my friends, and we all traveled to the main hall and sat around relaxing for more personal conversations. I opened the champagne bottle, and Peter passed out cigars to a few of us. I took one, inhaling a deep puff before exhaling smoke lost in translation. I avoid drinking except on special occasions, and today is a special day for all of us. As we sipped champagne and some enjoyed the Havana special cigars, the conversation turned to key events and trends in the **ESG (Environmental, Social, and Governance)** sector over the past year. We had some time before our rock show and took this time to summarize a few of our thoughts on how the social impact sector had panned out over the year. These are highly selective cases of discussion and by no means comprehensive.

I began, "Well, sustainable finance is huge now. The *GSS+ bonds have crossed $5 trillion*, with green bonds making up the major portion of the GSS+ bond market. Other types of bonds, like sustainability-linked and transition bonds, are increasingly used, especially by corporates within the sustainable finance sector. The complexity of social financing has increased over the years, with more structured products and structured finance investment products used to add socio-economic outcomes. Pay-for-performance structures are more common, with a few rolled out by multilateral organizations this year. Outcome-driven financial structures are nowadays ubiquitous. The explosion in electric vehicles is another major milestone. The impetus given to the renewable sector surged in the last few years partly due to the ongoing conflict in Europe. Carbon pricing through the ETS mechanism is significant with major coverage in China in recent years."

Adriana mentioned, "I read about outcome-driven bonds. The World Bank came out with an outcome-driven bond linked to Amazon Reforestation." I nodded in agreement.

Caroline added, "Do not forget the EU directive on **Corporate Sustainability Due Diligence Directive (CSDDD).** Implemented in 2024, the directive will enforce better human rights for companies across the global value chain. Large companies now have to report adverse impacts of their actions on human rights and the environment. The regulation brings a level playing field for players in the European Union.

➤ Xu asked how you think it will impact other markets.

Caroline: "Excellent question! This will greatly benefit emerging and frontier markets, which are major players in the global value chain. It will bring more transparency and better access to capital for the company and its value partners. Furthermore, it is better for ESG rating companies, as more information will lead to more due diligence and better ratings."

"How about the impact of absorbing new sustainability and climate disclosure standards?" I asked.

"Yes, true. Another important milestone is in the sustainability and climate disclosure accounting standards," Caroline added. Separately, there is a nudge toward disclosing scope three emissions in the United States. The ISSB introduced two standards, **IFRS S1** and **IFRS S2**, in 2023. By 2024, many companies have begun adopting these standards.

Adriana added – "Do not forget TISFD. The **Taskforce on Inequality and Social-related Financial Disclosures (TISFD),** launched in 2024, is a global initiative aimed at addressing the systemic risks posed by inequality and its social impacts. It brings together a diverse set of stakeholders, including institutional investors. The initiative seeks to address inequality and social issues through a comprehensive approach, examining both their financial materiality and systemic impacts while also focusing on idiosyncratic factors."

We all agreed that TISFD is a step in the right direction. "What about impact investors?" I asked Peter.

➤ Peter "This will be excellent for impact investors. We now have more data to judge the impact made by companies. Also, the size of assets under the management of impact investors has increased by 21 percent CAGR over the last 5 years. In 2024, **GIIN** reported $1.571 trillion in impact investing assets under management (AUM) worldwide, over 3907 organizations globally. GIIN also published a statistical analysis taking a sample size of 1593 impact investors. Interestingly, there is a significant variation between the average size of the portfolio ($986 million) and the median investment size ($42 million)."

"The impact investment sector is growing but still pales in comparison to the global capital markets' assets under management," Xu commented.

As the discussion lingered on, our conversation shifted to artificial intelligence. Xu and Solomon spoke at length about its impact on businesses, emphasizing that it will bring both positive and adverse effects. This year, the EU launched a framework for managing artificial intelligence. Xu explained how drones are taking on increasingly advanced roles in our lives, from delivering goods to customers to functioning as flying taxis – known as low altitude economy.

The discussion then turned to a "just transition," exploring how people displaced by rapid technological advancements could remain part of the labor force. The **World Bank** came out with a Just Transition framework in 2024. **Asian Development Bank (ADB)** launched a *Just Transition platform in 2022*, **The European Commission** established *the "Just Transition Mechanism,"* a key tool in mobilizing socio-economic outcomes of the transition by deploying €55 billion capital from 2021 to 2027. The United Nations also came out with similar guidelines. "This is based on my knowledge of some of the guidelines, but I might have missed a few; I'm not sure," Xu mentioned, concluding his thoughts. In addition, I know IDB is promoting transition principles within Latin America and the Caribbean. Yun added that reskilling and upskilling will be key skills in riding the wave of Just Transition. Yun shared her thoughts on reskilling, highlighting how technology could serve as a powerful enabler for this process.

I eventually concluded the discussion by pointing out that it was time for our musical show. Feeling energized and excited, we headed outdoors toward the musical setup. Finally, the last act of the evening is the much-anticipated rock show we had all planned for weeks. Our group, **"The Crackpots,"** received a thunderous welcome as we stepped onto the stage. I took the stage as our group's frontman and lead vocalist, with Yun Tang providing backing vocals. After introducing the band members, I started the show with the timeless classic *"Summer of '69"* by Bryan Adams, a crowd favorite. The audience sang along enthusiastically, creating an euphoric atmosphere. We followed up with a series of iconic tracks, including *"Sweet Child O' Mine," "Creep," "November Rain," "Smells Like Teen Spirit," "Cats in the Cradle,"* and *"I Wish It Would Rain Down"* by Phil Collins. As the show progressed, everyone's energy soared.

The audience joined in, their voices blending with ours in perfect harmony. I poured my best into *"Creep"* by Radiohead, stretching out the iconic line *"I wish I was special"* to the delight of the crowd, who went wild. Adriana and Peter shone during several tracks, especially their rendition of *"Secret Place"* by Megadeth. Adriana stood out as the lead guitarist, while Peter excelled on rhythm guitar. Solomon delivered groovy basslines, and Xu commanded the drums. Caroline, Yun and Élise added depth as background singers. Caroline performed a few country songs to add variety, including a heartfelt version of Eric Church's *"Springsteen"*, leading to rapturous applause from the audience. Our group became an instant hit. My stage antics and the group's showmanship, paired with brilliant dancing by Yun, Caroline, and Élise, kept the energy alive. A spectacular fireworks display lit up the sky as the clock struck midnight. A tech wizard, Xu collaborated with Solomon to arrange a breathtaking drone show. The drones painted the night sky with messages of "Happy New Year 2025".

As the audience clapped, hugged, and danced into the new year, I took Caroline in my arms and gave her the kiss of my life. As I released Caroline from my romantic hold, I realized how beautiful she is—shining in radiance. I shared my heartfelt wishes for 2025—a year filled with *holistic achievements, peace, harmony, and increased productivity*—and took time to reflect.

I expressed a hopeful yet wishful sentiment: that ongoing wars would end, poverty would diminish, and global values would improve. Though idealistic, hope is what keeps us going. Looking at everyone having the time of their lives, I smiled, feeling incredibly fortunate. I silently wished to marry Caroline in 2025. Despite the growing global awareness of ESG issues, many still have a sense of despondency. Yet, as a firecracker rocket soared into the sky and burst into a dash of bright lights, glowing in the darkness, framing the *Seattle skyline, Puget Sound, and Mount Rainier* in an awe-inspiring backdrop. The bright deflagration falling toward the

Earth filled me with pride and positivity. Whatever the future held, its OK. I closed the night with a tribute to **Jane "Nightbirde" Marczewski**, performing her moving song, *"It's OK."* As the final chords echoed into the night, I felt elevated, hopeful, and grateful.

"It's OK, it's OK...."

Note: Data is also covered in some instances for 2025.

Annexure

Chapter 1: Introduction Understanding Sustainable Development Sector

References

1. **Global Sustainable Investment Alliance (GSIA)** (2022). *Global Sustainable Investment Review 2022.* Retrieved from *https://www.gsi-alliance.org/members-resources/gsir2022/.*

2. **Organization for Economic Co-operation and Development (OECD). Official development assistance: Definition and coverage.** Retrieved from https://web-archive.oecd.org/temp/2024-06-21/61752-officialdevelopmentassistancedefinitionandcoverage.htm

3. **Organization for Economic Co-operation and Development (OECD).** *Net ODA indicators.* Retrieved from *https://www.oecd.org/en/data/indicators/net-oda.html*

4. **Organization for Economic Co-operation and Development (OECD).** *Official Development Assistance (ODA).* Retrieved from *https://www.oecd.org/en/topics/policy-issues/official-development-assistance-oda.html*

5. **European Commission (2021).** *Impact assessment report accompanying the document Commission Delegated Regulation (EU).../... supplementing Regulation (EU) 2020/852 of the European Parliament and of the Council by establishing the technical screening criteria for determining the conditions under which an economic activity qualifies as contributing substantially to climate change mitigation or climate change adaptation and for determining whether that economic activity causes no significant harm to any of the other environmental objectives.* Retrieved from *https://ec.europa.eu/finance/docs/level-2-measures/taxonomy-regulation-delegated-act-2021-2800-impact-assessment_en.pdf*

6. European Parliament and Council of the European Union. (2019). *Regulation (EU) 2019/2088 of the European Parliament and of the Council of 27 November 2019 on sustainability--related disclosures in the financial services sector.* Retrieved from *https://eur-lex.europa.eu/legal-content/EN/TXT/PDF/?uri=CELEX:32019R2088*

• ! **World Bank.** *Toward a Livable Planet in 2050: Making the Right Choices Now.* Retrieved from *https://blogs.worldbank.org/en/climatechange/towards-a-livable-planet-in-2050—making-the-right-choices-now*

   a. **United Nations Climate Change. (1997).** *Kyoto Protocol to the United Nations Framework Convention on Climate Change* (FCCC/CP/1997/L.7/Add.1). *https://unfccc.int/documents/2409*

   b. **Task Force on Climate-related Financial Disclosures.** *Publications. Retrieved from* https://www.fsb-tcfd.org/publications/

   c. **European Investment Bank (2022, November 14). 15 years of EIB green bonds: Leading sustainable investment from niche to mainstream.** *Retrieved from* https://www.eib.org/en/press/all/2022-308-15-years-of-eib-green-bonds-leading-sustainable-investment-from-niche-to-mainstream

   d. **Climate Bonds Initiative (2025, January). Climate Bonds publishes provisional 2024 numbers and key factors.** *Retrieved from* https://www.climatebonds.net/resources/press-releases/2025/01/climate-bonds-publishes-provisional-2024-numbers-and-key-factors

- **International Finance Corporation. (2023).** Blended finance for climate investments in India. World Bank Group. *https://www.ifc.org/content/dam/ifc/doc/2023/Report-Blended-Finance-for-Climate-Investments-in-India.pdf*

- **European Commission.** *Sustainability-related disclosure in the financial services sector. Retrieved from* https://finance.ec.europa.eu/sustainable-finance/disclosures/sustainability-related-disclosure-financial-services-sector_en

- **World Bank (2019, March 18). 10 years of green bonds: Creating the blueprint for sustainability across capital markets.** A note on the first green bond issued by the World Bank. *Retrieved from* https://www.worldbank.org/en/news/immersive-story/2019/03/18/10-years-of-green-bonds-creating-the-blueprint-for-sustainability-across-capital-markets

- **Development Assistance Committee (DAC).** *Working Party on Development Finance Statistics: Converged statistical reporting directives for the Creditor Reporting System (CRS) and the annual DAC questionnaire.* Organization for Economic Co-operation and Development (OECD). *Retrieved from https://one.oecd.org/document/DCD/DAC(2024)40/FINAL/en/pdf*

- **Organization for Economic Co-operation and Development (OECD) (2024).** *Flows by donor (ODA+OOF+Private) [DAC1]. Retrieved from* https://data-explorer.oecd.org/

- **Organization for Economic Co-operation and Development (OECD).** *ODA trends and statistics. Retrieved from* https://www.oecd.org/en/topics/oda-trends-and-statistics.html

- Techstars. *Homepage. Retrieved from* https://www.techstars.com/

- Y Combinator. *Homepage. Retrieved from* https://www.ycombinator.com/

- Slush. *Homepage. Retrieved from* https://slush.org/

- **Task Force on Climate-related Financial Disclosures** (2017). *Recommendations of the Task Force on Climate-related Financial Disclosures.* Financial Stability Board. *https://www.fsb-tcfd.org/publications/*

- **European Commission.** *Corporate sustainability reporting. Retrieved from* https://finance.ec.europa.eu/capital-markets-union-and-financial-markets/company-reporting-and-auditing/company-reporting/corporate-sustainability-reporting_en

Wikipedia as a reference for a few sources.

- *MSCI KLD 400 Social Index – Wikipedia*

- *Dow Jones Sustainability Indices – Wikipedia*

- *An Inconvenient Truth – Wikipedia*

- *Synthetic Fuels Corporation – Wikipedia*

Chapter 2: The Story Begins

References

a. U.S. Bureau of Economic Analysis, Per Capita Personal Income in Seattle-Tacoma-Bellevue, WA (MSA) [SEAT653PCPI], retrieved from FRED, Federal Reserve Bank of St. Louis; https://fred.stlouisfed.org/series/SEAT653PCPI, 20 February 2025.

- **World Bank (2023, December 1).** *Climate action game changers: Carbon markets.* Retrieved from *https://www.worldbank.org/en/news/immersive-story/2023/12/01/climate-action-game-changers-carbon-markets?cid=ccg_tt_climatechange_en_ext&s=03*

- **Kim Y, Tanaka K, Matsuoka S. Environmental and economic effectiveness of the Kyoto Protocol.** PLoS One. 2020 Jul 21;15(7):e0236299. doi: 10.1371/journal.pone.0236299. PMID: 32692765; PMCID: PMC7373286.

- **United Nations Climate Change.** (1997). *Kyoto Protocol to the United Nations Framework Convention on Climate Change* (FCCC/CP/1997/L.7/Add.1). *https://unfccc.int/documents/2409*

- European Environment Agency. *Atmospheric greenhouse gas concentrations.* Retrieved from *https://www.eea.europa.eu/en/analysis/indicators/atmospheric-greenhouse-gas-concentrations*

- World Bank Group. *Forest area (% of land area).* Retrieved from *https://data.worldbank.org/indicator/AG.LND.FRST.ZS*

b. IEA (2024), *Renewables 2023*, IEA, Paris. https://www.iea.org/reports/renewables-2023, Licence: CC BY 4.0

- **MSCI.** *MSCI KLD 400 Social Index (USD).* Retrieved from *https://www.msci.com/indexes/index/700727*

- **EU Emissions Trading System (EU ETS),** retrieved from *https://climate.ec.europa.eu/eu-action/eu-emissions-trading-system-eu-ets_en*

- **European Commission.** *European Climate Law.* Retrieved from *https://climate.ec.europa.eu/eu-action/european-climate-law_en*

- **International Union for Conservation of Nature.** *International Union for Conservation of Nature.* Retrieved from *https://iucn.org/*

Free data sources like Wikipedia are used.

Disclaimer: "This is a work derived by Nishant Malhotra from IEA material, and Nishant Malhotra is solely liable and responsible for this derived work. The derived work is not endorsed by the IEA in any manner."

Disclaimer: This work is for informational purposes only and does not constitute financial, legal, or professional advice. While every effort has been made to ensure accuracy, the author makes no representations or warranties, express or implied, regarding the content's completeness, reliability, or accuracy. Any forward-looking statements are based on current data and assumptions and are subject to change. The author is not liable for any direct, indirect, or consequential damages arising from the use of this work. Additionally, references to third-party data or materials do not imply endorsement or affiliation. Readers should independently verify all information before making any decisions based on this content.

Disclaimer: "This book is intended for informational and educational purposes only. While every effort has been made to ensure accuracy, the author and publisher make no representations or warranties regarding the content's completeness, reliability, or accuracy. The opinions expressed are solely those of the author and do not reflect the views of any organization, institution, or entity. This book does not constitute financial, legal, or professional advice. Readers are encouraged to verify information with primary sources and consult professionals where necessary. The author and publisher disclaim any liability for any direct, indirect, or consequential loss arising from the use or reliance on the information presented in this book."

Additional Reads

- Heinzer, I., & Mezzanzanica, A. *Does a company's ESG score have a measurable impact on its market value?* Deloitte.

- National Aeronautics and Space Administration (NASA). (2024). *Temperatures rising: NASA confirms 2024 warmest year on record.* Retrieved from *https://www.nasa. gov/news-release/temperatures-rising-nasa-confirms-2024-warmest-year-on-record/*

Chapter 3 : Understanding Asset Classes and Asset Managers

References

- **Kiva.org.** *Kiva.* Retrieved from *https://www.kiva.org*

- **a. The World Bank.** *Impact report: Sustainable development bonds & green bonds.* Retrieved from *https://thedocs.worldbank.org/en/doc/667f95939700497452d00a1544 ba2d01-0340022024/original/World-Bank-IBRD-FY23-IMPACT-REPORT.pdf*

- **b. World Bank.** (2016). *IFC: The first six decades—Leading the way in private sector development, a history.* World Bank Group. *https://documents.worldbank.org/en/publication/documents-reports/documentdetail/668851478627391927/*

- **International Finance Corporation.** *Press release.* Retrieved from *https://pressroom.ifc.org/all/pages/PressDetail.aspx?ID=16544*

- **World Bank Group.** *World Bank data.* Retrieved from *https://data.worldbank.org/indicator/AG.LND.FRST.ZS*

- **Investopedia.** *Eurocurrency market.* Retrieved from *https://www.investopedia.com/terms/e/eurocurrencymarket.asp*

- **World Bank (2024, May 8).** *World Bank prices 4-year SOFR index-linked floating rate bond.* Retrieved from *https://www.worldbank.org/en/news/press-release/2024/05/08/world-bank-prices-4-year-sofr-index-linked-floating-rate-bond*

- **World Bank.** *Our organization.* Retrieved from *https://www.worldbank.org/en/about/annual-report/our-organization*

- **Hand, D., Ulanow, M., Pan, H., & Xiao, K. (2024, October 23).** *Sizing the Impact Investing Market 2024.* Global Impact Investing Network. *https://link.edgepilot.com/s/de6468ac/W5jiBTEPIEugUZCFswrN_g?u=https://thegiin.org/publication/research/sizing-the-impact-investing-market-2024/*

- **Perold, André F. 2004.** *"The Capital Asset Pricing Model." Journal of Economic Perspectives, 18(3): 3–24.*

- Copyright American Economic Association; reproduced with permission from the Journal of Economic Perspectives.

Note: Long-term credit ratings image derived from Wikipedia page of ratings.

All values are rounded off to the respective digits.

Additional Suggested Reads and Books

- **Bernstein, P. L. (1992).** *Capital Ideas: The Improbable Origins of Modern Wall Street. Free Press.*

- **Todaro, M. P., & Smith, S. C. (2020).** *Economic Development* (13th ed.). Pearson.

- **Fabozzi, F. J. (2021).** *Bond Markets, Analysis, and Strategies* (10th ed.). Pearson.

- **Koller, T., Goedhart, M., & Wessels, D. (2020).** *Valuation: Measuring and managing the value of companies* (7th ed.). McKinsey & Company.

- **Jackley, J. (2015).** *Clay Water Brick: Finding Inspiration from Entrepreneurs Who Do the Most with the Least.* Spiegel & Grau.

- **Dalio, R.** (2017). *Principles: Life & Work.* Simon & Schuster.

- **Prahalad, C. K. (2004).** *The Fortune at the Bottom of the Pyramid: Eradicating Poverty Through Profits.* Wharton School Publishing.

- **Greene, B. (1999).** *The Elegant Universe: Superstrings, Hidden Dimensions, and the Quest for the Ultimate Theory.* W. W. Norton & Company.

- **Patterson, S. (2010).** *The Quants: How a New Breed of Math Whizzes Conquered Wall Street and Nearly Destroyed It.* Crown Business.

- **Bachelier, L. (1900).** *Théorie de la spéculation.* Gauthier-Villars.

- **Hull, J. C. (2022).** *Options, futures, and other derivatives* (11th ed.). Pearson.

- **Fama, E. F. (1965).** *Random Walks in Stock Market Prices.* Financial Analysts Journal, 21(5), 55-59.

- **The New Yorker.** *Jim Simons: The numbers king.* Retrieved from *https://www.newyorker.com/magazine/2017/12/18/jim-simons-the-numbers-king*

- **Office of the United States Trade Representative.** *Small business issues.* Retrieved from *https://ustr.gov/issue-areas/small-business*

- **Sharpe, W. F. (1964).** *Capital Asset Prices: A Theory of Market Equilibrium Under Conditions of Risk.* The Journal of Finance, **19**(3), 425-442. *https://doi.org/10.2307/2977928*

- **Mankiw, N. G. (2022).** *Macroeconomics* (11th ed.). Worth Publishers.

Chapter 4: Artificial Intelligence, and Startups – Innovation, Productivity and Economic Growth

References

- **World Bank. GDP per capita (current US $)** - Israel. *The World Bank.* Retrieved March 20, 2025, from *https://data.worldbank.org/indicator/NY.GDP.PCAP.CD?locations=IL*

- **European Commission.** *European Climate Law.* European Commission. Retrieved from *https://climate.ec.europa.eu/eu-action/european-climate-law_en*

    - SXSW. *Austin culture. https://www.sxsw.com/attend/*

    - European Climate, Infrastructure and Environment Executive Agency (CINEA). (2024, June 18). *Innovation Fund: 18 cleantech projects to receive €173 million in EU funding. https://cinea.ec.europa.eu/news-events/news/innovation-fund-18-cleantech-projects-receive-eu173-million-eu-funding-2024-06-18_en*

    - European Commission. (2021, November). *Innovation Fund pre-selected projects. https://climate.ec.europa.eu/system/files/2021-11/policy_if_pre-selected_projects_en.pdf*

- European Commission. *Innovation Fund.* European Commission. Retrieved from *https://commission.europa.eu/funding-tenders/find-funding/eu-funding-programmes/innovation-fund_en*

- Allen Institute. *Seattle hub for synthetic biology. https://alleninstitute.org/division/seattle-hub-for-synthetic-biology/*

- European Parliament. (2023, June 1). *EU AI Act: First regulation on artificial intelligence.* European Parliament. *https://www.europarl.europa.eu/topics/en/article/20230601STO93804/eu-ai-act-first-regulation-on-artificial-intelligence*

- Echoing Green. *Mission.* Retrieved from *https://echoinggreen.org/mission/*

- Techstars. *Global startup network: Better for founders.* Retrieved from https://www.techstars.com/

- Slush. *Most founder-focused event on Earth: Nov 19–20, 2025.* Retrieved from https://slush.org/

- Library of Congress. (2019). *National Film Registry: Jerry Maguire (1996).* Retrieved from *https://www.loc.gov*

- Schlitz, D. (1976). *The Gambler* [Recorded by Kenny Rogers]. United Artists.

- Petty, T., & Lynne, J. (1989). *Free Fallin'* [Recorded by Tom Petty]. MCA Records.

- **Malhotra, N.** (2020, February 25). *Atal Innovation Mission & Ramanan Ramanathan: Enabling world-class holistic innovation & entrepreneurship.* The Middle Road. *https://themiddleroad.org/atal-innovation-mission/*

- European Commission. *What is the Innovation Fund?* European Commission. Retrieved from *https://climate.ec.europa.eu/eu-action/eu-funding-climate-action/innovation-fund/what-innovation-fund_en*

YouTube Video:

- **Kawasaki, G.** YouTube videos.

- Kawasaki, G. [Guy Kawasaki]. *Videos.* YouTube. Retrieved from *https://www.youtube.com/@GuyKawasaki/videos*

- **Kawasaki, G.** *The only 10 slides you need in a pitch* [Video]. YouTube. Retrieved from *https://www.youtube.com/watch?v=WqnLU-Izy9g*

- **Kawasaki, G.** *How to start a startup: The art of the start* [Video]. YouTube. Retrieved from *https://www.youtube.com/watch?v=6tYiL6v8N8o*

- **Kawasaki, G. (2015).** *The Art of the Start 2.0: The Time-Tested, Battle-Hardened Guide for Anyone Starting Anything.* Portfolio/Penguin.

- **TEDxBerkeley Kawasaki, G.** (2014, November 26). *The Art of Innovation | Guy Kawasaki | TEDxBerkeley* [Video]. YouTube. *https://www.youtube.com/watch?v=Mtjatz9r-Vc*

Charts

Total Factor Productivity at Constant Prices for the US and UK (Jan 1, 1954, to Jan 1, 2019)

Data Source: University of Groningen and University of California, Davis, Total Factor Productivity at Constant National Prices for the United States [RTFPNAUSA632NRUG], retrieved from FRED, Federal Reserve Bank of St. Louis; https://fred.stlouisfed.org/series/RTFPNAUSA632NRUG, July 16, 2024. University of Groningen and University of California, Davis, Total Factor Productivity at Constant National Prices for the United Kingdom [RTFPNAGBA632NRUG], retrieved from FRED, Federal Reserve Bank of St. Louis; https://fred.stlouisfed.org/series/RTFPNAGBA632NRUG, July 16, 2024.

Reference Feenstra, Robert C., Robert Inklaar and Marcel P. Timmer (2015), "The Next Generation of the Penn World Table," American Economic Review, 105(10), 3150-3182, available for download at *www.ggdc.net/pwt*.

Units: Index 2017=1, Not Seasonally Adjusted, **Frequency:** Annual; Chart; Author

Additional Suggested Reads and Books

- Mishkin, F. S. (Year). *Macroeconomics: Policy & Practice*. Publisher.

- Senor, D., & Singer, S. (Year). *Startup Nation: The Story of Israel's Economic Miracle*. Publisher.

- Mankiw, N. G. (Year). *Macroeconomics* (12th ed.). Worth Publishers.

- Romer, P. M. (1994). *The origins of endogenous growth. Journal of Economic Perspectives, 8*(1), 3-22. *https://doi.org/10.1257/jep.8.1.3*

- Schwartzfarb, A., & Boehm, T. (2021). *Levers: The framework for building repeatability into your business*. Lioncrest Publishing.

- Todaro, M. P., & Smith, S. C. (2020). *Economic development* (13th ed.). Pearson.

- City of Bellevue. *Official website of Bellevue, Washington*. Retrieved from *https://bellevuewa.gov/*

- **Miller, C.** (2022). *Chip war: The fight for the world's most critical technology*. Scribner.

Chapter 5: Let's Order Sustainable Finance

References

a. ***Climate Bonds Initiative:*** *5 for 25 - Delivering £5 trillion of climate investment annually by 2025. Retrieved from https://www.climatebonds.net/files/releases/cbi_5_for_25_01b.pdf*

b. **World Bank.** *5 ways to unlock private capital to tackle climate change.* Retrieved from *https://blogs.worldbank.org/en/voices/5-ways-to-unlock-private-capital-to-tackle-climate-change*

c. **Climate Bonds Initiative (2023).** *Green bond pricing in the primary market: H1 2023.* Retrieved from *https://www.climatebonds.net/files/reports/cbi_pricing_h1_2023_01f.pdf*

- **International Capital Market Association (ICMA).** (2024). *Guidance Handbook and Q&A.* Retrieved from *https://www.icmagroup.org/sustainable-finance/the-principles-guidelines-and-handbooks/guidance-handbook-and-q-and-a/*

- **International Capital Market Association (ICMA).** *New guidance on blue-themed bonds to help unlock finance for a sustainable ocean economy.* Retrieved from *https://www.icmagroup.org/News/news-in-brief/new-guidance-on-blue-themed-bonds-to-help-unlock-finance-for-a-sustainable-ocean-economy/*

- **Social Finance. Reducing reoffending in Peterborough. Social Finance UK. Retrieved from https://www.socialfinance.org.uk/work/reducing reoffending in peterborough**

- **International Capital Market Association (ICMA).** *Sustainable Finance Database.* Retrieved from *https://www.icmagroup.org/sustainable-finance/sustainable-bonds-database/*

- **International Capital Market Association (ICMA).** *Social Bond Principles.* Retrieved from *https://www.icmagroup.org/sustainable-finance/the-principles-guidelines-and-handbooks/social-bond-principles-sbp/*

- **International Capital Market Association (ICMA).** *Green Bond Principles (GBP).* Retrieved from *https://www.icmagroup.org/sustainable-finance/the-principles-guidelines-and-handbooks/green-bond-principles-gbp/*

- **European Union.** (2019). *Regulation (EU) 2019/2088 of the European Parliament and of the Council of 27 November 2019 on sustainability-related disclosures in the financial services sector.* Official Journal of the European Union. Retrieved from *https://eur-lex.europa.eu/eli/reg/2019/2088/oj*

- **European Commission (2021).** Communication from the Commission to the European Parliament, the Council, the European Economic and Social Committee, and the Committee of the Regions: Strategy for Financing the Transition to a Sustainable Economy. **EUR-Lex.** Retrieved from *https://eur-lex.europa.eu/legal-content/EN/TXT/HTML/?uri=CELEX:52021DC0390*

- **World Bank.** (2021). *Sustainable Development Bond Framework.* Retrieved from *https:// thedocs.worldbank.org/en/doc/43b360bfda1e6e5b8a094ef2ce4dff2a-0340012021/ original/World-Bank-IBRD-Sustainable-Development-Bond-Framework.pdf*

- **World Bank.** *Sustainable Development Bonds for Impact [Video].* YouTube. Retrieved from *https://www.youtube.com/watch?v=WBSLXKZwtrE*

- **International Finance Corporation (IFC).** *Banking on Women.* Retrieved from *https://www.ifc.org/en/what-we-do/sector-expertise/financial-institutions/gender-finance/banking-on-women*

- **European Union.** (2023). *Summary report of the open and targeted consultations on the SFDR assessment 14 September 2023 - 22 December 2023.* Retrieved from *https:// finance.ec.europa.eu/document/download/0f2cfde1-12b0-4860-b548-0393ac5b592b_ en?filename=2023-sfdr-implementation-summary-of-respons*

- **International Platform on Sustainable Finance.** (2023). *Strengthening clarity in social finance: Scaling up social bonds.* Retrieved from *https://finance. ec.europa.eu/document/download/9d8bfe51-3969-4e3d-8369-a73c1f7cf941_ en?filename=231204-ipsf-social-bonds-report_en.pdf*

- **European Union Innovation Fund.** (2024). *Innovation fund: 18 cleantech projects to receive €173 million EU funding.* Retrieved from *https://cinea.ec.europa.eu/ news-events/news/innovation-fund-18-cleantech-projects-receive-eu173-million-eu-funding-2024-06-18_en*

- **International Finance Corporation (IFC).** (2019). *New IFC report explains how to unlock $25 trillion in green building investments in emerging markets.* Retrieved from *https://www.ifc.org/en/pressroom/2019/new-ifc-report-explains-how-to-unlock-25-trillion-in-green-building-investments-in-emerging-markets*

- **Hong Kong Mortgage Corporation (HKMC).** *Sustainable finance.* Retrieved from *https://www.hkmc.com.hk/eng/investor_relations/sustainable_finance.html*

- **ReNew.** *ReNew signs MoUs for INR 640 billion (US $7.8 billion) green energy projects.* ReNew Investor Relations. Retrieved from *https://investor.renew.com/news-releases/ news-release-details/renew-signs-mous-inr-640-billion-us-78-bn-green-energy-projects*

- **Global Sustainable Investment Alliance (GSIA).** (2022). *Global Sustainable Investment Review 2022.* Retrieved from *https://www.gsi-alliance.org/members-resources/gsir2022/*

- **World Bank.** (2018, October 29). *Seychelles launches world's first sovereign blue bond.* Retrieved from *https://www.worldbank.org/en/news/press-release/2018/10/29/ seychelles-launches-worlds-first-sovereign-blue-bond*

- **International Finance Corporation (IFC).** (2023). *IFC invests in PEPT's first securitization to support access to electricity in Côte d'Ivoire.* Retrieved from *https:// www.ifc.org/en/pressroom/2023/ifc-invests-in-pepts-first-securitisation-to-support-access-to-e*

- **International Finance Corporation (IFC).** (2025). *Côte d'Ivoire nears universal access to electricity.* Retrieved from *https://www.ifc.org/en/stories/2025/cote-divoire-nears-universal-access-to-electricity#:~:text=IFC's%20anchor%20investment%20of%20%2448.8%20million%20to%20support%20the%20poorest%2C%20most%20vulnerable%20citizens*

- **International Finance Corporation (IFC).** (2024, February 27). *Green and Social Bond Impact Report - Financial Year 2023.* Retrieved from *https://www.ifc.org/en/insights-reports/2024/green-social-bond-impact-report-fy23*

- **World Bank (2019, March 18).** *10 years of green bonds: Creating the blueprint for sustainability across capital markets.* **Retrieved from https://www.worldbank.org/en/news/immersive-story/2019/03/18/10-years-of-green-bonds-creating-the-blueprint-for-sustainability-across-capital-markets**

- **European Investment Bank (EIB).** *Sustainable finance.* **Retrieved from https://www.eib.org/en/investor-relations/sustainable-finance/index**

- **Climate Bonds Initiative (2023).** *Global State of the Market Report 2023.* Retrieved from *https://www.climatebonds.net/resources/reports/global-state-market-report-2023*

- **International Finance Corporation (2023). IFC annual report 2023 highlights. World Bank Group. https://www.ifc.org/content/dam/ifc/doc/2023/ifc-annual-report-2023-highlights-en.pdf**

- European Commission. (2021). *Strategy for financing the transition to a sustainable economy* (COM/2021/390 final). Publications Office of the European Union. *https://eur-lex.europa.eu/legal-content/EN/TXT/?uri=CELEX%3A52021DC0390*

* Data is calculated using Climate Bonds Initiative until 2024

Additional Recommended Reads

- OECD (2016), "Social impact bonds: State of play & lessons learned", *OECD Local Economic and Employment Development (LEED) Papers*, No. 2016/05, OECD Publishing, Paris, *https://doi.org/10.1787/3064b396-en.*

- Export options: *EndNote, Zotero, BibTeX, RefWorks, Procite, Import into RefWorks, Mendeley*

- OECD (2016), "Understanding Social Impact Bonds", OECD Local Economic and Employment Development (LEED) Papers, No. 2016/06, OECD Publishing, Paris, *https://doi.org/10.1787/7e48050d-en.*

- *Export options: EndNote, Zotero, BibTeX, RefWorks, Procite, Import into RefWorks, Mendeley*

Answers to Quiz Questions

- 1. Green Bonds.

- 2. Just Transition

- 3. Sustainability-Linked Bonds.

Chapter 6: Workout Day

References

- **CrossFit Games**. *CrossFit Games*. Retrieved from *https://games.crossfit.com*

- **Fraser, M.** *Matt Fraser – CrossFit Champion*. CrossFit Games. Retrieved February from *https://games.crossfit.com/athlete/153604*

Recommended Additional Reads

- Lee, B., & Little, J. (Eds.). (2016). *Bruce Lee's Fighting Method: The Complete Edition.* Tuttle Publishing.

- McDougall, C. (2009). *Born to Run: A Hidden Tribe, Superathletes, and the Greatest Race the World Has Never Seen.* Knopf.

Chapter 7: Carbon Pricing

References

- **European Parliament; The EU Emissions Trading System: Method and Effects of Free Allowance Allocation. European Parliament. Policy Department for Budgetary Affairs Directorate-General for Internal Policies PE 755.098 - October 2023.** Retrieved from *https://www.europarl.europa.eu/RegData/etudes/IDAN/2023/755098/IPOL_IDA(2023)755098_EN.pdf*

1. **World Bank. 2024. State and Trends of Carbon Pricing 2024. © Washington, DC: World Bank**. *http://hdl.handle.net/10986/41544* License: *CC BY 3.0 IGO.*

   https://openknowledge.worldbank.org/entities/publication/b0d66765-299c-4fb8-921f-61f6bb979087

2. **Joseph E. Stiglitz et al., "Report of the High-Level Commission"** on Carbon Prices," High-Level Commission on Carbon Prices, May 29, 2017, *https://doi.org/10.7916/d8-w2nc-4103*

3. **Carbon Pricing Database.** Retrieved from https://carbonpricingdashboard.worldbank.org/about#download-data

4. **Institute for Climate Economics (I4CE). (2022).** *Global carbon accounts in 2022.* Retrieved from *https://www.i4ce.org/en/publication/global-carbon-accounts-2022-climate/*

5. The World Bank. 2022. "State and Trends of Carbon Pricing 2022" (May), World Bank, Washington, DC. DOI: 10.1596/978-1-4648-1895-0. License: Creative Commons Attribution CC BY 3.0 IGO

- **Climate Action Game Changers:** *Carbon Markets,* Retrieved from *https://www. worldbank.org/en/news/immersive-story/2023/12/01/climate-action-game-changers-carbon-markets?cid=ccg_tt_climatechange_en_ext&s=03*

- **EU Emissions Trading System (EU ETS),** Retrieved from

- *https://climate.ec.europa.eu/eu-action/eu-emissions-trading-system-eu-ets_en*

- **Carbon Border Adjustment Mechanism,** Retrieved from

- https://taxation-customs.ec.europa.eu/carbon-border-adjustment-mechanism_en

- **"The Quest" by Daniel Yergin**

- Yergin, D. (2011). *The Quest: Energy, Security, and the Remaking of the Modern World.* Penguin Press.

- **United Nations Climate Change.** (1997). *Kyoto Protocol to the United Nations Framework Convention on Climate Change* (FCCC/CP/1997/L.7/Add.1). UNFCCC. *https://unfccc.int/documents/2409*

Chart

- Data Source: World Bank. (2024). Carbon Pricing Dashboard. Retrieved from *https://carbonpricingdashboard.worldbank.org/.* The figure is converted into a percentage and rounded off to two digits. Last update: 1 April 2024. Chart: Author

- Chart & Data Source: World Bank. (2024). *Carbon pricing instruments around the world, 2024* [Map]. Carbon Pricing Dashboard. Retrieved from *https:// carbonpricingdashboard.worldbank.org/*

- Data: European Environment Agency. "EU Emissions Trading System (ETS) Data Viewer." 2024,*https://www.eea.europa.eu/en/analysis/maps-and-charts/emissions-trading-viewer-1-dashboards.*

Chart Author

- Note: Some other factors in the market failure section include a low fertility rate, reduced funding for healthcare, and conflict.

Chapter 8: Are your investments Smart Beta?

References

- Ielasi, F., Ceccherini, P., & Zito, P. (2020). Integrating ESG Analysis into Smart Beta strategies. *Sustainability, 12*(22), 9351. *https://doi.org/10.3390/su12229351*

- Global Sustainable Investment Alliance (GSIA). (2022). *Global Sustainable Investment Review 2022*. Retrieved from *https://www.gsi-alliance.org/members-resources/gsir2022/*

- Note: For the US" revised methodology identified $8.4 trillion in sustainable investment assets under management in 2022, a material change from the $17 trillion reported in the previous Global Sustainable Investment Review."

- Perold, André F. 2004. "The Capital Asset Pricing Model." Journal of Economic Perspectives, 18(3): 3–24

Wikipedia contributors

- *Arbitrage pricing theory*. Retrieved from *https://en.wikipedia.org/wiki/Arbitrage_pricing_theory*

- *Capital Asset Pricing Model*. Retrieved from *https://en.wikipedia.org/wiki/Capital_asset_pricing_model*

- *Multiple-factor models*. Retrieved from https://en.wikipedia.org/wiki/Multiple_factor_models

- *Fama-French three-factor model*. Retrieved from *https://en.wikipedia.org/wiki/Fama%E2%80%93French_three-factor_model*

- *S&P 500*. Retrieved from *https://en.wikipedia.org/wiki/S%26P_500*

- *Performance Attribution*. Retrieved from https://en.wikipedia.org/wiki/Performance_attribution.

- S&P 500. Chart comparison of S&P GSCI Gold and S&P 500 TR. Link: https://www.spglobal.com/spdji/en/indices/commodities/sp-gsci-gold/?currency=USD&returntype=T-#data

Total Financial Assets of ETFs in billions

- Data: Board of Governors of the Federal Reserve System (US), Exchange-Traded Funds; Total Financial Assets, Level

- [BOGZ1FL564090005Q], retrieved from FRED, Federal Reserve Bank of St. Louis; https://fred.stlouisfed.org/series/BOGZ1FL564090005Q,

- January 15, 2025. Billions of Dollars, Quarterly, Not Seasonally Adjusted; Chart: Author.

Suggested Additional Readings

- Bernstein, P. L. (1992). *Capital Ideas: The Improbable Origins of Modern Wall Street*. Free Press.

- Damodaran, A. (2012). *Investment Valuation: Tools and Techniques for Determining the Value of Any Asset* (3rd ed.). Wiley.

- Sharpe, W. F. (1964). Capital Asset Prices: A Theory of Market Equilibrium under Conditions of Risk. The Journal of Finance, 19(3), 425–442.https://doi.org/10.2307/2977928

- Gary P. Brinson, L. Randolph Hood, & Gilbert L. Beebower. (1986). Determinants of Portfolio Performance. Financial Analysts Journal, 42(4), 39–44. *http://www.jstor.org/stable/4478947*

- Roll, R., & Ross, S. A. (1980). An Empirical Investigation of the Arbitrage Pricing Theory. *The Journal of Finance, 35*(5), 1073–1103. *https://doi.org/10.2307/2327087*

- Graham, B. (2006). *The intelligent investor: The definitive book on value investing* (Rev. ed.). Harper Business.

- Treynor, J. L. (1961, 1962). Toward a Theory of the Market Value of Risky Assets.

- Lintner, J. (1965). The Valuation of Risk Assets and the Selection of Risky Investments in Stock Portfolios and Capital Budgets. Review of Economics and Statistics.

- Mossin, J. (1966). Equilibrium in a Capital Asset Market. Econometrica.

- Markowitz, H. (1952). Portfolio Selection. Journal of Finance.

Images: Author

Chapter 9: Blended Finance

References

1. **OECD (2021),** *The OECD DAC blended finance Guidance*, **Best Practices in Development Co-operation, OECD Publishing, Paris, https://doi.org/10.1787/ded656b4-en.**

2. **FI Working Group on Blended Concessional Finance for Private Sector Projects. (2023).** *Joint report, March 2023 update.* **International Finance Corporation. https://www.ifc.org/en/insights-reports/2020/bf-dfi-ifc-annual-reports.**

How blended finance Works

- **International Finance Corporation. (n.d.).** How blended finance works. IFC. Retrieved August 31, 2025, from *https://www.ifc.org/en/what-we-do/sector-expertise/blended-finance/how-blended-finance-works*

- **Habbel, V. et al. (2021), "Evaluating blended finance instruments and mechanisms: Approaches and methods",** *OECD Development Co-operation Working Papers*, **No. 101, OECD Publishing, Paris,<u>https://doi.org/10.1787/ f1574c10-en.</u>**

- Link: https://www.oecd.org/en/publications/evaluating-blended finance-instruments-and-mechanisms_f1574c10-en.html

- Chart: Concessional and DFI New Commitments by Country Income Level, 2021 ($Millions)

- Chart: Total DFI concessional finance project costs by region in 2021

- Chart: Concessional Commitment Volume by Blended Concessional Finance Instrument, 2021 (Percentage)

- All the above chart data is from the FI Working Group on Blended Concessional Finance for Private Sector Projects. (2023). Joint report, March 2023 update. International Finance Corporation. https://www.ifc.org/en/insights-reports/2020/ bf-dfi-ifc-annual-reports.

- This can be assessed through other websites of multilaterals.

Chart: Growth of Annual blended finance Activities

- **Convergence.** Blended finance. Retrieved August 31, 2025, from https://www. convergence.finance/blended-finance

- Convergence. *Blended finance.* Retrieved August 31, 2025, from HYPERLINK https://www.convergence.finance/blended-finance?utm_source=chatgpt. com"https://www.convergence.finance/blended-finance

Chart Vehicle Types for blended finance

- Link: *https://www.convergence.finance/blended-finance*

- "Certain data and insights in this book are derived from publicly available reports by Convergence. All rights and credit belong to the respective authors and organizations."

Additional Suggested Reads

- **The Nature Conservancy.** *Belize debt conversion: A case study.* **The Nature Conservancy.** *https://www.nature.org/en-us/about-us/who-we-are/how-we-work/ finance-investing/naturevest/belize-debt-conversion-case-study/*

Chapter 10
Results-Based Climate Finance RBCF

References

a. **World Bank Emission Reduction-Linked Bond Uses Voluntary Carbon Market to Provide Clean Water to Children in Vietnam**

World Bank (2023). *World Bank Emission Reduction-Linked Bond uses voluntary carbon market to provide clean water to children in Vietnam. https://thedocs.worldbank. org/en/doc/d7d99578840ed938c52b08f6b9831f16-0340012023/original/Case-Study-Vietnam-Emission-Reduction-Linked-Bond.pdf*

• **The World Bank's Financial Model: How Much Do You Know About It?**
Carbon Credits (2023). *The World Bank's Financial Model: How Much Do You Know About It? https://carboncredits.com/new-world-bank-trust-fund-for-projects-that-cut-emissions/*

• **Scaling Climate Action by Lowering Emissions (SCALE)**
World Bank (2023). *Scaling Climate Action by Lowering Emissions (SCALE). https:// www.worldbank.org/en/programs/scale/overview*

• **Case Study: Vietnam Emission Reduction-Linked Bond**
The World Bank. (2023). *Case study: Vietnam emission reduction-linked bond. https:// thedocs.worldbank.org/en/doc/d7d99578840ed938c52b08f6b9831f16-0340012023/ original/Case-Study-Vietnam-Emission-Reduction-Linked-Bond.pdf*

• **Emission Reduction-Linked Bond – Achieving Wide-Ranging Development Outcomes by Enabling the Private Sector**
World Bank (2023). *Emission reduction-linked bond – Achieving wide-ranging development outcomes by enabling the private sector. https://www.worldbank.org/en/ news/feature/2023/02/14/emission-reduction-linked-bond-achieving-wide-ranging-development-outcomes-by-enabling-the-private-sector*

• **World Bank Emission Reduction-Linked Bond Uses Voluntary Carbon Market to Provide Clean Water to Children in Vietnam: Questions & Answers**
World Bank (2023). *World Bank emission reduction-linked bond uses voluntary carbon market to provide clean water to children in Vietnam: Questions & Answers. https:// thedocs.worldbank.org/en/doc/a550207090350837a902c49e00e93568-0340022023/ original/World-Bank-IBRD-Emission-Reduction-Linked-Bond-Q-A-Final.pdf*

• **Scaling Climate Action by Lowering Emissions (SCALE)**
World Bank. (2023). *Scaling climate action by lowering emissions (SCALE). https:// www.worldbank.org/en/programs/scale*

• **New World Bank Trust Fund for Projects that Cut Emissions**
Carbon Credits (2023). *New World Bank trust fund for projects that cut emissions. https://carboncredits.com/new-world-bank-trust-fund-for-projects-that-cut-emissions/*

- **Board of Governors of the Federal Reserve System**
  Board of Governors of the Federal Reserve System. (2023). *H.15 – Selected Interest Rates. https://www.federalreserve.gov/releases/h15/*

Charts

- Board of Governors of the Federal Reserve System (US), Market Yield on U.S. Treasury Securities at 5-Year Constant Maturity, Quoted on an Investment Basis [DGS5], retrieved from FRED, Federal Reserve Bank of St. Louis; https://fred.stlouisfed.org/series/DGS5, 25 November 2024.

- Federal Reserve Bank of New York, Secured Overnight Financing Rate [SOFR], retrieved from FRED, Federal Reserve Bank of St. Louis; https://fred.stlouisfed.org/series/SOFR, 25 November 2024. Percent, Not Seasonally Adjusted.

- Board of Governors of the Federal Reserve System (US), Market Yield on U.S. Treasury Securities at 5-Year Constant Maturity, Quoted on an Investment Basis [DGS5], retrieved from FRED, Federal Reserve Bank of St. Louis; https://fred.stlouisfed.org/series/DGS5, November 25, 2024. Board of Governors of the Federal Reserve System (US), Market Yield on U.S. Treasury Securities at 10-Year Constant Maturity, Quoted on an Investment Basis [DGS10], retrieved from FRED, Federal Reserve Bank of St. Louis; https://fred.stlouisfed.org/series/DGS10, November 27, 2024. DGS5 - Market Yield on U.S. Treasury Securities at 5-Year Constant Maturity; DGS10 - Market Yield on U.S. Treasury Securities at 10-Year Constant Maturity

- Federal Reserve Bank of New York, Secured Overnight Financing Volume [SOFRVOL], retrieved from FRED, Federal Reserve Bank of St. Louis; https://fred.stlouisfed.org/series/SOFRVOL, 27 November 2024. Billions of U.S. Dollars, Not Seasonally Adjusted. DGS5: Market Yield on U.S. Treasury Securities at 5-Year Constant Maturity, quoted on an Investment Basis, Percent, Daily, Not Seasonally Adjusted; DGS10 Market Yield on U.S. Treasury Securities at 10-Year Constant Maturity, Quoted on an Investment Basis, Percent, Daily, Not Seasonally Adjusted

- Data: Blue Gamma; One-month Euribor; Chart: Author Link: https://app.bluegamma.io/interest-rate-curves/usd

Additional Reference Reads and Books

- **Hull, J. & Basu, S.** (2023). *Options, Futures, and Other Derivatives* (11th ed.). Pearson.

- Articles from Risk.net

- **Fabozzi, F. J.** (2021). *Bond Markets, Analysis, and Strategies* (10th ed.). Pearson.

- **An Updated User's Guide to SOFR - The Alternative Reference Rates Committee**

- **Alternative Reference Rates Committee**. (2021). *An updated user's guide to SOFR. https://www.newyorkfed.org/medialibrary/Microsites/arrc/files/2021/users-guide-to-sofr2021-update.pdf*

Disclaimer

Blue Gamma Ltd is not an investment adviser, financial adviser, nor a securities broker. None of the data and information constitutes investment advice nor an offering, recommendation, or solicitation by Blue Gamma Ltd to buy, sell, or hold any security or financial product. All data and information are provided "as is" for informational purposes only and are not intended for trading, financial, investment, tax, legal, accounting, or other advice. Blue Gamma Ltd makes no representation and has no opinion regarding the advisability or suitability of any investment.

Chapter 11: Understanding Complex Investment Products within the Global Development Sector

References

- **World Bank (2023)**. *World Bank executes its largest single-country catastrophe bond and swap transaction to provide Chile with $630 million in financial protection against earthquakes.* [Case study]. Retrieved from *https://thedocs.worldbank.org/en/doc/bbe8fec1c061681e55f765239ae1c979-0340012023/original/Case-Study-Chile-2023-CatBond.pdf*

- **Artemis (2024)**. *Catastrophe bond market: Record issuance in 2024 pipeline completes.* Retrieved from *https://www.artemis.bm/news/catastrophe-bond-market-record-issuance-2024-pipeline-completes/*

World Bank Documents

a. **International Debt Report 2024:** World Bank (2024). *International Debt Report 2024.* Retrieved from *https://openknowledge.worldbank.org/entities/publication/f1700aa0-cc73-42b7-8ceb-630c5528a574*

b. World Bank (2023). *Poverty and Shared Prosperity 2023: Poverty, Prosperity, and the Planet.* Retrieved from *https://www.worldbank.org/en/publication/poverty-prosperity-and-planet*

- **World Bank Structured Notes:**
  World Bank (2021). *Structured notes.* Retrieved from *https://thedocs.worldbank.org/en/doc/0d89f46261f0c19cb57126365d17b824-0340022021/original/Structured-Notes.pdf*

- **Taking the Risk out of Interest Rate Risk:**
  World Bank (2018). *Taking the Risk out of Interest Rate Risk: Protecting Countries against Interest Rate Risk with IBRD Flexible Loans (Case Study).* Retrieved from *https://documents1.worldbank.org/curated/en/163801546962452164/Taking-the-Risk-out-of-Interest-Rate-Risk-Protecting-Countries-against-Interest-Rate-Risk-with-IBRD-Flexible-Loans-Case-Study.pdf*

- **Suspending the Offer of the Fixed-Spread Terms of IBRD Flexible Loan:**
  World Bank (2017). *Suspending the offer of the fixed-spread terms of IBRD flexible loan.* Retrieved from *https://thedocs.worldbank.org/en/doc/161391507314945324-0340022017/original/noteinterestrateriskmanagement201708.pdf*

Charts

Eurekahedge ILS Advisers Index

The Eurekahedge ILS Advisers Index is ILS Advisers and Eurekahedge's collaborative equally weighted index of 26 constituent funds. The index is designed to provide a broad measure of the performance of underlying hedge fund managers who explicitly allocate to insurance-linked investments and have at least 70% of their portfolio invested in non-life risk. The index is base weighted at 100 as of December 2005, does not contain duplicate funds, and is denominated in local currencies. For more information about ILS Advisers, please visit *http://www.ilsadvisers.com*. Link to the data: *https://www.eurekahedge.com/Indices/IndexView/Special/635/Eurekahedge-ILS-Advisers-Index*; Chart: Author

Additional Suggested Reads and Books

- Fabozzi, F. J. (Year). *Bond Markets, Analysis, and Strategies* (Edition). Pearson.

Chapter 12: Structured Finance

References

- **Structured and Securitized Products – Partial Credit Guarantees**
  Link: *https://www.ifc.org/content/dam/ifc/doc/2023/ifc-product-description-partial-credit-guarantees.pdf*

- **IFC Structured Finance Solutions: Securitization**
  Link: *https://documents.worldbank.org/en/publication/documents-reports/documentdetail/099103207102496015/idu11b6e0c1611e4114fcd19e4d195948661a875*

Chapter 13: New Year Wrap Up

References

- **European Commission**. *Corporate sustainability due diligence*. Retrieved from *https://commission.europa.eu/business-economy-euro/doing-business-eu/sustainability-due-diligence-responsible-business/corporate-sustainability-due-diligence_en*

- **IFRS**. *International Sustainability Standards Board (ISSB)*. Retrieved from *https://www.ifrs.org/groups/international-sustainability-standards-board/*

- **World Bank. (2024).** *Just Transition Taxonomy 2024*. Retrieved from *https://thedocs.worldbank.org/en/doc/4170363805a08d5eaca17fbd62db45d2-0340012024/world-bank-just-transition-taxonomy-2024*

- **Asian Development Bank. (2024).** *ADB launches just transition support platform*. Retrieved from *https://www.adb.org/news/adb-launches-just-transition-support-platform*

- **Inter-American Development Bank**. (2024). *Advancing a just transition in Latin America and the Caribbean*. Retrieved from *https://publications.iadb.org/en/advancing-just-transition-latin-america-and-caribbean*

- **European Commission**. *Just Transition Fund (JTF)*. European Commission. *https://ec.europa.eu/regional_policy/funding/just-transition-fund_en*

- **Hand, D., Ulanov, M., Pan, H., Xiao, K. (2024). Sizing the Impact Investing Market 2024.** The Global Impact Investing Network (GIIN), New York.

- **Taskforce on Inequality and Social-related Financial Disclosures.** *TISFD: Taskforce on Inequality and Social-related Financial Disclosures. https://www.tisfd.org/*

Video:

- America's Got Talent. (2021, June 8). *Jane "Nightbirde" Marczewski | America's Got Talent 2021* [Video]. YouTube. Retrieved from *https://www.youtube.com/watch?v=CZJvBfoHDk0*